Blo

By the same author

Edinburgh: A Capital Story (with Francis Jarvie), 1991
Scottish Names, 1992
Chambers Punctuation Guide, 1992

As editor

The Wild Ride and other Scottish Stories, 1987
The Genius and other Irish Stories, 1988
Scottish Folk and Fairy Tales, 1992
Irish Folk and Fairy Tales, 1992
A Friend of Humanity: Selected Stories of George Friel, 1992
Scottish Short Stories, 1992
The Scottish Reciter, 1993
Great Golf Stories, 1993

Bloomsbury
Grammar
Guide

GORDON JARVIE

BLOOMSBURY

Dedication
In affectionate memory
of my grandfather
Daniel Beattie 1879–1952
who led me to grammar and
to the dictionary

First published 1993

Bloomsbury Publishing Ltd, 38 Soho Square,
London W1V 5DF

Copyright © 1993 by Gordon Jarvie

The moral right of the author has
been asserted

A CIP catalogue record for this book is
available from the British Library

ISBN 0 7475 1385 6

10 9 8 7 6 5

Typeset by Hewer Text, Edinburgh
Printed in Great Britain by
Clays Ltd, St Ives plc

Contents

Introduction

This book is for that marvellous person: 'the average reader'. It is not for academic linguists, or advanced students of language. Rather it is aimed at those generations of readers who have passed through the British school systems without being able to say quite what a verb, or a preposition, or a clause, is. Those generations now extend – unbelievably perhaps – to include a generation of schoolteachers of English, many of whom cannot themselves say exactly what a verb, or a preposition, or a clause, is; and who are now rightly being asked to inform their pupils about such basic aspects of the language.

It is not that we do not know what grammar is; we have all been using language, in all its complexity, from early childhood. It is merely that we have not for several generations of British schooling felt its articulation to be worth while. The National Curriculum for English is now changing all this, and grammar is once again being taught in British schools.

What is grammar? Grammar is the study of a language. Students of grammar are interested in dismantling language – and putting it together again – to see how it works. So grammar is the study of the mechanics and dynamics of language. In a way, we are all students of language from the cradle to the grave. Five-year-old children are particularly keen students of grammar, and can pronounce authoritatively and often correctly: 'That's wrong,' or 'That isn't how you say it.' We all know grammar therefore, but we are not all able to describe its nuts and bolts. This book tries to help us with these nuts and bolts. Technical terms are therefore included, but I try to keep them to a minimum and to define them along the way in clear and consistent terms.

As part of our general knowledge, grammar should of course be taught in schools. A good knowledge of grammar should help us use language more effectively, both in our writing and in our speaking. It should encourage us to be precise and measured in our utterances. And, of course, knowledge of our own grammar will be especially helpful to us when we come to study foreign languages and their grammars. Much of the grammar we study in our own language turns out to be useful with foreign languages – they too have verbs, tenses and clauses. And surely one of the reasons for Britain's appalling record in foreign-language provision has something to do with our refusal over several generations to teach the basics of our own language. That, after all, is where everything starts.

How to use this book

In setting out to prepare this project, I was reminded of the oriental wisdom that there are sixty-three different ways to climb a mountain. So it is with grammar. Where to begin?

I have begun with **words** in Part 1 of the book, because we all know – or think we know – what a word is. From there I have gone to **phrases**, as the next building block in the hierarchy. Part 2 deals with **clauses** and **sentences**. I realise that there are those who believe that grammar should be approached the other way about. But I felt that to start with the sentence would offer a harder route to the summit – the North Wall of the Eiger rather than the Cook's Tour of the Alps. And as part of my aim was to make the approach as simple as possible, this route seemed less appropriate for me.

I have tried in Part 1 to avoid using terms that are not defined till Part 2, so in that sense I assume the book will be used consecutively. But I hope it will also be used for reference, and to that end a detailed index is provided.

Parts 3–6 of the book are autonomous and may be read in any order. Part 7 offers a few simple exercises, where readers may check up on how much they know.

Gordon Jarvie
Edinburgh, January 1993

one
Words and phrases

The investigation of words is the
beginning of education.

> Antisthenes the Sophist

Every name is called a NOUN,
As *field* and *fountain*, *street* and *town*;
In place of noun the PRONOUN stands,
As *he* and *she* can clap their hands;
The ADJECTIVE describes a thing,
As *magic* wand or *bridal* ring;
The VERB means action, something done–
To *read* and *write*, to *jump* and *run*;
How things are done the ADVERBS tell,
As *quickly, slowly, badly, well*;
The PREPOSITION shows relation,
As *in* the street or *at* the station;
CONJUNCTIONS join, in many ways,
Sentences, words, *or* phrase *and* phrase;
The INTERJECTION cries out, '*Hark!*
I need an exclamation mark!'

> An old children's rhyme for
> remembering the parts of speech

Nouns

Traditionally, **nouns** are defined as 'naming words', or the names of persons, animals, places or things. This is still a useful definition, as far as it goes. But modern grammarians are interested in describing the function of a word, as well as defining its meaning. They like to clarify what a word does in a sentence before assigning a part of speech to it. For example, look at the nouns in these:

Stop the watch!   Watch the stop!
They threw out the rubbish.   They rubbished his throw.

Stop, *watch*, *throw* and *rubbish* may be verbs and they may also be nouns – their function in the sentence dictates their part of speech. It is important to remember that the same word can do different things in different places.

Types of noun – proper or common

The words *city* and *country* are called **common nouns**; there are lots of cities and countries in the world. But words like *Moscow* and *Russia* are called **proper nouns**, because there is only one particular country called *Russia* and only one *Moscow*. Similarly, *woman* and *man* are common nouns; there are lots of them too. But *Eliza* and *Augustus* are proper nouns (and also proper names), and *Eliza Doolittle* and *Augustus Montague Toplady* are proper names too, because they refer to very particular individuals. They are specific, or proper, to them alone. Proper nouns require the use of an initial capital letter, common nouns do not.

Sometimes proper nouns have found their way into the language as common nouns:

He is a proper *Scrooge*.
This isn't the *Paris* I used to know.
I used to know three different *John Smiths*.

Types of nouns – abstract or concrete

Nouns may be either **concrete**, when they refer to things you can touch (*nails, cabbage, chocolate, table, tyres*), or they may be **abstract**, when they refer to ideas or concepts (*beauty, truth, Marxism, theology*).

Types of nouns – singular or plural

Most English noun endings indicate a difference between 'one' (**singular**) and 'more than one' (**plural**). The vast majority of them add *-s* or *-es* to show the plural form. If they end in a consonant + *y*, they change that to *-ies*:

Singular	Plural
book	books
dog	dogs
banana	bananas

tree	trees
bush	bushes
kiss	kisses
berry	berries
fairy	fairies

A few English nouns are **irregular**, and form their plurals in other ways, by changing their vowel, by adding -*en*, or by following a foreign rule:

Singular	Plural
man	men
woman	women
child	children
ox	oxen
foot	feet
tooth	teeth
goose	geese
mouse	mice
stimulus	stimuli
bacillus	bacilli
larva	larvae
criterion	criteria
automaton	automata

A few nouns ending with -*f* form plurals with -*ves*:

Singular	Plural
loaf	loaves
wolf	wolves

Similarly with words like *leaf, thief, scarf, hoof*.

Some nouns have two plural forms. *Brother* has *brothers* or the older form *brethren*. The latter form is now used only in a religious context. Other words with two plural forms are:

■

Singular	Plural
appendix	{ appendixes (anatomical) { appendices (literary)
formula	{ formulas { formulae
focus	{ focuses { foci

Some nouns are used only in the singular:

news   chemistry
snooker   mathematics
music   physics

and other scientific subjects. Other nouns are used only in the plural:

scissors   trousers
jeans   thanks
congratulations   police
cattle   vermin

To refer to any of the latter in the singular, use constructions such as:

a pair of scissors/jeans/trousers
a police*woman*

Types of noun – countable or uncountable

- Nouns are **countable** if:

  they can be preceded by *a*: *a car*
  they can be both singular and plural: *a dog, dogs*
  they can be counted: *one taxi, two taxis, twenty taxis*

- Nouns are **uncountable** if:

  they are preceded by *some* rather than *a*: *some salt, some marmalade*
  they are not normally counted or pluralised: *two butters, eleven flours*

Most uncountable nouns denote commodities or notions that tend not to be counted out as individual objects. We say *two oranges* or *six apples* (countable), but we don't normally say *two butters* or *six breads* (uncountable). For uncountable commodities we have to bring in other forms of measurement, such as:

a *bag/spoonful/ton* of flour
one/two/three *grains* of sand
a *piece* of information/music

a *slice* of bread/cake/beef
a *ton* of rice/cement/rubbish
an *ounce* of curry powder

Occasionally, nouns may be either countable or uncountable, depending on the context. Look at these:

I need *a pound of sugar.* (uncountable)
One sugar or two? (countable)
I never eat *cake.* (uncountable)
Here are *two nice chocolate cakes.* (countable)
Light travels faster than *sound.* (uncountable)
Please switch off *the lights.* (countable)

Noun gender

Unlike many other languages (such as French or German or Latin), the English language makes little use of grammatical **gender**. English nouns are grouped according to the three 'natural' genders, and classified accordingly. So *a man* is classified as **masculine**, *a woman* as **feminine**, and *a table* as **neuter**.

The gender of the noun demands the use of the appropriate pronoun:

The man was wounded. *He* had been shot.
The woman was unhurt. *She* had had a lucky escape.
The car was a write-off. *It* had crashed into a large beech tree.

Some nouns have **dual gender**. They refer to categories of people or animals without indicating gender. Nouns like *artist, singer, cousin, baby, adult, child, parent, dog, student, teacher, engineer, secretary* are all in this category. Without additional context clues, it is difficult to know which singular pronoun should accompany these nouns.

Traditionally, *he* was an acceptable pronoun for both sexes, but nowadays many people label this as **sexist language**. So now it is best not to say:

Each passenger must ensure that *he* has all *his* hand luggage with *him.*
Each applicant must sign *his* name at the bottom of the page.
Each student must check that *he* has answered three questions.

Writers nowadays either put these kinds of sentence in the plural, and use *they/their* instead of *he/his*; or they use a rather clumsy but non-sexist construction which is now widespread:

Passenger*s* must ensure that *they* have all *their* hand luggage with *them.*
Each passenger must ensure that *s/he* has all *her/his* hand luggage with *her/him.*

It is also increasingly common to meet this kind of blatant change from singular noun to plural pronoun:

Each passenger must ensure that they have all their hand luggage with them.

This is not recommended. It is far better to rephrase your statements completely.

There is more on this subject under **pronouns**, p. 12.

Noun case

The **case system** of noun endings comes from Latin grammar, where nouns were described as having six cases: **nominative**, **vocative**, **accusative**, **genitive**, **dative** and **ablative**. Latin noun endings were very important, because it was these which showed the noun's relationship to the other words in the Latin sentence.

English nouns can of course do everything that Latin nouns could do, but in English it is mainly word order and prepositions which signal a noun's function in the sentence. Unlike Latin, therefore, there is no need in English to learn case tables like the following:

Case	English	Latin	Latin
Nom.	girl/boy	puella	puer
Voc.	O, girl/boy	puella	puer
Acc.	girl/boy	puellam	puerum
Gen.	girl's/boy's	puellae	pueri
Dat.	to/for a girl/boy	puellae	puero
Abl.	by/with/from a girl/boy	puella	puero

English, as the table shows, has only two case endings: the **common** case ending and the **genitive**.

The genitive case signals possession or ownership. In most singular nouns, it is made by adding *s* preceded by an apostrophe. For plural nouns already ending with *s*, it is made by the addition of an apostrophe:

Barbara's bike
the boys' bikes

The alternative genitive construction is to use *of*:

the ship's crew
the crew *of* the ship

The choice between using the genitive case or the *of* construction is based on factors of gender and personal style. Proper names and animate beings tend to take the genitive ending, and inanimate objects the *of* construction. Usually, you would not say *the bike of Fred* or *the book's pages*; *Fred's bike* and *the pages of the book* would be commoner. In a case like *the ship's crew* versus *the crew of the ship*, you can grammatically distinguish a stronger emphasis on *crew* in the former, on *ship* in the latter.

There is more on case under **possessive pronouns**, pp. 11–12.

Collective or mass nouns

Collective nouns refer to groups of animate beings, such as *class, committee, council, government* or *herd*. They are singular nouns, but they carry a plural connotation. They are used when the whole group or gathering is being considered (rather than individual members of the group).

Being singular, collective nouns usually take singular verbs or pronouns:

The team played *its* heart out. *It was* magnificent.
The jury reached *its* verdict, and pronounced *its* view.

This agreement should be consistent, and singulars and plurals should not be mixed. Avoid, for example:

The team played *their* heart out . . .
The jury reached *its* decision, and pronounced *their* view.

Mass nouns such as *grass, hair, timber* are like collective nouns, but they refer to inanimate entities.

There is a large stock of collective nouns specific to certain animals and groups. Some of the best known include:

A drove of ponies
A flock of sheep
A herd of cattle, pigs
A gaggle of geese (when they are on the ground)
A skein of geese (when flying)
A nest of vipers, ants, rabbits
A troop of lions, monkeys, cavalry, fairies
A pack of wolves, hounds, submarines
A team of oxen, mules, horses
A shoal of herring, mackerel
A school of whales, porpoises
A brood of chickens
A litter of puppies, kittens, piglets
A congregation of church-people
An audience of concert-goers
A crowd of spectators

A horde of savages
A company of actors, artists
A gang of workmen, prisoners
A carillon of bells

Suffixes that indicate a noun

Certain word endings, or **suffixes**, are often used to form nouns, with some of the commonest being the following:

-age mile*age*, us*age*, wast*age*
-al arriv*al*, committ*al*, dismiss*al*, rebutt*al*, remov*al*
-ant combat*ant*, contest*ant*, entr*ant*
-ation admir*ation*, connot*ation*, explan*ation*, irrig*ation*
-dom bore*dom*, duke*dom*, king*dom*, star*dom*, wis*dom*
-eer mutin*eer*, profit*eer*, racket*eer*
-ency complac*ency*, insolv*ency*
-er explor*er*, foreign*er*, New York*er*, runn*er*, speak*er*
-ery green*ery*, knav*ery*, slav*ery*
-ese Chin*ese*, Japan*ese*, Vietnam*ese*
-ess enchantr*ess*, host*ess*, waitr*ess*
-ette kitchen*ette*, laundr*ette*, usher*ette*
-ful belly*ful*, jug*ful*, spoon*ful*
-hood child*hood*, father*hood*, spinster*hood*
-ian Arcad*ian*, Canad*ian*, Orcad*ian*
-ion act*ion*, express*ion*, suggest*ion*
-ing carpet*ing*, floor*ing*, moor*ing*
-ism ideal*ism*, loyal*ism*, national*ism*
-ist commun*ist*, Mao*ist*, social*ist*, union*ist*
-ite Ludd*ite*, social*ite*, Stalin*ite*, Thatcher*ite*, Trotsky*ite*
-ity advers*ity*, hostil*ity*, pervers*ity*, stupid*ity*
-let book*let*, flat*let*, pig*let*
-ling duck*ling*, gos*ling*, under*ling*
-ment employ*ment*, enjoy*ment*, excite*ment*, pay*ment*
-ness cleanli*ness*, good*ness*, happi*ness*, wicked*ness*
-ocrat bureau*crat*, demo*crat*, Euro*crat*, merito*crat*, pluto*crat*
-or object*or*, prospect*or*, surviv*or*
-ship friend*ship*, owner*ship*, steward*ship*
-ster gang*ster*, trick*ster*, young*ster*
-ty beau*ty*, cruel*ty*, pover*ty*

For **suffix spelling rules**, see pp. 100–1.

Compound nouns

One of the commonest types of word formation occurs with the joining together of two words to make a **compound noun**. These may be:

- pairs of words:

biscuit tin	beer bottle
fairy tale	face towel
breakfast time	bear cub
coffee jug	shoe polish
plant pot	

- hyphenated words:

passer-by	knuckle-duster
holiday-maker	engine-driver
bull's-eye	mid-air
spin-off	tin-opener
hanger-on	fire-eater

- single words:

babysitter	doorstep
battlefield	housewife
bearskin	seaweed
clergyman	teapot

All these words are at different stages in the process by which *ground sheet* becomes *ground-sheet* and finally *groundsheet*. Even dictionaries disagree about which of these words require a hyphen and which do not, with Americans slightly less keen on hyphens than UK writers. Generally, hyphens are favoured for longer words, or to avoid an odd spelling like *fire-eater*. Single, hyphenless words tend to indicate a well-established, frequently used word often made up of two short one-syllable words (*bedroom, bloodshed, teaspoon*).

Perhaps the best advice to give with compound nouns in these circumstances is to check their spellings with a dictionary, to be consistent in one's own practice, and to be watchful of other writers' practices.

Other compounds are:

- combinations of two or more words into longer **noun phrases** (see below):

down-and-out	colonel-in-chief
mother-in-law	Berwick-upon-Tweed
man-of-war	Stow-on-the-Wold
whisky-and-soda	

- combinations of letters and words:

S-bend	U-turn
T-junction	X-ray
T-square	

For more on compounding, see **hyphenation**, pp. 129–32.

Noun phrases

A group of words centring on a noun is called a **noun phrase**. It can appear at the beginning, the middle or the end of a sentence, and as **subject**, **object** or **complement** (see p. 74). Noun phrases consist of the noun on its own or accompanied by other words that modify its meaning.

Headword	Rest of sentence
<u>**Trees**</u>	live a long time.
<u>Many **trees**</u>	live a long time.
<u>Most of those pine **trees**</u>	live a long time.
<u>All the coniferous **trees** in that gully</u>	live a long time.

The noun phrases in the above examples are underlined. It will be noted that they can be extremely varied in their make-up. In the following extract, all the noun phrases are underlined:

When <u>the rains</u> stopped at <u>Wimbledon yesterday evening</u>, <u>the grunting</u> began, and <u>Monika Seles</u>, <u>who reached the women's semi-finals here for the first time</u>, was accused by <u>her beaten opponent</u> of putting <u>her fellow players at a disadvantage</u> when <u>her grunting</u> reaches <u>a crescendo</u>. <u>Seles</u> was called over by <u>the umpire after the eighth game of the second set</u>, and asked to keep <u>the noise</u> down. <u>The crowd behind the umpire's chair</u> cheered when <u>the warning</u> was issued.

There is more on phrases, including noun phrases, on pp. 60–5.

Pronouns

John Brown is very tall. *He* is a big lad now.
Sally has arrived. *She* is here at last.
The house is very old. *It* is falling down.

A **pronoun** substitutes for a noun. It is usually defined as a word that stands for a noun, or a noun phrase, or something relating to one. The meaning expressed by a sentence containing pronouns tends to be less specific than the meaning of a sentence containing nouns.

Personal and possessive pronouns

John took the stone and threw *it*.
Then *he* phoned Sally and invited *her* to supper.
'Where shall *we* meet?' *he* asked.
Here are the drinks. *This* is *mine*. *Hers* is the sherry.
Theirs is the third house on the left.

These are **personal pronouns**. Of all the different types of pronouns they occur most frequently. You use personal pronouns to refer back to something or someone that has already been mentioned. You also use them to refer to people and things directly. They are called 'personal' because they refer to the people or things involved in the text.

There are three types of personal pronouns: **subject pronouns**, **object pronouns** and **possessive pronouns**. As the names imply, subject pronouns are used as the subject of a sentence; object pronouns as the object of a sentence; and possessive pronouns are used to say that a person or thing belongs to or is connected with another person or thing:

	Singular			Plural		
subject pronouns	I	you	he/she/it	we	you	they
object pronouns	me	you	him/her/it	us	you	them
possessive pronouns:						
used with nouns	my	your	his/her/its	our	your	their
used instead of nouns	mine	yours	his/hers	ours	yours	theirs

Pronouns indicate **person**. The **first person** in the sentence is, or includes, the speaker/writer referring to himself or herself. Thus *I*, *me*, *my*, *mine*, *we*, *us*, *ours*, are the **first-person pronouns**.

You and *yours* are the **second-person pronouns**. The second person in the sentence is the person or thing being addressed, and excludes the speaker/writer.

He, *she* and *it* are the **third-person pronouns**. The third person in the sentence includes all third parties and excludes speaker and addressee. (Note that 'person' in this context can refer to things as well as persons.)

Pronouns can also reflect the possessive case, as the table on p. 11 shows. The **possessive pronouns** are *mine, yours, his, hers, its, ours* and *theirs*. Note that no apostrophe is used in writing a possessive pronoun: *it's* is not a pronoun, but an abbreviation of 'it is'. (*Her's* and *your's* are also very common spelling errors.) The only exception to this rule is the formal pronoun *one*, meaning 'people in general':

One should listen to *one's* conscience, shouldn't *one*?

Pronoun gender, sexist language and generic 'he'

he/she	his/hers
him/her	himself/herself

Two of the third-person pronouns reflect **gender**. This is not normally a problem area unless a writer refers to *he* or *him* when in fact the reference should be to men and women both. As we have seen, in certain contexts gender-specific pronouns are avoided nowadays:

The applicant must pay *his* own travelling expenses.
If a pupil fails the test, *he* will receive extra tuition.
Everyone must do *his* best.

Unless it is known that all the applicants and pupils and people referred to in the above sentences are indeed male, these sentences would nowadays tend to be rephrased. The easiest way to do this may be to render the sentences in the plural, or to say 'his or her':

Applicant*s* must pay *their* own travelling expenses.
Pupil*s* failing the test will receive extra tuition.
Everyone must do *his or her* best.

But idiomatic sayings like 'Everything comes to him who waits', 'He who hesitates is lost', 'He laughs best who laughs last' (and many others) should perhaps remind us that the generic pronoun *he* was an acceptable English usage for several hundreds of years – and that it cannot simply be expunged retrospectively from the language.

Reflexive pronouns

Tell me all about *yourself*.
He should be ashamed of *himself*.
John told the boy to get *himself* a haircut.
She has just bought *herself* a new computer.
They are making fools of *themselves*.

These are all **reflexive pronouns**. They refer back to a noun or pronoun elsewhere in the sentence. The complete list of reflexive pronouns is:

singular	myself	yourself	himself/herself/itself
plural	ourselves	yourselves	themselves

Sometimes a reflexive pronoun is used for emphasis:

The house *itself* was little more than a shack.
The prime minister *himself* is going to pay us a visit.
I saw him *myself*, with my own eyes.

Sometimes a reflexive pronoun is used to show that someone has done something alone and/or without any help:

He cooked the meal *himself*.
Did you build it *yourself*?
She was sitting in a quiet corner *all by herself*.

Reciprocal pronouns

They accused *each other* of the betrayal.
The Browns and the Smiths were always getting at *one another*.

These pronouns are used to convey a two-way relationship.

Demonstrative pronouns

This looks like an interesting book.
Those are John's shoes. *These* are mine.
Where on earth did you get *that*?

The **demonstrative pronouns** are *this, that, these* and *those*. They are used mainly to point to things. *This* and *these* usually refer to something nearby; *that* and *those* to something farther away.

Remember that these words can also function as **determiners** (see pp. 24–6):

Where did you get *that* hat?

Demonstrative pronouns are also frequently used to introduce or refer to particular people:

Who's *this*?
These are my daughters, Judith and Joan.
Was *that* Elizabeth on the telephone just now?

Demonstrative pronouns may refer back or forward in a conversation:

These are some of the topics I hope to cover next week . . .
That was an interesting comment John made just now.

The one or *this one* are used to stand in for a subject or object and function as a sort of demonstrative pronoun:

I'd like *this one*/*This one* will do.
Take *this one* here, not *that one* over there.
His car is *the old green one*.

Indefinite pronouns

He waited an hour before *anybody* came.
Is *anything* the matter?
Is *anyone* there?
Someone's been sitting in my chair.
Would you care for *something* to eat?
There was *nothing anyone* could do.

Indefinite pronouns refer to people or things without specifying exactly who or what they are. The list of indefinite pronouns is:

anybody	everybody	nobody	somebody
anyone	everyone	no one	someone
anything	everything	nothing	something

Note that *no one* is usually written as two words. All the others are compound words.

Occasionally words like *so* and *such* function as indefinite pronouns:

I hope *so*.
Such is life!

Interrogative pronouns

Who said that? (subject)
What happened to you? (subject)
Whose are those filthy shoes? (possessive)
Which of these books did you most enjoy? (object)
To whom did you give that book? (indirect object)

These are the main **interrogative pronouns**. They are used interrogatively, to ask questions, and are sometimes called *wh*-words.

Who, whom

The subject pronoun is *who* and the object pronoun is *whom*:

Who is there?
I can't see *who* is there.
To *whom* did you speak?
There's the man to *whom* I spoke.

This rule is breaking down in informal spoken English, where we often hear:

Who did you speak to?
There's the man *who* I spoke to.

Whose, who's

These forms are confused because they sound the same. *Who's* is the contracted form of *who is*:

Who's afraid of the big bad wolf?
I sent a fax to my boss *who's* abroad.

Whose is a pronoun, or a possessive adjective:

Here's the man *whose* house was burgled.
Whose is it?

What, which

What and *which* are used to ask questions about things:

What on earth was he talking about?
Which of the two cars do you prefer?

If *what* or *which* are immediately linked to a noun, they become **interrogative adjectives**:

Which car did he prefer?
What topics were on yesterday's agenda?

Relative pronouns

There was an old woman *who* lived in a shoe.
The shoe *that* she inhabited was, fortunately, enormous.
Here's the boy *whose* bicycle was stolen.
She destroyed all the letters *which* she had been sent.
She was the only person *in whom* I could confide.

The five **relative pronouns** are used to introduce **subordinate clauses** (see p. 78).

Distributive pronouns

These refer to members of a group or class:

All (of them) went to the pop concert.
Both of you should go along too.
Each of us received a reward.
Either of them might fall off the rock.
Neither of them will forget that climbing experience.

The distributive pronouns are usually followed by *of* + *pronoun*.

I and me [the first-person pronouns]

There is uncertainty in many speakers about when to use *I* (subject) and when to use *me* (object). This probably stems from the childhood recollection of being corrected for answering the question *Who is there?* with the words *It's me.* Strictly speaking, we should say *It is I.*

It is correct to say *John gave it to me*, and so it is also correct to say *John gave it to Sally and me.*

It is correct to say *I have been playing tennis*, and so it is also correct to say *Sally and I have been playing tennis.*

To decide which is right in the following, leave the other person out of the sentence and imagine it in the singular. Then you will know whether to use *I* or *me*:

John, Tom, Wajid and ―― were all born in September.
You and ―― are the only ones who can speak French.
Can Sally and ―― sit here?
Joan and Maureen are playing against Pam and ――.
In front of my wife and ―― sat the Browns.
This go-cart was made by Andrew and ――; Tom and ―― are going to make another one.

Pronouns misplaced

Writers often fail to check what they have written. One of the commonest errors they make is to fail to put the pronoun in the correct place – as near as possible to the noun to which it refers. The results can be quite ludicrous:

We met an old man and a little boy whose beard was long and white.
Complete the form with the required information about your house, which should then be sent to the town clerk.
We have a cupboard for storing bread that was made a hundred years ago.

Norfolk has many quiet and unfrequented villages to which thousands of visitors go each year.

Nelson was greatly feared by the French, in whose honour Trafalgar Day is still celebrated.

How should these sentences be written? Here are some alternatives, which make the sense clearer:

We met an old man, whose beard was long and white, and a little boy.

Send the form to the town clerk after completing it with the required information about your house.

We have a cupboard — for storing bread — that was made a hundred years ago.

Each year thousands of visitors go to Norfolk, which has many quiet and unfrequented villages.

Nelson, in whose honour Trafalgar Day is still celebrated, was greatly feared by the French.

Suitable punctuation, in addition to well-placed pronouns, helps get the meaning across. See also the sections on the **comma** (p. 122) and **dash** (p. 127) to mark off parentheses.

Adjectives

Adjectives are words that describe or give information about nouns or pronouns. They are therefore often said to **modify**, or limit, nouns and pronouns. Adjectives are usually easy to recognise in a sentence, often describing or modifying an object's size, colour or amount, as in:

Size: a *huge* ship, a *tiny* flower, a *narrow* window

Colour: a *blue* balloon, *white* bread, a *red* alert

Amount or number: *twelve* months, *one* year, *second* prize, *many* problems, *few* assets (these last examples are also called **determiners**; see p. 27 for more on this)

A second feature of adjectives is that they can have **comparative** and **superlative** forms, formed in one of two different ways:

Adjective	Comparative form	Superlative form
fat	**fatt**er	**fatt**est
black	**black**er	**black**est
fattening	**more** fattening	**most** fattening
intelligent	**more** intelligent	**most** intelligent

There is more on this in **Comparison of adjectives**, below.

Thirdly, adjectives can be modified by an adverb, as in:

a *very* old man
He is *extremely* old.

Position of adjectives

Adjectives can occur in various positions. They can be placed immediately before a noun:

a *delightful* evening
an *endless* journey through a *darkened* landscape
a *long* drink of *cool* water for a *thirsty* camel

These are called **attributive adjectives**.

Adjectives can also be joined to their nouns by a verb:

The dogs were *noisy*.
They seemed *hungry*.
The result of the game looks *doubtful*.

These are called **predicative adjectives**, so called because they help the verb to form the predicate of a sentence (the predicate being everything but the subject; for more on **predicates**, see p. 72).

Less frequently, adjectives can go directly after the noun:

The people *concerned* should notify the police.
the president-*elect*
'The River Weser, *deep* and *wide* . . .' (Browning)
'Something *old*, something *new*, something *borrowed*, something *blue* . . .'

These are called **post-modifiers**.

Certain fixed terms and technical designations also have adjectives following their noun:

letters patent	body politic
heir apparent	time immemorial
poet laureate	lords temporal and spiritual

These fixed terms tend to be **borrowings** (see p. 86) from other languages, but they have extended to certain other fixed phrases:

Friday next/last	for the time being
the sum outstanding	motivated by greed pure and simple
the amount accruing	whisky galore

Very occasionally a plural is required for one of these forms, and it is the noun – not the adjective – which pluralises, as in court*s* martial.

Comparison of adjectives

Most adjectives can be used comparatively in one of three ways. The qualities they describe may be compared to a higher degree, to the same degree, or to a lower degree.

Comparison of adjectives to a higher degree is shown by adding *-er* and *-est*, or *more* and *most*, to the absolute or base form of the adjective. The **comparative** form is used to compare two items (e.g. *older, more beautiful*), and the **superlative** form compares three or more items (e.g. *oldest, most beautiful*):

Andrew has an *old* car.
It is *older* than John's. (comparative)
It is the *oldest* car in the rally. (superlative)
It was a *beautiful* day.
It was a *more beautiful* day than Monday. (comparative)
It was the *most beautiful* day of the holiday. (superlative)

Comparison of adjectives to the same degree is shown by using the phrase *as . . . as*, or *so . . . as*:

His car is not *as* old *as* all that. It's not *so* old.

Comparison to a lower degree is indicated by the use of *less* and *least*:

Her contribution was *useful*.
John's contribution was *less useful* than Joan's.
Neil's was the *least useful* contribution to the whole debate.

Most adjectives are regular when it comes to forming comparatives and superlatives, and the choice between *-er/-est* and *more/most* is dictated by how long the adjective is. For example, one-syllable adjectives (*slim, bold, shy, black*) tend to take *-er/-est*. Two-syllable adjectives may appear in either form, with some preferring the *-er/-est* form: *clever, gentle, narrow, happy*, etc. Three-syllable adjectives (or longer) almost always use *more/most*; only if they begin with *un-* (*unlikely, unhappy*) do they sometimes take *-er/-est*.

Remember that some adjectives are irregular, including *good/better/best, bad/worse/worst, little/less/least, much* or *many/more/most*.

Some adjectives do not normally compare. They have only an absolute meaning. These include words like *real, right, perfect, unique, elder* (statesman), *mere, utter* (idiot), *late* (president), *former, occasional*, etc.

Sequencing adjectives

If several adjectives are wanted to modify a noun, they tend to be placed in certain sequences or patterns. Look at the following, but remember too that English is very flexible, and that different emphases can permit all sorts of permutations:

> 5   4   3   2   1
> a brand-new green Japanese enamel birdcage
>
> 5   4   3   2   1
> an enormous nineteenth-century New York brownstone office building
>
> 3   2   1
> a small monthly cash payment

Working back from the noun:

1 Closest to the noun would go any other noun used adjectivally, almost as a compound noun, to indicate purpose (*office building*).
2 In second position from the noun would go any other noun used adjectivally, indicating materials (*brownstone, enamel*).
3 Third from the noun would go indications of nationality or origin (*Japanese, New York*).
4 Then comes colour, or vintage, or frequency (*brand-new, nineteenth-century, monthly*).
5 Last come adjectives indicating age, size, shape, temperature (*enormous, small*).

Multiple adjectives can also be found after the verb, as postmodifiers:

> The house was *old, damp* and *smelly*.
> We felt *cold, tired* and *hungry*.

Interrogative adjectives

Which? and *what?* are the **interrogative adjectives**. They ask for information about their nouns:

> *What* plans do you have for the holidays?
> *Which* book are you reading just now?
> I saw a dog. *Which* dog did you see?

Interrogative adjectives often appear to be asking a speaker to 'fill in' the qualities of a noun. So they have been called 'blank cheque' adjectives:

> Q: *Which* dress did you buy?
> A: The *tie-dyed, blue and purple African cotton* one.

Demonstrative adjectives

This, that, these and *those* are called **demonstrative adjectives**. As their name indicates, they are used for pointing out or demonstrating the nouns which they modify:

That cottage was Wordsworth's.
These daffodils are most unusual.
This view of Windermere is my favourite.
Those hills in the distance are the Pennines.

Adjectives or nouns?

Sometimes adjectives can be used as nouns. This mostly happens when they appear with the definite article:

They have joined the ranks of *the unemployed* and *the homeless.*
We pray for *the sick* and *the poor* of all nations.
Give me *your tired, your poor,* your huddled masses . . . (Emma Lazarus)

Sometimes colour adjectives function as nouns:

She won't wear *green.*
Green is a restful colour.
A brighter shade of *green*

Conversely, nouns can function as adjectives:

the *city* hall, the *town* clock, the *ocean* liner

Nouns used adjectivally do not usually require to take a hyphen. (For more on **hyphenation**, see pp. 129–32.)

Adjectives or adverbs?

Several words function as both adjectives and adverbs. The context will indicate to which part of speech they belong:

Adjective	Adverb
It was **early** morning.	They left **early.**
It was a **wet** morning.	It looks **wet.**
They took a **late** bus.	They left **late.**

Adjectives or participles?

Again, there are some words which function as both adjectives and verb participles, and we have to examine the context before deciding to which part of speech they belong:

Adjective	Participle
We sat by the **roaring** fire.	The fire was **roaring** fiercely.
Her argument was **confusing**.	You are **confusing** two separate issues.
The news is **worrying**.	The dog was **worrying** the sheep.

Adjectives with prepositions

Some adjectives are used with a prepositional phrase in the following ways:

She is very *good at* languages.
I was *upset at* the decision.
He was *afraid of* his enemies.
He's terribly *fond of* you.
It was *rude of* them to walk out.
They were *rude to* her for no obvious reason.
She was pretty *angry about* the result.
You are *responsible for* this mess.

These are sometimes called postmodifying adjectives, because they come after the verb.

Common adjectival word endings

Certain word endings (or suffixes) commonly indicate an adjective. These include:

-ish redd*ish*, green*ish*, young*ish*, small*ish*, round*ish*, child*ish*, fever*ish*, styl*ish*, fool*ish*, owl*ish*, devil*ish*, Brit*ish*, Span*ish*, Ir*ish*

-ful use*ful*, meaning*ful*, wonder*ful*, bash*ful*, sin*ful*, plenti*ful*, fear*ful*, skil*ful*, beauti*ful*, fright*ful*

-ing bor*ing*, charm*ing*, middl*ing*, shock*ing*

-less use*less*, meaning*less*, fear*less*, hat*less*, sun*less*

-like war*like*, glass-*like*

-ly king*ly*, saint*ly*, god*ly*, scholar*ly*, mother*ly*, hour*ly*, queen*ly*

-y sunn*y*, rain*y*, dust*y*, sand*y*, ston*y*, blood*y*, dirt*y*, tast*y*, hast*y*, nast*y*

-ous danger*ous*, glori*ous*, plente*ous*, courte*ous*, chivalr*ous*, tempestu*ous*, nutriti*ous*, delici*ous*, poison*ous*

-ic volcan*ic*, magnet*ic*, hero*ic*, microscop*ic*, systemat*ic*, (a)pathet*ic*, asthmat*ic*, atom*ic*, athlet*ic*, histor*ic*, dramat*ic*

-en flax*en*, wood*en*, molt*en*, braz*en*, wax*en*

-able/-ible charit*able*, hospit*able*, break*able*, indescrib*able*, defin*able*, eat*able*, incompar*able*, ed*ible*, vis*ible*, aud*ible*, tang*ible*, terr*ible*, ac-cess*ible*

-al herb*al*, region*al*, industri*al*, centr*al*, coloni*al*, music*al*, logic*al*, critic*al*, commerci*al*, provinci*al*, confidenti*al*, habitu*al*, vit*al*, norm*al*, dism*al*, abysm*al*

-ar circul*ar*, angul*ar*, molecul*ar*, muscul*ar*, sol*ar*, lun*ar*

-worthy blame*worthy*, news*worthy*, air*worthy*

-proof rain*proof*, bomb*proof*, water*proof*

There is more on adjective suffixes in Chapter 3, on **word formation**. For **suffix spelling rules**, see pp. 100–1.

Compound adjectives and hyphens

The main thing to note here is that adjectives are usually hyphenated when they precede a noun, to remind readers of their function. So:

Compound adjective	Other use
It was a first-class performance.	She is in the first class.
He broke his six-inch ruler.	His ruler was six inches long.
Ninth-grade students	Students in the ninth grade
He uses state-of-the-art equipment.	What is the current state of the art?

The adjective phrase

These are adjective-equivalents, and they operate just like adjectives in that they qualify or describe nouns. For example:

The shoes are not *the right size*.
The way *through the woods* is dark and long.
Her eyes were *the size of saucers*.
That car is *smaller than mine*.
What part of speech are these words?

There is more on this under **phrases** (pp. 63–4).

Abuse of adjectives

Adjectives have been described as the enemy of the noun. That is to say, at the hands of wordy writers and speakers they often add nothing of substance to the nouns they modify. (A verbose writer might have written, 'nothing of *real* substance'.) We know how common it is to hear references to a subject being 'under *active* consideration at this *precise* point of time'. And how often do we hear that there is no cause for *undue* alarm (as if a modicum of alarm is appropriate), or that the outbreak of X poses no *serious* threat to our safety (perhaps just a teensy-weensy threat?). It is one thing to talk about a *diplomatic* crisis or a *naval* disaster; it is quite another to talk about a *serious* crisis or a *dreadful* disaster. Crises are serious and disasters are dreadful by definition. All these popular usages are examples of waffle; they are superfluous, and better avoided.

Determiners

Determiners, like adjectives, give information about nouns and pronouns. But they do not strictly speaking *describe* nouns and pronouns – which is one of the definitions of an adjective – and that is one reason why modern grammarians like to distinguish them from adjectives.

Determiners were so named because they *determine* the number and definiteness of the noun phrase to which they are attached. The commonest determiners are in the following categories:

- articles: *a, an, the*
- demonstratives: *this, that, these, those*
- possessives: *my, your, his/her/its, our, their; mine, yours, theirs*
- numbers: *one, two, three . . . first, second, third . . .*
- indefinite determiners: including *all, any, both, each, either, every, few, less, more, enough, neither, no, several, some, only*

Determiners are sometimes called 'function words', because they have very little meaning in themselves – they merely perform a function in the sentence. True adjectives, on the other hand, are called 'content words' – because they have some sort of finite content, or meaning, when they stand alone.

The article

There are two articles in English – the **definite article** (*the*), and the **indefinite article** (*a*, or, preceding a word beginning with a vowel, *an*).

The definite article

The definite article in English has the following functions:

- It refers back to a person or thing already identified:

  You described a man with a beard. Is this *the* man?
  Jason built a special ship for his voyage. *The* ship was called Argo.

This is called **anaphoric** reference. An author's use of something as apparently insignificant as the definite instead of the indefinite article can have a major impact on the resonance of a text. (See **Notes on 'the'**, p. 28.)

- It defines or marks someone or something as the only one:

the Bible　　　　　　　　　*the* House of Commons
the Lord God　　　　　　　　*the* Leader of *the* Opposition
the prophet Muhammad　　　*the* Prime Minister
the holy Koran　　　　　　　*the* Tsar of Russia

- It indicates a whole class or group or clan:

the Reptile family　　　　　*the* English
the working class　　　　　*the* Armstrongs and *the* Percys

- When stressed (and pronounced *thee*), it indicates uniqueness:

Callas was *the* soprano of her generation.
It was *the* pub for live folk music and real ale.

The indefinite article

The indefinite article *a/an* has the following functions:

- It is a form of *one*:

A hundred years ago (not two hundred)
A mile wide
Wait *a* minute

If you wish to stress *one* – rather than a lot – you exaggerate the pronunciation, *ay*:

Take *a* biscuit, not a fistful!

- It singles out a particular and specific person or thing:

I'm going to tell you *a* story about *a* girl called Sally. She lived in *a* red sandstone terraced house . . .

- It has the indefinite meaning of *any*:

It was as big as *a* horse.
A peninsula is surrounded by water on three sides.

- It is distributive:

Fifty pence *a* kilo (= per kilo, each kilo)
Ten pence *a* slice

A is used before an initial consonant sound, *an* before an initial vowel sound, a rule which applies regardless of spelling:

A chair, *a* seat, *a* bed, *a* horse
An igloo, *an* egg, *an* ostrich, *an* heir, *an* SOS, *an* LP

There has been some disagreement in the past about words like *hotel*, *hereditary*, *habitual* and *historic* – should the 'h' sound be pronounced, thus requiring the words to be preceded by *a*? Or should it not be pronounced, leaving the words to be preceded by *an*? The consensus nowadays seems to favour *a hotel* over *an hotel*, though the latter is not wrong.

The zero article

The absence of an article is sometimes referred to as the **zero article**, and it helps us to refer to generic qualities. Thus:

Lions are dangerous animals.
(*Compare* **The lion is** *a* **dangerous animal.**)

The zero article is also used idiomatically:

They went by train/car/bus.
Have breakfast/dinner/lunch.
Go to bed/hospital/church.
At sea/work/home
In class/hospital

Demonstratives

The **demonstratives** are *this/that* (singular) and *these/those* (plural). *This/these* indicate nearness to the speaker, and *that/those* indicate distance from the speaker. The demonstratives are called determiners only if they precede a noun. If they stand alone, standing in place of a noun, then they are described as pronouns:

Determiners	Pronouns
Give me **that** gun.	Give **that** to me.
This girl is my best friend.	**This** is my best friend.

A special use of *this* is as a time marker:

Let's try and meet *this* **week.**
Can we fix a time? *This* **Friday?**

Possessives

Possessive markers may be either determiners (if they qualify a noun), or pronouns (if they are standing in for a noun). It all depends on their use in the sentence:

Possessives as determiners	Possessives as pronouns
This is my car.	The car is mine.
his	his.
her	hers.
your	yours.
our	ours.
their	theirs.

Numbers

One, two, three, etc. are called **cardinal numbers**, and they answer the question, *How many?* The **ordinal numbers** are *first, second, third,* etc., and they indicate an order. Numbers usually precede adjectives in a sentence:

ten green bottles
the *six* rowdy youngsters
my *third* shot

Indefinite determiners

These words function as determiners only when they modify a noun. The versions that stand alone are pronouns:

Determiners	Pronouns
All the good work is ruined.	**All** is not lost.
Both climbers are missing.	**Both** are safe and well.
Either bus goes into town.	**Either** is possible.
Neither answer is right.	**Neither** is right.
We see her **every** Tuesday. We have **no** bread.	(These have no equivalents.)
Each man had a gun.	**Each** had a gun.
Few people take holidays here.	**Few** come here on holiday.
Have you **enough** food?	I've had quite **enough**.

Notes on 'the'

- Study this use of the definite article in the opening two paragraphs of Betsy Byars' novel for young people, *The Eighteenth Emergency* (1976):

The pigeons flew out of *the* alley in one long swoop and settled on *the* awning of *the* grocery store. A dog ran out of the alley with a torn Cracker Jack box in his mouth. Then came *the* boy.

The boy was running hard and fast. He stopped at *the* sidewalk, looked both ways, saw that the street was deserted and kept going. The dog caught the boy's fear, and he started running with him . . .

This use of *the* cannot be anaphoric reference – reference back to something which has gone before – since nothing has gone before these opening paragraphs of the novel. But does the reader sit back and wonder 'What pigeons?' or 'What alley?' or 'What boy?' No: the author's skilful use of *the* instead of the more obvious *a* has made the text especially gripping from the very start – which is part of the reason for the novel's appeal.

- Always look at the context of the words you are analysing. *The* looks very simple, and of course usually it is. But what about this sentence:

There's not a single *the* in this sentence.

Here *the* functions as a noun.

Verbs

In many ways the **verb** is the most important of all the parts of speech. This was certainly the Romans' point of view: *verbum* in Latin meant '*the* word', so in this way its pre-eminence is still articulated in all the Romance languages as well as in English.

From school, we remember that verbs are 'doing' words or 'action' words, and for the vast majority of verbs this is a fair description. But we should remember that in addition to the main verbs of 'doing' (*run, jump, walk, stand, shake*), there are also auxiliary or 'helping' verbs (*be, have, do will, can, may, shall, would, could, might, should, must*; see pp. 29–31). Indeed, main verbs and auxiliary verbs are the two key classes of verb.

The following sections look at the verb from a variety of grammatical perspectives.

Verb agreement or concord

The girl *speaks* good English.
The girls *speak* good English.

Concord, or agreement, is the rule that ensures the harmonisation of different grammatical units. **Number concord** is the most important type of concord in English, and ensures that a singular subject is always followed by a singular verb, a plural subject by a plural verb.

The following sentences are wrong because they break the rules of number concord:

The *girl speak* good English.
The *girls speaks* good English.

Apart from the rule of adding -*s* or -*es* in the third-person singular (he, she, it) of English verbs, there is not much left of verb concord in English. We used also to mark the second-person singular (you, or thou) for subject–verb concord:

The day *thou* gavest, Lord . . .
Where art *thou*, Sylvia?

This use has almost died out, and is now found only in poetry, in biblical writing and in certain dialects.

Auxiliary verbs

She *is* planning a visit to India.
I *haven't* seen her since last Tuesday.
Which bus *do* you plan to take?

The main **auxiliary**, or 'helping', verbs are *be*, *have* and *do*. They are used with main verbs to help them form specific tenses, as well as negatives and questions.

Be is used as an auxiliary with the -*ing* form of the main verb to form the continuous:

She *is living* in Poland.
We *were going* to the cinema.

Be is used with the past participle of the main verb to form the passive (see p. 36):

The street *was covered* in mud.
These computers *are made* in America.

Have and *had* are used as auxiliaries along with the past participle to form the past tenses:

I *have changed* my mind.
She *has completed* her course.
I wish we *had visited* St Petersburg.

Be and *have* are also used as auxiliaries to form negative sentences, question forms and the passive:

She *isn't finished* yet.

Haven't you *finished* yet?
Was the wallet *found* in the street?

Do is used as an auxiliary to make negative and question forms:

I *don't smoke. Do* you?
Do you *like* my new shoes?
He *didn't get* the job, *did* he?

See also **modal auxiliary verbs** (below).

Modal auxiliary verbs

Modal verbs are a category of the auxiliaries: they too are 'helping' verbs. They help the main verb to express a range of meanings: possibility, probability, certainty, permission, requests, instructions, suggestions, offers and invitations, wants and wishes, obligation and necessity. The modal verbs are:

can, could	must, ought
shall, should	need to
will, would	be able to
may, might	have (got) to

Modals are very easy in one respect: they have only one form. Below are some examples of modals in use:

● Negatives and questions:

You *may not* walk on the grass.
He *couldn't* stop laughing.
Would you give me a lift into town?

● Possibility (*can, could, may, might*):

Can you unlock this door for me?
This *might* come in useful.
It *could* have been a disastrous accident.
When *may* she get up?

● Probability and certainty (*cannot/can't, must, ought, should, will*):

You *must* be Dr Livingstone.
He *can't* have told me the whole story.
We *ought* to arrive home by noon.
That *must* be the postman now.

● Ability (*can, could, be able to*):

He *cannot* sing for toffee.
He *could* read and write from a very young age.
She *was able* to sign her name with difficulty.
She *couldn't* stop laughing.

- Permission (*can, could, may*):

  You *can* use my car if you want.
  You *may* speak now, John.
  Can I ask a question?

- Instructions and requests (*can, could, will, would*):

  Would you give John a message for me, please?
  Would you do me a favour?
  Could you explain that again for me?
  I *would* like this work finished by Friday.

- Suggestions (*could, may, might, shall*):

  You *could* try again later.
  You *might* like to try this new shampoo.
  You *may* as well start again.
  Shall we change the subject?

- Offers and invitations (*can, could, shall, will, would*):

  Will you have a cup of tea?
  Would you like a biscuit?
  I *could* give you a lift to the shops.

- Obligation and necessity (*must, mustn't, have to, have got to*):

  I *have* to go now.
  I *must* get to the interview in good time.

Finite and non-finite verbs

The dog *barks* when hungry.
It *is barking* now.
It *has been barking* for hours.

A **finite** verb is sometimes called a 'tensed' verb, because it varies for present and past tense. Auxiliaries and modals are finite, as are verb phrases which contain them: *eats, is eating, has eaten, has been eating, was eating, was being eaten* are all finite verb phrases.

Finite verbs have a subject with which they agree in person and number. Clauses with finite verbs are called **finite clauses**, while clauses with non-finite verbs are called **non-finite clauses**:

When I *was first looking* into the matter . . . (finite clause)
After Caesar *had crossed* the Rubicon . . . (finite clause)
On looking into the matter . . . (non-finite clause)
Having crossed the Rubicon . . . (non-finite clause)

There are three **non-finite** verb forms: the **infinitive** form, with or without *to*; the *-ing* form (or **present participle**, or **gerund**); and the *-ed* form (or **past participle**). Non-finite verbs do not have a subject, and they show no variation for tense.

All verbs have non-finite forms, except for **modal auxiliaries** (see pp. 30–1).

Infinitives, participles and gerunds

These are the **non-finite** parts of the verb (see above).

The infinitive

This is the part of the verb often prefixed by *to*:

I remembered *to lock* the door.
I wish *to see* him immediately.
To sleep, perchance *to dream* . . .
To err is human, *to forgive* [is] divine . . .

The infinitive, without the *to*, is often called the **base form** of the verb.

Split infinitives

There used to be a taboo dear to the hearts of grammatical purists which said that adverbs should never be inserted between *to* and the infinitive: as in *to boldly go, to fully understand,* etc. Sometimes, however, sense requires the splitting of infinitives. 'Completely failing to recognise' and 'Failing to completely recognise' are not quite the same thing, as Sir Ernest Gowers long ago pointed out.

Participles and gerunds

Verbs have **present participles**, formed with *-ing* (*running, jumping, standing*); and **past participles**, formed with *-ed* in regular verbs or with *-en* or in other ways for irregular verbs (*finished, given, thought, forsaken*).

Participles are sometimes used adjectivally:

the *gusting* wind
the *forsaken* merman
A *rolling* stone gathers no moss.

To distinguish between participles and gerunds, look at the following:

A: He was *smoking* an enormous cigar.
B: *Smoking* is bad for your health.

In the A-type sentence, *smoking* is the participle in the verb phrase *was smoking*. In the B-type sentence, *smoking* functions as a noun, and this is the key characteristic of a gerund.

Linking verbs, or copular verbs

Linking verbs are so called because they link a subject with a complement. Unlike regular verbs, they do not denote an action so much as record a state. They are sometimes called **copula** or **copular verbs**, from Latin *copula*, 'a bond'. The main linking verb is *be* (see below, and also the section on **complements**, p. 74):

He *is* a Frenchman.
He *is* very ill.

The other main linking verbs are *appear, become, feel, get, grow, look, remain, seem*:

She *appears* distressed.
The room *became* quiet.
The condition *is getting* serious.
Andrew *grew* tall. (But not as in: Andrew grew radishes.)
She *looks* unconvinced.
She *seems* a very sincere person.

The verb 'to be'

Be is the most frequently used verb in the English language. It is also the most irregular. *Be* has three very important roles:

- It is a copula, or linking verb (see above). Instead of taking an object, it introduces a complement linked to the subject:

He *is* a bus driver.
She *was* very shy.
They *are* my next-door neighbours.
It *is* the River Nile.

Sometimes this use is called **equative *be***, because the subject and the complement are the same thing:

He = bus driver
She = very shy
They = my next-door neighbours
It = the River Nile

- *Be* indicates the continuous or progressive aspect of a main verb:

They *are working* for charity.

He *was living* in France.
She *is being trained* to succeed the present director.

- *Be* indicates the passive voice:

The child *was named* Joseph.
I *am asked* for an explanation.

- A fourth use of *be* might be called the 'existential' use, because it conveys the meaning 'to exist'. This use is not now common:

When I have fears that I may cease *to be* . . . (Keats)
To be or not *to be*, that is the question. (Shakespeare)
A poem should not mean but *be*. (Archibald MacLeish)
I *am* – yet what I am, none cares or knows. (John Clare)
Whoever thinks a faultless piece to see, Thinks what ne'er *was* nor *is* nor e'er *shall be*. (Pope)

Moods of the verb

These are verb categories which tell us about the degree of reality conveyed by the verb. There are three types of mood in English: showing whether a sentence is making a statement (the **indicative mood**), giving an order (the **imperative mood**), or expressing a wish or supposition or other non-factual utterance (the **subjunctive mood**).

Indicative or declarative mood

He *speaks* German.
She *was walking* on the grass.
He *is* rather noisy.

Imperative mood, or command

The verbs in these requests and commands all give an order; they are in the imperative mood:

Speak to him in German, please.
Keep off the grass.
Be quiet. *Sit* in the corner.

Note that imperatives need not necessarily be imperious:

Excuse me.
Have a beer.
Take the first turning on the right.

Subjunctive mood

The subjunctive mood is used in modern English only for certain hypothetical statements:

If I *were* you . . .
If this *be* true . . .
She wished she *were* dead.

Or for fixed forms:

So *be* it!
Be that as it may . . .
God *save* the Queen.
Good luck *be* with you.

Or as formal *that* subordinates:

I insist that Tom *pay* his debt.
I demand that he *write* me an apology.

The word **mood** comes from Latin *modus*, meaning 'way' or 'manner'. So in its original meaning it was said to indicate the verb's 'attitude' or manner of speaking.

Subjunctive was also a Latin term, used to describe a mood confined to verbs in subordinate clauses. Latin grammarians described these clauses as dependants or subordinates of the main clause of the sentence, and marked the verbs accordingly. The main clause of a Latin sentence usually took the indicative mood and dealt in facts, while the *sub*ordinate clause took the *sub*junctive mood to express qualifications, conditions, suppositions, ideas and hypotheses dependent on those facts.

Transitive and intransitive

Subject	Verb	Object
He	**saw**	the crash.
She	**made**	a lovely meal.
They	**wrote**	an angry letter to their MP.

A **transitive verb** is one which takes a direct object. An **intransitive verb** does not:

Subject	Verb
Torrential rain	**fell**.
The volcano	**erupted**.

Many verbs can function transitively and intransitively:

John *played* the cello in the garden. (transitive)
John *played* in the garden. (intransitive)
The army *exploded* the bomb. (transitive)
The bomb *exploded*. (intransitive)

The word transitive is from Latin *transire*, 'to pass over', and in transitive verbs the action was thought to pass over to the object immediately following – like a spark jumping a break in an electrical circuit.

Active and passive

A: The Romans *invaded* Britain.
B: Britain *was invaded* by the Romans.

Transitive verbs occur in these two kinds of sentences. A-type sentences are called **active**, because the subject performs the action described by the verb. B-type sentences are called **passive**, because the subject is the recipient of the action.

The **passive auxiliary** is generally a form of the verb *to be*:

He *was* wounded in the leg.
They *were* told to take him to hospital.

Often, however, *get* performs a similar function (especially if the action received is disagreeable):

They *got* beaten up by some thugs.
She *got* run over at the pedestrian crossing.
He'll *get* knocked to smithereens.

Passive constructions are found much less frequently than active constructions. They are found in scientific writing, for instance, where we are not interested in who performs the action:

A sample of soil *is placed* in a weighted evaporating basin which *is* then *reweighed*. The basin *is heated* over a water-bath for some hours or days according to the weight and nature of the sample, to drive off the soil water. The basin *is* then *allowed* to cool in a desiccator and *weighed* again. Heating and reweighing *are continued* until two weighings give identical results, showing that all the soil water has evaporated . . . (D. G. Mackean, *Introduction to Biology*, John Murray 1962)

Another common use of the passive is when the subject performing the action is unknown:

The woman was struck on the head.

A third frequent use of the passive requires a measure of vigilance on the part of the reader:

Thousands of civilians were tortured and executed. (By whom? The rebels? The government?)

A new tax called the poll tax is to be introduced.

Verb tense

The word tense is from Latin *tempus*, 'time', and it is used to show the time when the action of a verb takes place. It is marked by inflection in English only for the **present tense** and the **past tense**:

Present tense

Here he *comes*.
She *likes* him very much.
The fighting in Bosnia *continues* unabated.

The **present tense** marks an action now going on, or a state now existing. It also has one or two other uses:

He *gets up* at six o'clock every morning.
I don't *take* sugar in coffee.
She *teaches* chemistry.

The above shows the **habitual present**, marking habitual (repeated or recurring) events. An extension of this is the use of the present tense to denote what is true at all times – the **stative present**:

Lions *are* carnivorous animals.
Salt *dissolves* in water.

Sometimes the present is used with an **adverbial** (see p. 74) to indicate future time:

Term *begins* next Monday.
We *leave* tomorrow morning.

Past tense

Columbus *crossed* the Atlantic in 1492.
When they *woke*, the sun *was shining*.
We *arrived* yesterday.

The **past tense** describes an action or state which has taken place at a particular time before the present. It is formed by adding *-ed* or *-d* to the base form of regular verbs: *cross/crossed, arrive/arrived, talk/talked*. With irregular verbs, it is formed differently: *wake/woke, begin/began, leave/left*, etc. (See pp. 40–3 for more on irregular verbs.)

Verb phrases can be made past by using the past tense of their finite verb:

When they woke, they *were rested* and the sun *was shining.*

The past tense is often used to mark reported speech:

I *am* ill.
He *said* that he *was* ill.
Did he *say* that he *was* ill?

It also describes habitual actions in the past:

Last term, we *got up* at seven o'clock.
Long ago, everything *was run* by the monks.

Future tense

Tomorrow *will be* wet and windy.
We *shall arrive* on the midday flight.

The **future tense** describes actions or states which will take place at some future time, and it is marked by the use of *will* and *shall.* Traditionally, *will* was used with second- and third-person subjects, and *shall* with first-person subjects:

You/he/she/it/they *will go*
I/we *shall go*

These combinations were reversed to indicate emphasis, refusal, insistence, etc.:

I *will* not do it.
They *shall* not pass.

A verbal equivalent of stamping the feet, and certainly expressive of deep intransigence, would be a construction such as:

I *will* not and *shall* not do it.

Other future time markers are *to be about to* or *to be going to* + the base form of the verb:

Hurry up – the train *is about to depart.*
I hope John Smith *is going to be* the next prime minister.

Other past tense forms

I *have visited* Paris several times.
I *had visited* New York when I was twelve years old.
By the time I am fifteen, I *shall have visited* Cairo.

These forms are called, respectively, the **perfect** (*have* + *-ed* form); the

past perfect, or 'past in the past', sometimes called the **pluperfect** (*had* + *-ed* form); and the **future perfect** or 'past in the future' (*will/ shall have* + *-ed* form).

Verb aspect

Aspect is a verb category indicating the point of time from which an action is seen to take place. Two contrasts of aspect are marked in English: **progressive aspect** and **perfect** (or **perfective**) **aspect**. The former states that the action is in progress, ongoing or continuous at that point of time; the latter states that the action is retrospective or has been completed.

Progressive/continuous aspect is marked by the use of *be* + present participle:

She *is driving* through the town.
She *was listening* to the car radio.

Perfect aspect is marked by the use of *have* + past participle:

He *has cooked* a splendid meal.
He *had fed* his guests by 10 o'clock.

Progressive and perfect aspect can be combined:

For years we *have been coming here* for our holiday.
We *had been looking* forward to a short break.

Verb suffixes and prefixes

Certain **prefixes** are associated with verbs. Here are some common verb prefixes:

a/ab- *ab*dicate, *ab*hor, *ab*ide, *ab*olish, *ab*ominate, *ab*ridge, *ab*rogate, *ab*sorb, *ab*stain

ac- *ac*celerate, *ac*cept, *ac*cede, *ac*company, *ac*count, *ac*cuse

ad-/af-/ap- *ad*here, *ad*mire, *ad*opt, *ad*ore, *ad*vance, *af*firm, *af*ford, *ap*peal, *ap*pal, *ap*pend

co- *co*exist, *co*habit, *co*produce, *co*operate

con- *con*cede, *con*cur, *con*cuss, *con*done, *con*fess, *con*fine, *con*firm, *con*form, *con*geal, *con*gratulate, *con*gregate, *con*nect, *con*sider, *con*struct, *con*sume, *con*tain, *con*tinue, *con*vene

com- *com*mit, *com*plain, *com*pile, *com*pose, *com*plete, *com*municate

de- *de*cide, *de*ceive, *de*clare, *de*cline, *de*corate, *de*cree, *de*cry, *de*fy, *de*ject, *de*liver, *de*molish, *de*mur, *de*nounce, *de*pend, *de*plore, *de*plete, *de*prave, *de*spair, *de*tect, *de*velop

dis- *dis*able, *dis*cover, *dis*miss, *dis*qualify, *dis*tress

en- *en*gulf, *en*chant, *en*case, *en*velop
in- *in*fringe, *in*vade, *in*trude, *in*troduce
inter- *inter*cede, *inter*fere, *inter*pret, *inter*vene
out- *out*do, *out*fight, *out*jump, *out*play, *out*run, *out*swim, *out*produce
over- *over*come, *over*do, *over*flow, *over*ride, *over*see, *over*work
sub- *sub*ject, *sub*join, *sub*merge, *sub*mit, *sub*sist, *sub*vert
tran-/trans- *trans*act, *trans*cend, *trans*cribe, *trans*fer, *trans*fix, *trans*gress, *trans*late, *trans*pose
un- *un*bend, *un*do, *un*earth, *un*loose, *un*button, *un*zip, *un*tangle, *un*tie, *un*dress, *un*hitch, *un*veil
with- *with*draw, *with*hold, *with*stand

Here are some common verb **suffixes**:

-ate chlorin*ate*, concentr*ate*, fascin*ate*, incapacit*ate*, orchestr*ate*, vener*ate*
-er batt*er*, clatt*er*, glitt*er*, mutt*er*, quav*er*, quiv*er*, sev*er*, shatt*er*, shiv*er*, stutt*er*
-ify beaut*ify*, de*ify*, glor*ify*, simpl*ify*
-ise/-ize advert*ise*, cauter*ise*, computer*ise*, final*ise*, hospital*ise*, modern*ise*, oxid*ise*, privat*ise*, real*ise*, sermon*ise*, verbal*ise*
-ish abol*ish*, establ*ish*, fam*ish*, fin*ish*, flour*ish*, nour*ish*, per*ish*, pol*ish*, pun*ish*
-mit ad*mit*, com*mit*, de*mit*, per*mit*, sub*mit*, trans*mit*

The *-ise/-ize* suffix is optional in some cases, and an occasional subject of debate. Some verbs are never spelt with *z* (*advertise, advise, arise, comprise, despise, exercise, revise, supervise, televise,* etc.), so for most British spellers *-ise* is the easier option. But American English prefers the *-ize* spelling for the remainder.

Regular and irregular verbs

The vast majority of English verbs are **regular** – that is, their forms can be established by rules. But there are about 300 **irregular** verbs, where some of the forms are unexpected. Instead of regular and irregular, we sometimes used to call them 'weak' and 'strong' verbs, because the weak ones toed the line and kept to the regular rules, while the strong ones were a law unto themselves!

All newly formed verbs are regular, or weak (e.g. *privatise, chlorinate*), and there has been a tendency over the years for certain strong verbs to become weak (e.g. *thrive* is listed below as following the same pattern as *drive*, but as well as *thrive/throve/thriven*, the weak *thrive/thrived/thrived* version is also used nowadays, especially by Americans).

There are four main forms of the **regular** verb, best indicated in the following table:

Infinitive or base form	-s form, or third-person singular	-ing participle	-ed past form and past participle
walk	walks	walking	walked
stop	stops	stopping	stopped
try	tries	trying	tried
love	loves	loving	loved
push	pushes	pushing	pushed
prefer	prefers	preferring	preferred

The **irregular** verb forms fall into three main types:

- Identical forms for the infinitive, past tense and past participle:

bet	hit	shut
bid	hurt	slit
burst	let	split
cast	put	spread
cost	quit	thrust
cut	set	

- Identical past tense and past participle:

Base form or infinitive	Past tense/participle	Other examples
burn	burned/burnt	learn, smell, spell, spill, spoil
bend	bent	build, lend, send, spend
bleed	bled	breed, feed, flee, hold, lead
sleep	slept	creep, keep, leap, sweep, weep
cling	clung	fling, sting, string, swing, wring
bring	brought	buy, catch, fight, seek, teach, think
bind	bound	find, grind, wind
get	got	
lose	lost	
shine	shone	
shoot	shot	
sell	sold	tell
(be)come	(be)came	
run	ran	
hear	heard	
light	lit	

make	made	
say	said	lay, pay
stand	stood	
spit	spat	

The two past tense forms of *burn* do not convey exactly the same meanings. The *-ed* form is used to convey the duration of the action, while the *-t* form conveys a completed action:

The fire burned for weeks.
Fetch me a bandage – I've burnt myself.

● Infinitive, past tense and past participle forms are all different:

Infinitive	Past tense	Past participle	Other examples
hew	hewed	hewn/hewed	mow, sew, saw, sow, show, swell
break	broke	broken	awake, choose, freeze, speak, steal, wake, weave
bear	bore	born/borne	
swear	swore	sworn	tear, wear
blow	blew	blown	grow, know, throw
bite	bit	bitten	
hide	hid	hidden	
take	took	taken	shake
drive	drove	driven	rise, ride, thrive, write
begin	began	begun	sing, sink, swim, shrink, drink, ring, spring
eat	ate	eaten	
fall	fell	fallen	
dive	dived/dove	dived	
do	did	done	
draw	drew	drawn	
fly	flew	flown	
forget	forgot	forgotten	
give	gave	given	
go	went	gone	
lie	lay	lain	
see	saw	seen	

Several irregular verbs are treated differently in the UK and USA. *Dove*, for example, as the past tense of *dive*, is an Americanism. The other common Americanism is *gotten* (for UK *got*).

Phrasal verbs

Many English verbs are made up of a simple verb followed by a preposition or adverb such as *about, in, off*. Some of these verbs are called **phrasal verbs**, because the words in them combine to give a single meaning. Sometimes this meaning is obvious, i.e. it can be guessed from the meanings of the individual parts. But often the meaning of a phrasal verb is idiomatic and cannot be guessed from the meanings of the parts.

Look at these pairs:

1 Tom *came off* the midnight train.
2 I don't think his plan will *come off*.

1 She *came round* to see us last night.
2 She didn't *come round* till a week after the accident.

The second sentence in the first pair has *come off* with the idiomatic meaning of 'succeed'; the second sentence in the second pair has *come round* with the idiomatic meaning of 'regain consciousness'.

Warning: Not all verbs followed by a preposition or adverb are phrasal verbs. Look at these pairs:

1 He *looked/ up* the road. (verb *looked* + prepositional phrase)
2 He *looked up* in the dictionary. (phrasal verb *looked up* = try to find a meaning)

1 She *came/ by* bus. (verb *came* + prepositional phrase)
2 She *came by* a valuable painting. (phrasal verb *came by* = acquired)

Phrasal verbs are especially common in spoken and colloquial English. People are more likely to say they have *climbed down* a ladder, rather than *descended* it; that they have *put up with* a noisy neighbour, rather than *tolerated* him or her, etc. Phrasal verbs are less pompous, less formal than verbs of classical origin. A list follows showing some of the commonest of the thousands of English phrasal verbs. Idiomatic meanings are also shown:

ask after   seek information about   *She phoned the hospital to ask after her father.*
back out (of)   withdraw from   *He backed out of the project when he realised what it would cost.*
back up   support   *Please back me up in this argument.*
bear up   keep strong   *He tried to bear up for the sake of his family.*
break down   **1** stop functioning   *The car broke down.* **2** cry, burst into

tears   *He broke down at the news of her death.* **3** reduce to its constituent parts   *Try to break this data down a bit.*

break in(to)   interrupt   *The demonstrators kept breaking into the proceedings.*

break off   sever   *Negotiations were broken off this morning.*

bring about   **1** cause   *The accident was brought about by careless driving.* **2** turn a boat around   *They managed to bring the ship about and head for port.*

bring in   introduce   *The government keeps bringing in new legislation.*

bring off   complete successfully   *The team brought off a famous victory.*

bring round   revive   *The lifeguard brought the child round after he'd been rescued from the water.*

bring up   raise, educate   *I was brought up by my grandmother.*

call for   demand   *The crisis calls for strong leadership.*

call in   summon   *They called in a doctor.*

call off   abandon   *The race was called off because of snow.*

care for   **1** like   *He didn't much care for her manner.* **2** look after   *He cared for his invalid parent for many years.*

carry on   **1** make a fuss   *These children have been carrying on all morning.* **2** continue   *Please carry on with your work.*

carry out   undertake   *The police will carry out a full investigation.*

check in   register   *She checked in at the Forest Lawn Hotel last night.*

check out   **1** leave   *We'll be checking out before noon.* **2** find out (about)   *You'll have to check out his alibi.*

check (up) on   investigate   *We've checked on his story and it seems to be true.*

clear up   **1** (of weather) get better   *The weather is clearing up nicely.* **2** solve   *The police are keen to clear the matter up quickly.*

come off   prosper, succeed   *His plans haven't come off very well.*

come round   recover consciousness   *Three hours after the operation, she still had not come round.*

count out   exclude   *Please count me out of your escapade.*

draw up   stop (a vehicle)   *The police drew up in front of the runaway car.*

get across   communicate ideas   *He got his message across to his audience with great force.*

get away with   **1** steal   *They got away with a million dollars.* **2** escape punishment   *That man gets away with murder.*

get by   cope, manage   *She gets by on her widow's pension.*

get down   depress   *Don't let them get you down!*

give away   betray confidences   *She plays her cards close to her chest – never gives anything away.*

give up   **1** stop, lose interest   *Don't just give up because it's difficult.* **2** renounce, stop   *He's been trying to give up smoking for years.*

go down with   contract, become ill with   *Half the class went down with flu.*

go in for   **1** enter for   *She went in for the Mastermind quiz.* **2** like   *All my friends go in for football in a big way.*

go off   **1** explode   *The bomb went off without warning.* **2** go bad   *Milk soon goes off in warm weather.* **3** dislike   *I used to like Mary, but I've gone right off her lately.*

go through   **1** endure, suffer   *She's gone through a lot lately.* **2** search, examine   *The police went through the scene of the crime with a fine-tooth comb.*

hang about   wait idly   *He spent his days hanging about street corners.*

hang back   hesitate   *He always hangs back when he is in her company.*

hang on   wait   *Hang on a minute and I'll be right with you.*

hang on to   retain   *You should hang on to that Picasso painting – it's worth a lot of money.*

hang up   end a phone conversation   *We were in the middle of a chat when she just hung up on me.*

hold on   wait   *The telephone operator asked me to hold on.*

keep at   persist with   *You can learn anything if you keep at it.*

knock out   stun, defeat   *The boxer knocked out his challenger.*

let down   disappoint   *Don't cancel the game and let the teams down.*

let off   **1** release   *The plane let off a deafening blast of air.* **2** forgive, excuse   *The culprit was let off with a warning from the magistrate.* **3** explode   *They let off hundreds of fireworks on Guy Fawkes Night.*

look after   take care of   *The hospital looks after about 200 patients.*

look in   call, visit   *The doctor will look in on you on his way home.*

look into   investigate   *The police will look into any complaints.*

look up   **1** improve, get brighter. *After the war, things started to look up a bit.* **2** consult   *Look it up in the dictionary/telephone directory.*

look up to   respect, admire   *He had no role model to look up to.*

make for   **1** go towards   *When it started raining, we made for shelter.* **2** provide a basis for   *Their management style doesn't make for good industrial relations.*

make out   **1** understand   *I can't make out his writing.* **2** write   *She made out a cheque for £100.* **3** get on   *How are you all making out?* **4** have sex   *The room was full of disco noise and kids making out.*

make up   **1** invent   *He makes up the most amazing stories.* **2** renew friendship, return to good relations   *They decided to kiss and make up.* **3** apply cosmetics   *The actors were making up their faces before the performance.*

make up for   compensate for   *He tried to make up for his earlier outburst.*

pass away   die   *He passed away in his sleep.*

pass off   **1** take place   *The performance passed off very successfully.* **2** masquerade   *He passed himself off as a Texan millionaire.*

pass out   faint   *He passed out in the crowded, airless compartment.*

press on   continue to work hard   *Regardless of all the interruptions, she pressed on with the job.*

pull up   halt   *The horses pulled up at the inn.*

put off   postpone   *The game was put off till Friday.*

put up   accommodate   *I can put you up for a couple of nights.*

put up with   tolerate   *She won't put up with any more nonsense.*

ring back   telephone again   *She'll ring you back in ten minutes.*

ring off   end a phone conversation   *She rang off when her boss came into the room.*

ring up   1 telephone   *She rang up to tell me she'd arrived safely.* 2 register cash in a till   *The assistant rang up £29.95 for the garment.*

run down   1 knock down with a vehicle   *He was run down by a speeding motorist.* 2 disparage   *She loves running people down behind their backs.* 3 slowly bring to a halt   *The Coal Board has been running that mine down for the last two years.*

run into   1 meet by chance   *I ran into an old school friend yesterday.* 2 add up to   *His income runs into millions of pounds.*

run out of   use up   *The car's run out of petrol.*

see off   say goodbye to   *They saw me off from the station.*

see through   1 help through a difficult period   *We'll see this problem through together.* 2 assess to be untrue   *We could see through most of their ploys and ruses.*

see to   attend to   *You'll need to see to that cut on your leg.*

set back   delay, hinder   *The fire has set back their plans for expansion.*

set off/out   1 start a journey   *The bus set off at nine o'clock.* 2 enhance   *The large painting sets off the great hall very effectively.* 3 ignite   *The kids have been setting off fireworks all night.*

show off   boast, display oneself   *Small children love to show off to adults.*

show up   1 appear   *Guess who showed up at the party?* 2 shame   *She enjoyed showing her boyfriend up in public.*

stand by   support, help   *We agreed to stand by the company and see it through its difficulties.*

stand for   tolerate   *He won't stand for any nonsense.*

stand up for   defend, support   *He always stands up for the underdog.*

take after   resemble   *Mary takes after her father.*

take in   1 dupe   *He was very plausible and took us all in.* 2 believe   *It was such a surprise that we couldn't take it all in.* 3 include   *The tour took in all the main tourist spots.*

take off   1 leave the ground   *The plane took off at 9 a.m.* 2 imitate, mimic   *He enjoys taking off Margaret Thatcher.*

take on   1 undertake, accept   *He has taken on a directorship of ICI.* 2 challenge   *We took on a strong team from America.*

take over   absorb   *Our company has been taken over by a multinational.*
think out   reason, plan   *We will have to think out our next move very carefully.*
turn down   reject   *The planning committee turned down his application.*
turn out   end, transpire   *His plan has turned out very well.*
turn up   be found, appear   *His baggage turned up a week late.*
wear off   lose power   *The power of the sedative began to wear off in the morning.*
work out   solve   *There was one clue I couldn't work out.*

When a phrasal verb is turned into a passive form, the preposition or adverb remains attached:

The result cannot be *wondered at.*
He was well and truly *done for.*
That practice has been *done away with.*
Try not to let yourself be *imposed upon.*

Adverbs and adverbials

Adjectives qualify nouns and pronouns. **Adverbs** modify the other parts of speech – verbs, other adverbs, adjectives, prepositions and conjunctions. Thus they are a very heterogeneous word-class. But probably the most important and frequent function of an adverb is to modify the main verb in a sentence – hence its name.

So the two key functions of adverbs are:

• To modify the main verb of a sentence, so that the whole meaning of the sentence is affected. Thus:

Subject	Verb phrase with **adverb**
Aunt Agatha	arrived **yesterday**.
The bus	travelled **slowly**.

• To modify individual words and phrases (verbs, adverbs, adjectives, prepositions, conjunctions). Thus:

He managed to rest, even to sleep *fitfully*. (verb modification)
The weather changed *very* suddenly. (adverb modification)
She is *seriously* ill. (adjective modification)
The train left *just* before noon. (preposition modification)
Let me show you *exactly* how it works. (conjunction modification)

An adverb is a single word. But there are many multi-word constructions which have the same role and perform the same function. These are called **adverbials**; they are introduced in this chapter along with adverbs, but their role and function is described in more detail elsewhere. (See p. 74.)

Kinds of adverbs

Adverbs are commonly defined according to the kinds of questions they answer about the verbs they modify. They usually come after the verb, or after the object if there is one.

Adverbs and adverbials of time

Adverbs of time say *when* something happened, and they include words like *then, now, sometimes, afterwards,* etc.:

They left the police station *later.*
Afterwards we all had dinner.

Many prepositional phrases may also be used as **time adverbials**:

I saw her *during the holidays.*
I saw her *for a brief five minutes.*
I talked to him *for a whole day.*
They stayed in London *over Christmas.*
They met us *before the match.*
She's been wearing glasses *since she was eleven.*

Some of the other commonest adverbial time constructions include *in the evening, last week, next year, in September, at 8 o'clock, for a fortnight, after three days, since 1945, a month ago,* etc.

Adverbs and adverbials of place

Adverbs of place say *where* something happened. They include words like *here, there, anywhere, nowhere, somewhere, hence, hither, thence, thither, upstairs, downstairs, away, abroad, indoors, outdoors, underground,* etc.:

John was *there* a moment ago.
Please go *downstairs* and answer the phone.

Adverbials of place include a range of notions of space, position, direction and distance:

She ran *to the house.* (direction to)
He came down *from the glen.* (direction from)
They drove *for 20 kilometres.* (distance)
He lives *in the end villa on the right.* (position)

Adverbs and adverbials of manner

They thanked us *fulsomely* for our hospitality.
The bad end *unhappily*, the good *unluckily*. That is what tragedy means. (Tom Stoppard)
The lava flowed *relentlessly* and *inexorably* downhill towards the village.

These adverbs tell us *how* something happened, and they are very often formed by adding *-ly* to an adjective:

Adjective	Adverb
absolute	absolutely
bad	badly
beautiful	beautifully
careful	carefully
exceptional	exceptionally
quick	quickly
quiet	quietly
soft	softly
sudden	suddenly

Some adjectives require modification before the addition of *-ly*:

Adjective	Adverb
automatic	automatically
easy	easily
full	fully (full + y)
gentle	gently (no e)
true	truly (no e)

A few other suffixes indicate an **adverb of manner**:

-ways: sideways
-wise: streetwise, clockwise
-wards: forwards, backwards, skywards, earthwards
-fashion: squirrel-fashion, Edwardian-fashion
-style: 1960s-style, English-style

Adverbials of manner also describe the way in which something happens or is done.

She listened *with great sadness* to his story.
The team did not play *well enough* to win the cup.
He looked at her *in the most furtive and nervous manner*.

Remember that not all words ending in -*ly* are adverbs of manner. Some adjectives also have this ending (*manly, elderly, friendly, lordly*, etc.).

Adverbs and adverbials of reason and purpose

These tell us something about the purpose behind an action, or *why* things have happened. They include adverbs like *purposely, deliberately, intentionally, accidentally*, etc. and adverbials like the following:

They went to France *for a holiday*.
He blares his stereo *to annoy*.

Adverbs and adverbials of frequency, degree and probability

These say *how often* something happens, *to what extent* something has happened, or *how sure* you are that something is going to happen. They include words like *always, ever, never, frequently, a lot, seldom, rarely, possibly, wholly, partially, thoroughly, probably, definitely, certainly, maybe, perhaps*. They usually come before the main verb (unless the main verb is *be*, when they come after):

I *definitely* saw him yesterday.
The taxi driver will *probably* know the quickest route.
I shall *never* forget that game.
Don't *ever* do that again!
I was only *partially* convinced by his story.

Adverbs of duration

These are words like *already, still, yet, any longer, any more, no longer*. You use them to say that an event is continuing, stopping, or not happening at the moment.

Is the sun out *yet*?
I can't stand this weather *any longer*.
Surely it can't *still* be raining?
Have they finished the job *already*?

Interrogative and conjunctive adverbs

Interrogative adverbs are words like *where, when, how, why, whence* and *whither* which ask the questions that are answered by adverbs of place, time, manner, etc.:

When did they leave the hotel?
Why do you ask that question?
How was she keeping?

Conjunctive adverbs are the same words as interrogative adverbs, but they perform a slightly different function in the sentence. Instead of asking a question, they join two clauses together:

He asked the receptionist *when* they had left the hotel.
I wonder *why* you asked that question.

Other everyday adverbs

Words like *yes* and *no* are almost like sentences, in the sense that they are often used as stand-alone words, or sentence equivalents. But they were traditionally classed as adverbs, because they modified verbs – even if those verbs were as often as not unspoken ones. Look at an exchange like the following:

Question: Are you coming?
Answer: *Yes.*

Yes here actually means 'Yes, I am coming.' So traditional grammarians said *yes* was an adverb.

Other common adverbs are that range of words used mainly to qualify adjectives and other adverbs – *very, terribly, frightfully, excessively, too, quite, almost, so, more, most, scarcely, not* and *less.*

'Special' adverbs

A number of words function as both adjectives and adverbs, with only their context to tell you which they are. They include words like *cheap, clean* (as in completely, e.g. he clean forgot), *dead* (as in utterly, e.g. she was dead cool), *easy, fast, fine, free, hard, high, just, late, loud, low, pretty, quick, real, sharp, slow, straight, sure, well, wide, wrong.*

Comparison of adverbs

Adverb comparison is very similar to adjective comparison (see p. 19), but to a higher degree; you use *-er/-est* or add *more/most* to the adverb to convey comparative and superlative forms.

The job was completed *more promptly* than last time.
John was affected *more seriously* by the accident than I was.
I object *most strongly* to these insinuations.

He drove the car *faster and faster*.
His cough sounded *worse and worse*.

Position of adverbs

Adverbs are extremely mobile in their deployment, and in many cases they can go at the beginning or in the middle or at the end of a sentence:

Suddenly I heard a noise upstairs.
I was *suddenly* aware of a noise.
He left the party quite *suddenly*.

A word like *originally* can be inserted at any of the points marked / in the following sentence:

/The dress/must/have/been/purchased/in Marks and Spencer's/.

Generally speaking, adverbs should be so positioned as to make quite clear which particular words they are intended to modify. Compare, for example:

She smiled at him *foolishly*. (i.e. she gave him a foolish smile)
Foolishly, she smiled at him. (i.e. it was unwise of her to do so)

The split infinitive

For a reason which was once perhaps more persuasive than it now is, many people professed an objection to the use of an adverb between *to* and the verb's infinitive form. They insisted that the 'unity' of the infinitive must be respected, and they objected to split infinitive constructions like the following:

He tended *to frequently interrupt* the conversation.
She intends *to really work* this semester.

Nowadays, it is perhaps enough to avoid split infinitives in formal writing, although most people would not object to the following even in writing:

He wants *to so organise* his agenda that . . .
He forgot *to fully extend* the aerial.

See also p. 32.

Prepositions

It was *on* the table.
He is *at* school.
We drove *to* the shops.
We had to be there *before* 5 o'clock.

Prepositions are words like *on, at, to* and *before*. They show the relation of a noun or noun equivalent to the rest of a sentence. As the name suggests ('pre[ceding] position'), they usually come before the words they complement. Most often, they show how two parts of a sentence are related in time or space.

Simple and complex prepositions

Simple prepositions consist of a single word. **Complex prepositions** consist of two or three words. Here are some of the commonest:

Simple prepositions

about	down	over
above	during	round
across	for	since
after	from	through
against	in	to
along	inside	towards
among	into	under
around	of	up
at	off	with
before	on	within
behind	onto	without
beneath	opposite	
by	out	

Complex prepositions – two words

ahead of	due to
apart from	except for
because of	instead of
close to	near to

Complex prepositions – three words

as far as	in spite of
by means of	in terms of
in accordance with	on account of
in addition to	on behalf of
in front of	with reference to

Preposition or adverb or conjunction?

Many of the simple prepositions listed above have several other possible functions. Before we can be sure they are indeed prepositions, we need to check the context in which the words are used:

- If the words are followed by nouns or noun equivalents, they are **prepositions**: 'I gave you that information *before* tea.'
- If they are used to link clauses, they are **conjunctions**: 'I gave you that information *before* you asked for it.'
- If they are not followed by nouns and don't link clauses, they are **adverbs**: 'I gave you that information *before*. Don't ask for it again.'

Prepositional meanings

Prepositions cover a wide range of meanings. First, they express **spatial meanings**. Many of these spatial meanings can be best illustrated diagrammatically (see page opposite).

Prepositions are also used to convey a sense of:

- time ('*at* 5 o'clock', '*for* six weeks', '*by* next Tuesday')
- cause ('He was sacked *for/on account of* his laziness', 'She did it *out of* kindness')
- manner ('I paid *by* travellers' cheque', 'He worked *like* a demon')
- accompaniment ('You must go *with* them')
- support or opposition ('I was *against* the plan', 'They are *with* you all the way')
- concession ('She came *despite* her illness')
- possession ('a musician *of* rare talent', 'a bag *with* a purple handle')
- addition and exception ('The car was a bargain *apart from* its rusty bonnet', 'We had a great time *except for* the weather')

Prepositional phrases

The combination of the preposition and its noun phrase complement is called a **prepositional phrase**. These can come after, or **post-modify**, a noun:

The villain was the man *in the blue suit.*

Or they can be adverbials:

*At 5 o'clock in the afternoo*n, the rain came on.

Or they can complement verbs or adjectives:

He fell *off the table.*

We were very sorry *for him.*

Or they indicate possession:

Two Gentlemen *of Verona*

Space prepositions

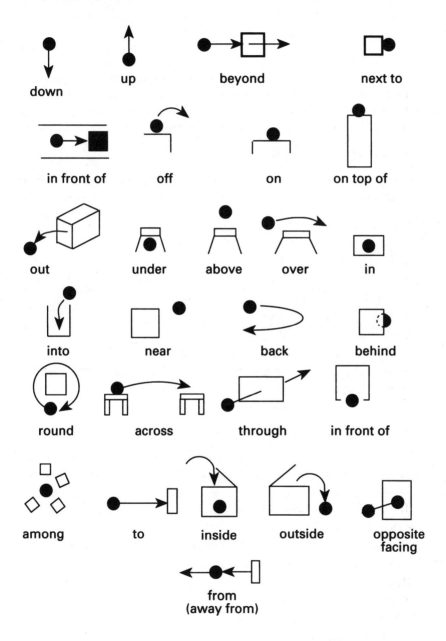

Prepositions governing two elements

A preposition need not be repeated if it has two complements:

An operetta *by* Gilbert and Sullivan, NOT *by* Gilbert and *by* Sullivan
He spoke *with* passion and humour, NOT *with* passion and *with* humour.

But you do need to repeat the preposition if there is a risk of ambiguity:

She was talking *about* health education and smoking cigarettes.
She was talking *about* health education and *about* smoking cigarettes.

Prepositions at the end of sentences

Because a Latin sentence could not end with a preposition, some English scholars used to claim that an English sentence shouldn't end with one either. If it ever was one, this is no longer a rule of English usage. A better rule is to place the preposition where it sounds most natural:

What hotel did you stay *in*?
In what hotel did you stay?

Either of these alternatives is acceptable, though the latter is more formal and sounds stiffer. In some examples, there is no alternative:

What was she looking *for*?
NOT: *For* what was she looking?

Winston Churchill poked fun at the former reluctance to put a preposition at the end of a sentence with the following example of contorted English:

This is the sort of behaviour *up* with which I shall not put.

Prepositional idioms

Many prepositions are embedded in **idioms**. There are no easy rules for deciding which preposition to use in such phrases. They just have to be learned. A person who is overcharged is said to pay *through* the nose; one who is made to do as we wish is led *by* the nose; and when we do something without a person noticing we say that we have done something *under* his very nose.

Other examples include:

off colour	an ear *for* music
against the grain	*with* the stream
stick *at* nothing	beating *about* the bush
straight *from* the shoulder	*above* board

beyond your means   *into* the bargain
soldiers *under* arms   *on* call

Conjunctions

Conjunctions are link words or 'joining together' words. There are two
types: coordinators and subordinators.

Coordinating conjunctions

The **coordinators** are so called because they join units of equal status.
The units may be words ('fish *and* chips', 'tired *but* happy', 'tea *or*
coffee'); or they may be sentences ('John is working in the garden *and*
Mary is working in the house', 'His name is Steven *and* he lives in
Leeds').

The coordinating conjunctions are:

and	both . . . and
but	either . . . or
or	neither . . . nor
then	
so	
yet	

Look at these:

The weather will be (*both*) dry *and* windy tomorrow.
The weather will be dry *but* windy tomorrow.
The weather will be dry *or* windy tomorrow.
The weather will be *neither* dry *nor* windy tomorrow.
She was born in Zagreb *and* raised in Philadelphia.
She didn't complain *or* even protest.
When she saw John she blushed, *then* walked away.

These sentences show some of the range of meanings afforded by
coordinating conjunctions. Note that in the last three examples, the
clauses have the same subject (*she*); when you use a coordinating
conjunction you do not always need to repeat the subject in the second
clause.

These are all examples of **linked coordination**. When there is no
conjunction, the coordination is said to be **unlinked**:

The weather was wet *and* windy *and* cold. (linked coordination)
The weather was wet, windy, cold. (unlinked coordination)

Subordinating conjunctions

The **subordinating conjunctions** join subordinate or dependent clauses to the main clause of a sentence. (For more on this, see under **sentence** structure, p. 77.) The main subordinators are:

after   He laughed *after* she cracked a joke.

(al)though   *Although* it is sunny now, the forecast is for rain.

as   The car banked hard *as* the dog ran across the road.

as . . . as   They left the scene *as* quickly *as* they could.

as if   He talked *as if* money were no problem.

because   He climbed the hill *because* it was there.

before   Tell me one thing *before* you go.

even if   I don't want to go *even if* you give me a free ticket.

except   I'd go *except* I've no time.

if   *If* you throw litter you'll get a £10 fine.

in case   We left some supper *in case* John dropped by.

in order to   She left early *in order to* get her train.

more . . . than   I've grown far *more* potatoes *than* I can use.

rather than   I'd starve *rather than* eat snails.

since   The business has flourished *since* it was taken over.

so that   The management worked hard *so that* it would succeed.

that   The reason *that* I am here today . . .

till/until   They drew no salaries till its prospects were secure.

when   They relaxed a bit *when* they got their first big contract.

whenever   They still work flat out *whenever* they have to.

where   They go *where* the good orders are.

whereas   They are real professionals *whereas* their competitors are a lot of amateurs.

wherever   You'll find them *wherever* there's business to be had.

whether   Now they have to decide *whether* they will consolidate or expand the business.

while   Nero fiddles *while* Rome burns.

Some subordinating conjunctions also function as prepositions:

Subordinator	Preposition
He arrived **before** I did.	He arrived **before** me.
He left **after** I did.	He left **after** me.

Most subordinating conjunctions can also be used to link sentences, rather than just to link a subordinate clause with a main clause in the same sentence:

'When can I have it?' – '*When* John's finished with it.'
'Can I take the car?' – '*So long as* it's back by tea time.'
'That goes by fax.' – '*Then* the client gets it right away.'

And as an idiom

Sometimes *and* has a special idiomatic use, and isn't really a conjunction at all:

- In expressions like 'You're looking fine *and* comfortable' or 'This towel is nice *and* soft', *and* is used almost as an adverb equivalent.
- In 'Try *and* remember where you put it' or 'Let's try *and* find it', *and* really equals *to*.
- In 'He ran *and* ran *and* ran', the repeated *and* functions as a sort of emphatic, or **intensifier**.
- In 'There are universities *and* universities', the idiomatic *and* carries the sense that there are various kinds of universities and only some of them are worthy of the name.

Interjections

Oh!	Ah!	Ooh!	Alas!
Help!	Ow!	Eh?	Sh!
Pooh!	Whew!	Tut-tut!	Look out!
Cheers!	Nice one!	Golly!	Gosh!
Hem!	Oh dear!	Look here!	Bless my soul!

These are exclamations, or emotional noises. As a part of speech, they are termed **interjections**. Sometimes they are formed by actual words, sometimes not. We use them to express sudden feelings of joy, pain, surprise, disgust, anger, etc. They are generally marked by an exclamation mark or a question mark. They stand alone, as above, or they may be loosely added on to a sentence.

Oh no – I can't bear to watch any longer!
Dear me – what has happened to your clothes!
There now – don't cry!

Many interjections or exclamatory statements are elliptical – that is, they refer to previous parts of a conversation or text, with words left out or implied:

What an ass/night/experience!
Poor fool/kid/lamb/lad!

Being colloquial, interjections are being generated all the time, different social groups favouring different expressions:

Gordon Bennett! Blimey! (Southern English)
Crivvens! Help-ma-boab! Jings! (Glasgow)
Cool! (US)

Phrases

So far in this book, we have looked at the traditional eight parts of speech, although by adding determiners we have made it nine. Part 2 of the book will examine larger chunks of meaning – sentences and clauses. But if words are the smallest building blocks of language, the next category in the hierarchy is **phrases** (about which a little has already been said). We will look now at phrases, before going on to consider sentences and clauses.

Basically, a phrase is a small group of words which function as a grammatical unit. If you look at a sentence you can usually break it up into phrases:

The cat / sat / on the mat / waiting / for its tea.

This sentence has been broken into five phrases. (In grammar, it is important to remember that a phrase may consist of one word or more than one word.)

What about this?

The / cat sat on the / mat waiting / for its / tea.

This example is made up of rather unnatural breaks. It has been broken into groups of words which do not function as grammatical units. Thus we see that not all groups of words make phrases. A certain internal structure is required.

In grammar, we distinguish five kinds of phrase. Each is named after the word class which plays the key part in its structure:

● **noun phrase:**

a great big balloon (main word: noun *balloon*)
the most ghastly accident (main word: noun *accident*)

● **verb phrase:**

may have been sleeping (main word: verb *sleeping*)
will have surrendered (main word: verb *surrendered*)

● **adjective phrase:**

frightfully smart (main word: adjective *smart*)
very very old (main word: adjective *old*)

● **adverb phrase:**

quite inadvertently (main word: adverb *inadvertently*)
very stupidly (main word: adverb *stupidly*)

- **preposition phrase:**

   in the river (main word: preposition *in*)
   for your private information (main word: preposition *for*)

Structurally, a phrase is analysed in terms of a main word and its modifiers. In grammar, as we have noted, a phrase may contain one word or several. The subject of each of the following sentences, for example, may be described as a noun phrase. This is true even of the first sentence, where the noun phrase is in fact a single noun:

   Balloons were bobbing about in the sky.
   The balloons were bobbing about in the sky.
   A great big blue and yellow balloon was bobbing about in the sky.

It is not uncommon for one phrase to embed another, or several other, phrases. So:

   on the edge of a busy street (prepositional phrase: main word *on*)
   the edge of a busy street (noun phrase: main word *edge*)
   of a busy street (prepositional phrase: main word *of*)
   a busy street (noun phrase: main word *street*)

A phrase may also embed a clause. So:

   the house that Jack built (noun phrase: main word *house*)
   that Jack built (relative clause, introduced by *that*)

Noun phrases

The main word – sometimes, as we have seen, the only word – of a **noun phrase** is usually a noun or pronoun:

   buds

Often there is a **determiner**:

   a bud   *the* buds

Then there are the **modifiers**:

   green buds   *darling* buds *of May*

If the modifiers come before the main word, they are called **pre-modifiers**; if they come after it, they are **post-modifiers**.
   The modifiers may themselves be modified:

   a *distinctly* ramshackle bus
   the red bus standing at platform 16 *with its engine running*

Apposition is not uncommon in noun phrases. The noun phrase is followed by a second, explanatory, noun phrase, which is said to be 'in apposition' to the first:

   Zagreb, *the capital of Croatia*, was once a peaceful place.
   A well-known media personality, *namely Terry Wogan*, is present.

Certain types of clauses feature commonly as modifiers in a noun phrase:

She has an Alsatian which barks constantly.
The man who spoke to me is an Egyptian.

The first sentence contains the noun phrase 'an Alsatian which barks constantly', in which is embedded the **relative clause** 'which barks constantly'. The second sentence contains the noun phrase 'the man who spoke to me', in which is embedded the relative clause 'who spoke to me'.

Appositive clauses are also commonly embedded in a noun phrase. They are introduced by *that*, functioning as a conjunction:

The fact that he insulted her . . .
The reason that he is here today . . .

Compound nouns (see pp. 9–10), especially multi-word technical terms, are best treated as noun phrases:

automatic speech output device
lexical stress assignment process
airport flight information systems

Sometimes a noun phrase is made up of adjectives: *the poor, the famous*.

Verb phrases

The main word of a **verb phrase** is a main verb, which may be preceded by up to four auxiliaries. Some of the verb phrases are:

see
have seen
shouldn't have been seeing
must have been being seen

The main verb of the verb phrase will be in one of these forms:

- the base form: *see, speak, run, jump*
- the -*s* form: *sees, speaks, runs, jumps*
- the -*ing* participle form: *seeing, speaking, running, jumping*
- the -*ed* past or participle form (regular or irregular): *saw, spoke, ran, jumped*

The verb phrase may be active or passive. Here are some active and corresponding passive verb phrases:

Active	Passive
sees	is seen
ate	was eaten

is cooking	is being cooked
has built	has been built
will elect	will be elected
may have affected	may have been affected
should be delivering	should be being delivered

The auxiliaries precede the main verb in a specified order or sequence:

- modals, such as *can, may, will, must*
- perfect auxiliary *have*
- progressive auxiliary *be*
- passive auxiliary *be*

These auxiliaries in turn specify the form to be taken by the main verb which follows:

- can *read*, may *speak*, must *work* . . .
- have *read*, have *spoken*, have *worked* . . .
- was *reading*, was *speaking*, was *working* . . .
- was *read*, was *spoken*, was *worked* . . .

Verb phrases which contain a phrasal verb or a multi-word verb may occasionally be interrupted:

He *has handed in* his resignation.
He *has handed* his resignation *in*.
You *should put off* your decision.
You *should put* your decision *off*.

A verb phrase is the essential and pivotal element of a **clause** (see p. 71).

Adjective phrases

The main word in an **adjective phrase** is an adjective. The other words are modifiers, which may precede the adjective (pre-modifiers) or follow it (post-modifiers):

happy	*sad*
ecstatically and deliriously *happy*	very obviously *sad*
happy to see you all	*sad* to the point of despair

Some adjectives need to have post-modifiers:

John is very *keen* (+) on cricket.
She is fully *aware* (+) of your criticism.
I'm very *fond* (+) of golf.

Adjective phrases function mainly in the following ways:

- they are pre-modifiers in a noun phrase:

  It was a *very eloquent and witty* speech.

- they are post-modifiers in a noun phrase:

  She has done something *rather silly*.

- they are subject complements:

  The job was *extremely difficult*.

- they are object complements:

  He made her *very happy*.

- they complete the meaning of certain adjectives:

  She is *afraid of the big bad wolf*.

Sometimes adjectives are used as the main word in what then becomes effectively a noun phrase. Adjectives of nationality do this:

the Americans
the Welsh
the Germans

So do classes of society:

the poor
the sick
the old

And so do certain superlatives:

the latest
the worst

Examples of these usages:

The wounded have now been evacuated from the war zone.
The French have pioneered this approach.
What's *the latest* from Downing Street?

Adverb phrases

The main word in an **adverb phrase** is an adverb. The other words are called modifiers, which may precede the adverb (pre-modifiers) or follow it (post-modifiers):

amazingly
so *amazingly*
amazingly for him
very *amazingly* indeed

There are two main functions for adverb phrases:

- they modify an adjective:

Her advice was *extremely and surprisingly* constructive.

- they modify an adverb:

She spoke *somewhat* inappropriately about the economy.

Prepositional phrases

The components of a **prepositional phrase** are the preposition and its complement. The prepositional complement is most commonly a noun phrase.

across the barricades
into the abyss

But it can also be certain types of clause:

He'll drive you *to wherever you want to go.*

Prepositional phrases function mainly in the following ways:

- they are post-modifiers in a noun phrase:
a man *in a brown suit*
the boys *in blue*

- they are adverbials:

He drove *to the city* (1) *in the early evening* (2).

- they are verb or adjective complements:

Tom was *in a great hurry.*
She was sitting *on the floor.*
I was very sorry *for them.*

Remember that prepositional phrases often occur in clusters:

He lives *in a bungalow* (1) *near a nice beach* (2) *in Cornwall* (3).

Remember too how prepositional phrases may be embedded in one another:

It was a disaster in the annals of international diplomacy.
in the annals of international diplomacy (prepositional phrase)
the annals of international diplomacy (noun phrase)
of international diplomacy (prepositional phrase)
international diplomacy (noun phrase)

two
Sentences and clauses

How to do things with words.

J.L. Austin,
William James Lectures
at Harvard University, 1955

Backward ran sentences until reeled the mind.

Wolcott Gibbs, satirising the
style of *Time* magazine in
the *New Yorker*, 1936

I will not go down to posterity talking bad grammar.

Benjamin Disraeli, correcting
proofs of his last parliamentary
speech, 1881

I don't want to talk grammar, I want to talk like a lady.

George Bernard Shaw,
Pygmalion, 1916

The sentence

It is helpful to think of the **sentence** as the largest unit of grammar. In the hierarchy of the nuts and bolts of language, we can say that:

A **sentence** consists of one or more clauses.
A **clause** consists of one or more phrases.
A **phrase** consists of one or more words.
A **word** consists of one or more **morphemes**.

We have looked at words and phrases in Part 1 of this book, and we will look at word formation in Part 3.

Grammar deals with the rules for combining words and phrases into sentences. We all think we know what we mean by a sentence in English, even if it is rather hard to define.

Some people say that a sentence is a group of words which begins with a capital letter and ends with a full stop (or one of the equivalents of a full stop, i.e. a question mark or an exclamation mark). This has been called the 'formal' definition of a sentence, because it defines the term by describing its form or shape. It is obviously a better definition of the written than of the spoken language!

Others tell us that a sentence is a 'complete expression of a single thought'. This is called the 'notional' definition, because it defines the term by the notion or idea it conveys. But it begs the rather large question of exactly what is a single thought.

According to these definitions, the following are all sentences:

Good morning!
No parking.
Come in.
For her last holiday, Jane took a trip to Tunisia, where she visited lots of interesting
    places, swam in a warm sea, ate some splendid meals, and contrived in the
    course of a hectic courtship to get herself married to the wealthy proprietor of a
    large ceramic-tile factory near Carthage.

They all comply with the 'formal' definition, although the last example seems rather to test the 'notional' definition.

Perhaps a simpler way to define a sentence in English is to apply three criteria to it:

- It is a construction that can stand alone, without people feeling it to be incomplete.
- It is constructed according to agreed rules of grammar; that is, it has a certain structure.
- It is the largest structure to which the rules of grammar apply. The unit beyond the sentence is the **paragraph** (see pp. 133–4), which is more accurately a part of the specialised topic of punctuation than grammar.

Following these rules, most people will probably be able to pick out the sentences from the non-sentences in the following list:

Time for bed, said Zebedee.
The car won't start.
Where are my football boots?
Go away.

Even for adults.
In the street.
Here I you wish were.
Them stop coming from.

The fifth and sixth items are incomplete, while the seventh and eighth are unstructured jumbles of words. They are not grammatical, so they are not sentences.

Major and minor sentences

Sentences come in all shapes and sizes, as the merest glance across the range of printed media will confirm. Students of grammar often divide them into 'major' and 'minor' types. **Major sentences** are often described as 'regular', and **minor sentences** as 'irregular'.

Major sentences are said to break down into certain structural patterns, like these:

John Brown	has scored	a winning goal	for Chelsea.
I	lost	the car keys.	
Tom and Yvette	went back	to Canada	yesterday.

(We will look at the patterns of the major sentence later.)

Minor sentences are the ones that cannot be broken down in this way. They include:

- Interjections (see pp. 59–60): *Shhhh! Oh dear! Ahem! Whew!*
- Proverbs (see p. 157): *Once bitten, twice shy. Easy come, easy go.*
- Phrases used as questions: *Milk and sugar? Feeling better?*
- Short forms: *Road closed. No smoking. Weather dreadful.*
- Formula expressions: *Well done! How do you do? Hello! Good evening. Nice to see you!*

Simple and multiple sentences and clauses

Consider this sentence:

It was a lovely day.

This is called a **simple sentence**. It cannot be broken into smaller sentences.

Now look at this sentence:

It was a lovely day and I golfed in the afternoon.

This second sentence can be broken into two sentences:

It was a lovely day. (+) I golfed in the afternoon.

This is said to be a **multiple sentence**, made up of *two clauses* joined by *and*. Thus simple sentences contain only one verb or verb phrase, and can be analysed into only one clause. Multiple sentences contain more than one verb or verb phrase, and can be analysed into more than one clause:

It *was* a lovely day, I *was* up to date with most of my work, my good friend John Brown *called* at the door unexpectedly with his golf clubs after lunch, and thus we *ended up* playing a pleasant afternoon game of golf.

This is a multiple sentence with four verb phrases (underlined) and four clauses.

Sentence types: declarative, interrogative, imperative, and exclamative

These are the four main types of sentence.

- **Declarative sentence** (conveying information):

She lives in Jamaica.
The capital city of the new republic, normally picturesque and prosperous, is at present a dispirited and shell-shocked shadow of its former self.

- **Interrogative sentence** (requesting information):

Where is the bus station?
Have you had a nice holiday?

- **Imperative sentence** (requesting action):

Take a letter, please.
Let's have a cup of tea.

- **Exclamative sentence** (expressing feelings):

Get you!
How wonderful!

Most of this chapter is about declarative sentences.

Positive and negative sentences

Sentences are either **positive** or **negative**. They are made negative by the use of *n't* or *not* after the auxiliary. If there is no auxiliary, a 'dummy auxiliary' *do/does* is incorporated:

Positive: Elizabeth speaks good French.
Negative: Elizabeth *doesn't speak* good French.

Positive: I'll send you the bill tomorrow.
Negative: I *won't send* you the bill tomorrow.
Positive: John is running a profitable business.
Negative: John *is not running* a profitable business.

Certain other words convey a negative meaning to a sentence:

He has *never* met her.
She saw *nothing*.
I can *by no means* condone this behaviour.

Active and passive sentences

Sentences are either **active**, with an agent doing something, or **passive**, with something being done to an agent:

Active: The man addressed the crowd.
Passive: The crowd was addressed by the man.

The first sentence is made passive by moving *the man* and *the crowd* to the opposite ends of the sentence, by adding *by* before *the man*, and by changing the active verb *addressed* to the passive form *was addressed*.

Other examples of active and passive sentences:

Active: Paul Azinger yesterday won the PGA Golf Championship at Pinehurst, North Carolina.
Passive: The PGA Golf Championship was won yesterday at Pinehurst, North Carolina, by Paul Azinger.
Active: The Tory whips have warned backbenchers that the PM will be finished if they do not tonight support the Government motion in the House of Commons.
Passive: Backbenchers have been warned by the Tory whips that . . .

Most of the examples in this chapter are of active sentences, which are very much commoner than passive ones.

Sentences and clauses

As we have seen, a **simple sentence** has a single verb phrase (underlined below), and is made up of a single clause:

John *is digging* his garden.

A **multiple sentence** is one which has more than one clause:

John *is digging* his garden and *whistling* a tune.

The second sentence has two verb phrases; so it has two clauses, joined by the linking word *and*.

Clause elements

Simple clauses are made up of certain elements, or components, each of which conveys a particular kind of meaning. The five elements of a clause are:

---

subject S

---

verb V
object O
complement C   } **predicate**
adverbial A

Clauses need not contain more than some of these elements, although some will contain all of them. All clauses contain a verb element:

He (S) is drinking (V).
He (S) is drinking (V) a mug of coffee (O).
Christopher Robin (S) is saying (V) his prayers (O).
The tax office (S) has sent (V) me (O) two reminders (O) this month (A).
US voters (S) recently (A) elected (V) Mr Clinton (O) the 42nd president (C).
Give (V) me (O) that book (O).

Unless the clause has an imperative function (as in the last example) or an interrogative one, the subject is usually the first element in the clause, and gives it its theme or topic. Then, usually, comes the verb element, the key to the clause in the sense that this is the one component that every major clause has. The object and complement elements usually follow the S + V in a clause. The adverbial element usually adds information about details like the time or the location of the action. It is highly mobile, and is placed closest to the element it modifies.

Subject (S)

Subjects of a declarative sentence are usually any of the following:

● noun phrases:

The people voted for a change of government.

● pronouns:

They have become disillusioned with the current regime.

● proper nouns:

Rome is the capital of Italy.

- *-ing* forms:

  Smoking is bad for you.

- *to* forms:

  To work hard is all you are asked.

- inverted finite clauses:

  That the PM should resign is clear for all to see.

The subject of a clause is important. Often therefore, in the absence of a meaningful subject, a 'dummy subject' is introduced:

There is a slight problem. (Where?)
It is wet and windy. (What is *it*?)

Predicate

This is a traditional grammatical term covering the part of the clause that makes a statement about the subject of the clause. As the box below shows, the **predicate** includes all the parts of the clause that are not contained in the subject:

Subject	Predicate
Elizabeth	slept.
Elizabeth	was ever so tired and sleepy.
Elizabeth	slept deeply if fitfully for upwards of fifteen hours.

Verb (V)

In English clause analysis, it is important to remember the two types of verb – the **'doing' words**, like *sing, jump, dance*; and the **copular verbs**, which are *be, appear, become, get, grow, look* and *seem*. Ordinary 'doing word' verbs – the vast majority of verbs – take an object:

S	V	O
John	has bought	a house in London.
Mary	gave	me a kiss.

Copular verbs take an object equivalent called a **complement**:

S	V	C
He	is	a fisherman.
She	seems	in a great hurry.

As already stated, the verb element is the most important and pivotal element of the clause. A few of the commonest verb patterns are listed below, with the verb in italics:

SVO	The post office *has opened* a new branch.
SV	Andrew's pet rabbit *has died*.
SVC	The dinner *was* a great success.
SVA	She *departed* secretly.
SVOO	Alison *cooked* him his favourite meal.
SVOC	Alison's cooking *is driving* him mad.

There is more on verbs on pp. 28–47 and 62–3.

Object (O)

The **object** of a declarative clause normally follows a verb. Sometimes two objects follow the verb:

James ate *his lunch*.
John passed *James* (1) *the salt* (2).

The verbs here are **transitive verbs**, or verbs which take an object. Some verbs can take both a **direct** and an **indirect object**:

S	V	O (indirect)	O (direct)
Paul	**brought**	Vicky	a bunch of flowers.
Vicky	**gave**	him	a kiss.

An indirect object is one which can be preceded by *to* or *for*.

Paul brought [*for*] Vicky a bunch of flowers.
Vicky gave [*to*] him a kiss.

The direct object of a declarative clause is usually either a noun, a noun phrase, or an object pronoun:

He plays *soccer*.

He has attended *two hundred league matches*.
The police followed *him* to a deserted house.

Occasionally a finite or non-finite clause functions as the object:

I explained *what I had done*.
He denied *that he was involved*.
He denied *being involved*.
He proposes *to build a house*.

Complement (C)

This is the name given to the object equivalent in a clause taking a copula or linking verb:

S	V	C
Mary	is	a vet. (noun phrase complement)
She	appears	very competent. (adjective phrase complement)
She	seems	in a great hurry. (prepositional phrase complement)
She	is	downstairs. (adverbial complement)

Adverbial (A)

Adverbials, as we have seen, are clause elements and function like adverbs and adverb phrases. They can be found more or less anywhere in the clause. They are often optional, and peripheral to the drift of the clause:

After ten days I began to suspect an accident.
We got the good news *last Friday*.

There may be several adverbials in one clause.

He left the house *very angrily* (1) *at 12.15* (2) *to meet his creditors* (3).

In spite of their name, adverbials do not necessarily contain adverbs. In the above case, they comprise an adverb phrase (1), a prepositional phrase (2), and a non-finite verb phrase (3). But they all answer adverbial questions:

How did he leave? – Very angrily.
When did he leave? – At 12.15.
Why did he leave? – To meet his creditors.

Compound and complex sentences

So far, most of the example sentences in this chapter have been patterned on simple sentences, containing only one clause. Sentences with more than one clause can be analysed into **compound** and **complex sentences**.

In compound sentences, the clauses are linked by coordinating conjunctions – usually *and, or, but* – and each clause can potentially stand on its own.

Main clause 1	Coordinator	Main clause 2
I travelled by bus	and	John went by taxi.
I liked Florence	but	I didn't like Rome.

These sentences are made up of two main clauses linked by coordinating *and* and *but*.

In complex sentences, there is a main clause and one or more subordinate clauses. Subordinate clauses lack the potential to stand on their own, and require a main clause before they can make much sense:

Main clause	Subordinate clause
I phoned the police	when I heard the shooting.

Subordinate clause	Main clause
After she'd completed the report	she went to a meeting.

Subordinate clauses may be **finite**, like the two examples above; that is, they have a finite verb. Or they may be **non-finite**:

I phoned the police *after hearing the shots.*
After completing the report, she went out.

In none of these versions can the subordinate clauses stand on their own.

Independent and dependent clauses

A main clause is sometimes called an **independent clause**. As the name indicates, this is a clause which can stand alone and is not dependent on another clause:

[The noise got louder] and [the children screamed].

The above sentence has two independent – or main – clauses joined by *and*. If we change it to read:

[When the noise got louder], [the children screamed].

we still have two clauses, but the first clause has now become **dependent** on the second, or subordinate to it. In this next example:

[She thought [that I was serious] [when I spoke to her]], [but she was wrong].

there are two independent clauses (*She thought* and *but she was wrong*) and two dependent clauses (*that I was serious* and *when I spoke to her*).

The terms independent and dependent are more or less synonymous with main and subordinate.

Coordination

In sentence grammar, **coordination** tells us that the elements that are joined have the same status. The joined elements may be words, phrases or clauses. Coordination is signalled by the use of the coordinating conjunctions – usually *and, but, or*:

She can speak to you *in German* or *in English* or *in French*.
He has lost *his cheque card* and *his driving licence*.
John worked all morning and *Alison worked all afternoon*.

Here phrases and clauses are coordinated. Sometimes the coordinating conjunctions are left out; the coordination is then said to be unlinked:

She speaks German, English, French.

Sometimes more than the coordinating conjunction is left out, and there is an ellipsis:

John worked all morning, Alison all afternoon.

Subordination

In **subordination**, we see that the joined elements do not have the same status. Subordination may be between clauses or phrases, and is usually marked by one of the subordinating conjunctions. When introducing an adverbial clause, these include *although, since, when, if, until*:

She'll help you *if you ask nicely.*
She talked on and on *until I nearly screamed.*

When introducing noun clauses, they include *that* and *what*:

It was clear *that he was badly hurt.*
He always gets *what he wants.*

When introducing 'adjective' or relative clauses, they include *that, which, who* and *whom*:

The present *that I received yesterday* is delightful.

There are also multi-word subordinators which introduce subordinate clauses, such as *in order that, as long as, insofar as, so that, assuming that* etc.:

He drives very competently, *given that* he has only one arm.
I'll see you next week, *as long as* you don't forget.

In all these clauses, the subordinate clauses depend for their meaning on the main clauses. That is why they are often also called dependent clauses.

Subordinate clauses

As we have seen, a **subordinate clause** is dependent on another clause, the main clause. There are four types of subordinate clause, depending on their position or function in relation to the main clause:

- **nominal** or **noun clauses**
- **adverbial clauses**
- **relative clauses**
- **comparative clauses**

Nominal or noun clauses

These are subordinate clauses with a function in the sentence similar to that of the noun phrase. They can act as the subject, object, or complement of the main clause:

[What you think] is of no interest to me. (subject)
I'm not asking [what you think]. (object)
The plan is [that we will fly to New York]. (complement)

There are finite and non-finite nominal clauses:

She tells me [that her father is in prison]. (finite *that* clause)
[What you need now] is a spot of good luck. (finite nominal relative clause)

[Giving him a bottle of whisky] is the same thing as [giving him a loaded pistol].
(non-finite nominal *-ing* clause)

Sometimes nominal clauses come after a preposition:

It depends on [what you think].

Adverbial clauses

These are subordinate clauses with a function in the sentence similar to adverbials. Thus they modify the main clause by adding information about time, location, concession, cause, etc. They are usually linked to the main clause by a conjunction. They can occur in most parts of a sentence:

She must phone the police [if she is bullied].
[If she is bullied], she must phone the police.

Adverbial clauses cover a wide range of structures and meanings:

He pulled the cord [to set off the alarm].
[Gasping audibly], he completed his speech.
She retired [heartily detested by the electorate].

These non-finite adverbial clauses all answer basic adverbial questions:

Why did he pull the cord?
How did he complete his speech?
How did she retire?

Relative clauses

These are subordinate clauses with an 'adjectival' function in the sentence, as modifiers of a noun phrase:

The car [*which* I bought] was a mini.
I talked to the people [*who* were selling it].

In these sentences, the relative clauses are joined to the main clauses by the relative pronouns *which* and *who*. They refer back to the noun phrases *the car* and *the people*, which are called the **antecedents** of the relative clauses.

Often, especially in speech, the relative pronoun is missed out:

The man [he works for] is American. (= *whom* he works for)
I won't reply to the letter [you wrote]. (= *which* you wrote)

Comparative clauses

These are subordinate clauses which modify comparative adverbs and adjectives. The main comparative adjectives are the ones with regular *-er* endings – *older, fatter, harder, simpler,* etc. Other comparative words are *more, less, better, worse,* etc.:

It's less difficult [than I thought].

This melon seems a bit riper [than the last one was].

She tried [as hard as she could].

Things are even worse [than you might have imagined].

Finite and non-finite clauses

Finite clauses are those with a finite verb:

When he's working, he chews gum.

Both clauses in the above sentence are finite, because their verbs are finite (*is working*; *chews*).

A **non-finite clause** has a non-finite verb:

He chews gum to help his concentration.

The second clause in the above sentence is non-finite, because its verb is the non-finite *to* form (an infinitive).

Restrictive and non-restrictive clauses

This is a subdivision of relative clauses in which punctuation (or, for spoken language, intonation) plays a crucial part. Look at these sentences:

My sister *who lives in Canada* is coming to stay.

My sister, *who lives in Canada,* is coming to stay.

In the first sentence, the relative clause *who lives in Canada* is **restrictive**, specifying which sister. The informant thus perceives a certain emphasis in the first sentence:

My sister who lives in *Canada* . . . Not the one who lives in *Rickmansworth* . . .

In the second sentence, the relative clause, which has been marked off in commas, is **non-restrictive**. The information between the commas is not restricted, and the sentence has two things to say: (1) the informant has a sister who is coming to stay; (2) that sister happens to live in Canada.

Punctuation – or intonation – thus conveys the information that the informant in the first sentence has more than one sister, while the informant in the second sentence has only one sister, and that sister is resident in Canada.

Dangling modifiers

We know that a modifier is a word, phrase or clause which is added to another word to specify more exactly what that word refers to. We talk about a **dangling**, or 'hanging', **modifier** when it has been misplaced in the sentence, often with ridiculous results. For example:

The explosive was found by a security man in a plastic bag.
The boy picked the flowers that his mother had been growing for a friend.
I have a canary in a cage that can talk.
Visitors with dogs who wish to enter the garden must keep them on a lead.
Children with parents who are under ten are admitted free.
You see few signposts driving across Dartmoor.
Although big enough, she did not take the apartment.

These sentences all need to be rethought. They all point out the moral that modifiers need to be carefully 'tucked in' to the sentence.

Reading difficulty

Academic studies of **readability** point to a number of specific constructions causing difficulty to the reader. Among these are areas such as the following:

● a high number of clauses per sentence
● use of the passive
● nominalisations deriving from verbs, e.g. *reduction* from *reduce*
● ellipsis, as in 'The car [. . .] I bought was red.'

It is of course impossible and inadvisable to completely avoid such constructions in writing. But it is sometimes useful to remember that certain constructions are known to give difficulty to the reader, and to double-check one's writing when such constructions have been used.

A few specific examples of 'difficult' constructions follow. Usually the difficulty is fairly obvious, and not always easy to avoid. This merely means that certain kinds of text – e.g. scientific or legal documents – have to be read more slowly and carefully than others:

● Extended noun phrase as subject:

The conversion of the products obtained from the crackers of the oil refineries into the basic raw materials of the plastics industry occupies a large part of the world chemical industry.

● Embedded relative clauses (or 'interrupting constructions'):

Meanwhile the Normans, *who earlier in the Confessor's reign had failed to gain a commanding position in the kingdom*, were now preparing a landing somewhere along the coast.

- Non-subject noun phrases in first position in the sentence:

  The clothes and personal effects we disposed of.

- Nominalisations:

  The *exploration* and *subjugation* of this coast were the work of Portuguese seamen.

- Use of multiple subordinate clauses in subject position:

  The fact *that the monomers and similar chemicals that are the starting materials for the manufacture of plastics can now be made cheaply in large quantities* is a result of extensive research and development.

- Adverbials in first position:

  Returning from its feeding grounds in the Antarctic Ocean, the emperor penguin leaps to a height twice its own length.

- Subordinators in first position:

  Had the journey been undertaken in the eighteenth century, they would have found the countryside far more open.

- Concealed or double negatives:

  These experts *seldom* made *any* affort actually to improve the quality of people's everyday lives.

- Ellipsis:

  The internationally renowned physicist forgot [*that*] his college tutor had suggested the key experiment in the first place.

three
Word
formation

Philologists who chase
A panting syllable through time and
space,
Start it at home, and hunt it in the dark,
To Gaul, to Greece, and into Noah's
Ark.

William Cowper,
'Retirement', 1782

Some word that teems with hidden
meaning – like Basingstoke.
W.S. Gilbert, *Ruddigore*, 1887

Word formation is the study of how words are formed, particularly of
how longer and more complex words are formed from shorter and
simpler ones.

Many words comprise only a **base form** (or 'root' or 'stem'). The
base form of a noun is the singular form (e.g. *cat* not *cats*); for an
adjective it is the positive (e.g. *old* not *older* or *oldest*); and for a verb it is
the infinitive or imperative (e.g. *speak* and not *speaks, spoke, spoken* or
speaking; walk and not *walks, walked* or *walking*). So words like *apple, house,
sad, big, learn, jump* and *go* comprise only the base form; words like
applejack, housekeeper, sadly, splendiferous, unlearn, jumping jack and *go-between*
are **complex forms**, with something added to the root.

The two key ways in which base words are changed are:

● Inflection, e.g.:

apple	apples		
house	houses		
sad	sadder	saddest	
big	bigger	biggest	
learn	learns	learned	learning

jump	jumps	jump**ed**	jump**ing**
go	go**es**		go**ing**

- Word formation, e.g.:

indigestible: in + digest + ible (affixation)
hyperinflationary: hyper + inflate + ion + ary (affixation)
scuba diver: *self-c*ontained *u*nderwater *br*eathing *a*pparatus + diver (acronym)
glitzy: *gl*amour + r*itzy* (blending)
birthday: birth + day (compounding)
eyeball: eye + ball (compounding)
street cred: street credibility (clipping)
café, restaurant: (borrowing, from French)
automate: automation (back formation)
enthuse: enthusiasm (back formation)

This chapter concentrates on word formation, the second of these aspects, the main inflections of English having been covered in Part 1. The biggest part of the present chapter is given over to lists of key prefixes and suffixes, the use of which has been and remains one of the main and most productive methods through which the stock of English words has grown and developed.

Affixation is a very long-standing process. Prefixes such as *an-* and *apo-*, *mis-* and *be-*, have been in full production for many centuries. *De-* is in similar mould, with an interesting flurry of contemporary creativity with coinages like *deskill, deregulate, decommission* and *destabilise,* etc. Even *mega-* has had a burst of glory in the 1980s. Other affixes, such as *ab-, exo-, -et* and *-id,* may look pretty dormant, but it is tempting fate to write off even the most classical and Latinate of affixes: their days of productivity may well come again.

It is important to remember that words are not invariably formed by tight adherence to formal rules. Language is much more dynamic and fluid than that. As Dwight Bolinger expressed it in his *Aspects of Language* (1968):

Practically all words that are not imported bodily from some other language . . . are made up of old words and their parts. Sometimes those parts are pretty well standardized, like the suffix *-ness* and the prefix *un-*. Other times they are only broken pieces that some inventive speaker manages to refit . . . *Hamburger* yields *-burger,* which is reattached in *nutburger, Gainesburger,* and *cheeseburger. Cafeteria* yields *-teria,* which is reattached in *valeteria, groceteria,* and *washeteria.* Trade names make easy use of almost any fragment, like the *-roni* of *macaroni* that is reattached in *Rice-a-Roni* and *Noodle-Roni.* The fabrication may re-use elements that have been re-used many times, or it may be a one-shot affair such as the punning reference to being a member of the *lowerarchy,* with *-archy* extracted from *hierarchy.* The principle is the same. Scientists and scholars may give themselves airs with high-bred affixes borrowed from classical languages, but they are linguistically no more sophisticated than the common speakers who are satisfied with leftovers from the vernacular.

The list of prefixes and suffixes is given on pp. 91–112. Some of the other main forms of word formation are listed below.

Acronyms

Acronyms are abbreviations pronounced as if they were words, and they are a fairly recent method of word formation. They have proliferated in the twentieth century alongside the many abbreviations of our time. Here are a few:

AIDS	Acquired *I*mmuno-*d*eficiency *S*yndrome (1982)
AWOL	Absent *W*ithout *L*eave (US military, 1919)
IATA	*I*nternational *A*ir *T*ransport *A*ssociation
NAAFI	*N*avy *A*rmy and *A*ir *F*orce *I*nstitutes
NATO	*N*orth *A*tlantic *T*reaty *O*rganisation
OPEC	*O*rganisation of *O*il *E*xporting *C*ountries
SALT	*S*trategic *A*rms *L*imitation *T*alks
SAM	*S*urface-to-*A*ir *M*issile
TEFL	*T*eaching *E*nglish as a *F*oreign *L*anguage
UFO	*U*nidentified *F*lying *O*bject
UNESCO	*U*nited *N*ations *E*ducational *S*cientific and *C*ultural *O*rganisation
dinky	*d*ouble *i*ncome *n*o *k*ids (1980s)
laser	*L*ight *A*mplification by *S*timulated *E*mission of *R*adiation (1957)
nimby	*n*ot *i*n *m*y *b*ack *y*ard (1980s)
quango	*q*uasi-*a*utonomous *n*on-*g*overnmental *o*rganisation (1970s)
radar	*R*adio *D*etecting *a*nd *R*anging (1941)
scuba	*s*elf-*c*ontained *u*nderwater *b*reathing *a*pparatus (1952)
snafu	*s*ituation *n*ormal *a*ll *f*owled *u*p (UK military, 1940s)
yuppie	*y*oung *u*rban [or *u*pwardly mobile] *p*rofessional (1980s)

Note that the first set of examples are spelled out as capital letters, while the second set are written as ordinary words. One of the earliest acronyms is found in both forms: OK, or okay (USA, 1830s, meaning 'ol korrect').

Analogy

Another, and a much more seminal and multifarious, method of word formation is **analogy**. Many words and expressions are formed in this way, whether one describes an unmemorable person as *underwhelming* (by analogy with *overwhelming*), or says that a person has *hidden shallows* (by analogy with *hidden depths*), or coins words like *motorcade* by analogy with *cavalcade*, *telethon* by analogy with *marathon*, or *technobabble* by analogy with *nukespeak*.

Back formation

This is the process whereby a new word is formed by removing an element from – rather than adding one to – an imagined root or base. A change of word class usually occurs. For example, the verbs *edit* and *psych* are back formations from the nouns *editor* and *psychology*. Or again, the noun *permutation(s)* has recently been observed attempting to back-form a verb, *permutate*, when the verb has in fact existed for many centuries, albeit little-used nowadays, as *permute*. More frivolously, *gruntled* (whatever that may mean) is a back formation from *disgruntled*. It is worth noting in passing that the verb *back-form* is itself a back formation. Here are a few common back formations:

automate	*from*	automation
burgle	*from*	burglar
craze	*from*	crazy
donate	*from*	donation
eavesdrop	*from*	eavesdropper
enthuse	*from*	enthusiasm
greed	*from*	greedy
henpeck	*from*	henpecked
intuit	*from*	intuition
televise	*from*	television
vivisect	*from*	vivisection

Blending

Blending is a form of word compounding where new words are formed from the overlap and amalgamation of two existing words. Lewis Carroll, himself rather fond of creating such words, called these creations 'portmanteau words'. Examples are:

beresk	*from*	bereaved / berserk
biodegradable	*from*	biologically / degradable
blooper	*from*	bloomer / pooper
breathalyser	*from*	breath / analyser
brunch	*from*	breakfast / lunch
camcorder	*from*	camera / recorder
chocaholic	*from*	chocolate / -aholic (analogy alcoholic)
chortle	*from*	chuckle / snort

electrocute	*from*	electro- / execute
Eurocrat	*from*	European / bureaucrat
Eurovision	*from*	European / television
ginormous	*from*	gigantic / enormous
glitzy	*from*	gleaming and glamour / ritzy
moped	*from*	motor / pedal bike
motel	*from*	motor / hotel
motorcade	*from*	motor / cavalcade
Oxbridge	*from*	Oxford / Cambridge
Oxfam	*from*	Oxford / famine relief
raunchy	*from*	rancid / paunchy
sitcom	*from*	situation / comedy
slithy	*from*	slimy / lithe
smog	*from*	smoke / fog
telecast	*from*	television / broadcast
televangelism	*from*	television / evangelism

Blending is popular with advertisers, with words like 'Schwepper-vescence' and 'Ricicles' (which we all know are 'twicicles' as 'nicicles').

Borrowing

This is one of the simplest kinds of word formation: a term is quite simply lifted from a foreign language. The new word may be needed in English because it describes something not previously known to English speakers. Hence nouns for much flora and fauna: *lemon, orange, lilac, yam, jute, tea, shamrock, paprika, yak, kangaroo, wombat.* Many borrowed words are from foreign diets and cuisine (itself a borrowed word from French): *frankfurter, pretzel, cinnamon, ginger, yogurt, chop suey, fricassee, patisserie, lasagne, pasta, vodka.* Walter Scott popularised in his novel *Ivanhoe* the realisation that while the names of many animals in their lifetime are English (*ox, cow, calf, sheep, swine, boar, deer*), they reach the table with French names (*beef, veal, mutton, pork, bacon, brawn, venison*). This is a relic from the time when Norman masters left the care of the living animals to the Anglo-Saxon lower classes, while the superior French *cuisine* was kept in the hands of Norman cooks and *chefs.* Many other borrowings testify to this superiority: *sauce, boil, fry, roast, toast, pastry, soup, sausage, jelly, dainty.* And while the humbler *breakfast* is English, the more sumptuous meals, dinner and *supper,* as well as *feasts* generally, are French.

Most of these borrowings date from the Norman Conquest and are no longer perceived to be foreign words. We tend to be more aware of certain recent borrowings, such as *pogrom, blitzkreig, glasnost* and *pere-stroika.* But how many of us are actually aware that when we say *nix* with a negative shake of the head, we are actually using the German negative word *nicht*? Or that a *shanty town* is a direct borrowing of French *chantier*, the name Quebec lumbermen gave to their log cabins in the forest, and more generally in standard French the name for a building site? Or that if we tell an unruly child to *vamoose*, or go away, we are using the Spanish verb *vamos* or *vamonos*, meaning 'let's go'? These are all fairly recent borrowings, and contribute to the ongoing patchwork called English.

A notorious old borrowing, dating to the Norman Conquest of England in the eleventh and twelfth centuries, is the expression *apple-pie order*. We all know this means 'neat and tidy', but what have apple pies to do with neatness and tidiness? The answer is: nothing at all. This borrowing too goes back to the French-speaking Norman lords and ladies at the dinner table and their lower-class English servants. The French-speaking lady of the house would have asked the English-speaking servant girl to put smart-looking clean white folded linen at each place at the high table – folded napkins, in other words, for important guests. The French for folded napkins is *nappes pliées*, and the English-speaking servant girl called that smart and tidy-looking table *apple pie*, because that's what the words sounded like to her. A thousand years later, we continue to use the expression for the most part without the slightest knowledge of its original meaning.

There follows a list of selected borrowings under the headings of the source languages. Latin, Greek, and French are not listed, since borrowings from these sources are wholesale:

Celtic languages ambassador, bijou, blarney, bog, breeches, brogue, bug, cairn, car, carriage, clan, corgi, crag, dolmen, flannel, galore, glen, hooligan, leprechaun, loch/lough, minion, peat, piece, shamrock, slogan, sporran, Tory, trousers, whisky

Dutch/Afrikaans apartheid, bluff, boss, brandy, bully, bumpkin, clamp, coleslaw, commando, cookie, cruise, dapper, dope, drill, drum, frolic, golf, grime, hunk, kink, landscape, loiter, poppycock, rant, skipper, sledge, slim, smack, smuggle, snap, snoop, spook, spoor, stoop, trek, yacht

German blitz, dachshund, Fahrenheit, flak, frankfurter, glockenspiel, hamburger, hamster, kindergarten, kitsch, leitmotif, nix, pretzel, quartz, schnitzel, strafe, waltz, yodel

Norse and the Scandinavian languages anger, auk, balderdash, bleak, blether, blink, bloom, blunder, blur, clamber, creek, crook, die, dirt, doze, dregs, egg, eider, fellow, flat, fleck, gasp, gaze, geyser, girth, glint, glitter, gloat, happen, harsh, inkling, kick, law, leg, meek, muck, nasty, nudge, oaf, odd, raise, roof, saga, scalp, scant, scold, scowl, seat, skewer, ski, skid, skill, skin, skull, sky, slalom, sniff, squall, squeal, take, they, thrift, thrust, tungsten, ugly, want, weak, window

North American languages anorak, caucus, chipmunk, igloo, kayak, moccasin, moose, papoose, persimmon, pow-wow, raccoon, skunk, squaw, toboggan

South American languages alpaca, avocado, barbecue, buccaneer, cashew, chilli, chocolate, condor, coypu, hammock, iguana, jaguar, petunia, poncho, potato, quinine, tobacco, tomato, toucan

Caribbean languages cannibal, canoe, hurricane, maize, papaya, vicuña, yucca

African languages chimpanzee, gnu, harmattan, impala, mumbo-jumbo, okra, quagga, raffia, tsetse fly, voodoo, yam, zombie

Arabic admiral, alchemy, alcove, algebra, alkali, almanac, apricot, assassin, aubergine, azimuth, bedouin, cypher, gazelle, ghoul, giraffe, hazard, henna, jasmine, jihad, Koran, lemon, magazine, minaret, mohair, monsoon, Muslim, safari, saffron, salaam, scarlet, sherbet, sofa, syrup, talisman, tariff, zero

Hebrew alphabet, cabal, camel, cinnamon, hallelujah, hosanna, Jehovah, leviathan, manna, maudlin, messiah, rabbi, sabbath, shibboleth

Indian languages anaconda, bungalow, carmine, cheetah, chintz, chutney, crimson, curry, dinghy, dungarees, gymkhana, juggernaut, jungle, jute, lacquer, mango, mantra, mongoose, mulligatawny, nirvana, pakora, pariah, pundit, sapphire, shampoo, sugar, sutra, swastika, tomtom, yoga

Chinese and Japanese bonsai, chopsticks, geisha, ginseng, kaolin, ketchup, kimono, kung-fu, sampan, samurai, shogun, tea, tycoon, yen, zen

Clipping

Clipping is a type of word formation which occurs when a word or group of words is abbreviated. The resulting terms are often colloquial, and found more often in spoken than in written English. Examples are:

ad	advertisement
amp	ampere
artic	articulated lorry
bus	omnibus
cello	violoncello
chimp	chimpanzee
demo	demonstration
disco	discotheque
fax	facsimile
fridge	refrigerator

gent	gentleman
goalie	goalkeeper
hippo	hippopotamus
lab	laboratory
mob	*mobile vulgus* (Latin: 'the masses')
phone	telephone
photo	photograph
piano	pianoforte
pram	perambulator
pro	professional
revs	revolutions
spec	specification
telly	television

Personal names are often subject to clipping:

Alexander	Alex, Sandy
Katherine	Kath, Kate
Elizabeth	Liz, Beth
William	Will, Bill

Coining

Given the enormous range of opportunities in English for creating new words from old, it is perhaps unsurprising that the actual **coining** of new words is comparatively rare. Inventive writers like Lewis Carroll and Roald Dahl give us polysyllabic *jabberwocky* or *frobscottle* or *snozzcumbers* from time to time, by a combination of known and novel elements. Others, like J.M. Barrie or William Sharp, 'create' new personal names like *Wendy* (1904, from reduplicative 'friendly-wendy') or *Fiona* (1880s, with careful attention to the rules of Gaelic). Advertisers and creators of brand names are prolific coiners, but few of their creations enter the language – *Hoover, Kodak* and *Kleenex* are rare exceptions. Probably the best-known coinages are *fun* and *pun*, both dating from around 1700.

Compounding

Compounding occurs with the joining up of two or more smaller words to form a bigger one. It is important because it has always provided many new words, from well-established items like *housewife, nostril* (*nose* + *thirl*, or 'hole'), *eyeball, birthday, cupboard, armchair, bookcase, butterfly, blackbird, sheepdog, breakwater, steamboat, limestone, headmaster, gentleman, clergyman, playboy*, etc., to more recent creations like *astronaut, biorhythm,* *skinhead, thermonuclear.* Compounds may be written as single, fused words, like the foregoing, or they may take hyphens: *men-at-arms, commander-in-chief.* Or they may be written as two words: *fairy tale, honey bee, time warp.* Some compounds, especially of abstract or technical English, form large clusters: *first-degree murder, photoelastic stress analysis, X-ray spectrometer, liquid-crystal display hand, short-range nuclear warhead.*

Some complete words affix particularly easily and yield numerous compounds. A selection of these (*news-, out-, -down, -head,* etc.) is listed under prefixes and suffixes below.

Reduplication

This is the name given to the process whereby words are created by partial or complete repetition. Some of the resulting words are commonest among children: *abracadabra, puff-puff* (for train, in the days of steam), *wee-wee, teeny-weeny, bye-bye.* Some of the creations are echoic: *tomtom, tut-tut, tick-tock.* Many involve contrasting sounds: *hanky-panky, helter-skelter, hocus-pocus, hugger-mugger, knick-knack, mish-mash, ping-pong, mumbo-jumbo.* The resulting words are often spelled with a hyphen.

Many of these reduplicative words involve an element of rhyme, which is what makes them memorable and ensures the contemporary colloquial popularity of this aspect of word formation. Nowadays we all seem to love a rhyme.

Other reduplications:

Rhyming	Nonrhyming
Ally Pally (for Alexandra Palace)	dilly-dally
argy-bargy	ding-dong
arty-farty	flimflam
backpack	shillyshally
Delhi belly	singsong
easy-peasy	
fat cat	**Repetitive**
heebie-jeebies	chin-chin
hi-fi	chop chop
hoity-toity	gaga
namby-pamby	go-go
pub grub	so-so
silly-billy	
sin-bin	
toy-boy	
willy-nilly	

Prefixes and suffixes

Affixation is the general name for the fixing of something in front of a word or base (when it is called a **prefix**), or after a word or base (when it is called a **suffix**). Affixation is by far the most prolific and enduring form of English word formation. English prefixes and suffixes are formed from a variety of source languages, including Old English, Old French, Latin and Greek. When a prefix contributes obviously to the meaning of the word (as *un-* does in *unkind* or *unclean* or *unfair*), it is sometimes called **productive**. Where it does not make an obvious contribution to the meaning of the word (as *ana-* does not in *anagram, anatomy* or *analysis* – unless one is a classical Greek scholar), it is sometimes called **unproductive**. Nowadays many affixes which were once productive have become unproductive, especially to users of the English language with scanty knowledge of Latin or Greek. The notorious example of *history/herstory* illustrates the point. Some members of the anti-sexist lobby took the view that world history as a subject was male-dominated, and that the very construction of the word illustrated this point nicely. They may have been entirely right about the subject, but they were wrong about the word, since it was taken into English from the Greek word *historia*, meaning 'knowing' or 'inquiry', and demonstrably not made up of 'story' as a base plus 'his' as a prefix or compound.

Other etymologically daft, if 'politically correct', constructions are nonwords like *efemcipate* and *femstruate* (for *emancipate* and *menstruate*). These terms may eliminate the (by some people) hated elements *man* and *men*, but they do no more than represent crude and rather ridiculous attempts at thought-policing by people who seem to have little feeling for how language evolves and works. They are the farther reaches of the movement that has tended to replace *mankind* with *humankind, spokesmen* with *spokespersons,* etc. That is one thing, of course; to threaten *Herman* with his *Walkman* is slightly different!

There follows a selective list of some of the more common prefixes and suffixes in modern English, with brief notes on their etymologies, and examples of some of the words formed. Some of the more common compounds are also listed:

Prefixes

a-, an- from Greek 'without' or 'not' or 'opposite to'. For example, an '*a*political' person is without views about politics. Other words formed from this prefix: *a*moral, *a*phasic, *a*tonal, *a*typical, *a*sexual, *a*gnostic, *a*narchy, *a*theist, *a*nonymous

a- from Old English 'on', as in *a*stern, *a*bed, *a*board, *a*foot, *a*live, *a*shore

ab- (a-, abs-) from Latin 'from' or 'away', as in *a*version, *a*vert, *ab*dicate, *abs*tract, *abs*tain, *ab*ound, *ab*use, *ab*duction

ad from Latin 'to' or 'towards', as in *a*dore, *a*dvise. This prefix generally assimilates before *b, c, f, g, l, n, p, r, s, t*, and converts into *ab*breviate, *ac*cident, *ac*cord, *ac*cuse, *ac*cede, *af*firm, *af*fix, *ag*grieve, *al*lude, *an*nounce, *an*nexe, *ap*pear, *ar*rive, *as*similate, *a*scribe, *as*sent, *as*sure, *as*sault, *at*tend, *at*tain, *a*vow

aero- from Greek 'air', as in *aero*dynamics, *aero*plane, *aero*naut, *aero*space, *aer*ial, *aer*obic, *aero*batics, *aero*foil

after- from the Old English preposition, giving compound nouns like *after*noon, *after*birth, *after*life, *after*thought, *after*math, *after*-effects. A wide range of adjectives is also derived: *after*-school, *after*-dinner, *after*-hours, etc. The adjectives usually take a hyphen, the nouns not.

agro-, agri- from Greek 'field', giving *agri*culture, *agri*business, *agro*nomy, *agro*chemical

am-, ambi- (1) from Latin 'around' or 'about', akin to **amphi-**, as in *am*bassador, *amb*ient, *amp*utate, *amb*ition, *ambi*guous, (2) from Latin for 'both', as in *ambi*dextrous, *ambi*valent

amphi- from Greek 'on both sides' or 'round', as in *amphi*bious, *amphi*theatre

ana- from Greek 'on', 'up', 'throughout', or 'backwards', as in *ana*tomy, *ana*lysis, *ana*chronism, *ana*gram, *ana*logy

ante-, anti- from Latin 'before', as in *ante*date, *ante*cedent, *ante*natal, *ante*diluvian, *ante*-room, *anti*cipate

anti-, ant- from Greek 'against', usually forming words indicating opposition or prevention, as in *anti*thesis, *anti*dote, *anti*pathy, *anti*biotic, *anti*freeze, *anti*-nuclear, *anti*-inflationary. Not to be confused with **ante-**, and vice versa.

apo- from Greek 'from' or 'off from', as in *apo*crypha ('things hidden from'), *apo*logy, *apo*stle, *apo*gee, *apo*strophe, *apho*rism (*apo* + *horizein*, 'within a limit', meaning a pithy definition)

arch- from Greek for a 'ruler' or 'chief', giving words like *arch*angel, *arch*bishop, *arch*duke, *archi*tect. The prefix also functions as a sort of intensifier, as with *arch*-enemy, *arch*-rebel, *arch*-competitor, etc. (See also the suffix **-arch**, below.)

astro-, astron- from Greek 'star', giving *astron*omy, *astro*dome, *astro*physics, *astro*logy, *astro*naut, *astr*al

at- from Old English, giving *at*one ('bring together into one'), *a*do ('at do'), *t*wit (verb, 'at wit')

audio-, aud- from Latin 'hear', as in *audio*cassette, *audio*-tape, *audio*-lingual, *audio*-visual, *audi*tion, *audi*tory

auto- from Greek 'of or by itself', as with (1) things that work '*auto*matically', such as *auto*mobile, *auto*mation, *auto*cue, *auto*-reverse;

(2) things to do with 'oneself', such as *auto*biography, *auto*nomy, *auto*graph, *auto*crat; (3) words to do with cars, or 'autos', such as *auto*sport, *auto*-industry

be- from Old English intensifier, giving (1) words suggesting a 'covering' or item of dress, such as *be*wigged, *be*spattered, *be*jewelled, *be*spectacled; (2) words suggesting a certain state, such as *be*calmed, *be*fuddled, *be*sotted, *be*trothed, *be*witched, *be*mused; and (3) various transitive verbs, such as *be*friend, *be*moan, *be*queath, *be*siege, *be*set, *be*hold. Also *be*head, *be*come, *be*have, *be*lieve, *be*ware.

bi- from Latin 'two', as in *bi*cycle, *bi*focal, *bi*ped, *bi*sect, *bi*annual, *bi*furcation, *bi*lingual, *bi*noculars, *bi*centenary, *bi*gamy, *bi*carbonate. There is some potential for confusion with this prefix, because it can sometimes mean 'half' and sometimes 'twice', with the result that words like *bi*weekly or *bi*monthly can mean 'twice a week/month', or 'once every two weeks/months'. These terms should therefore be avoided.

bio- from Greek for 'life', as in *bio*chemistry, *bio*graphy, *bio*logy, *bio*degradable, *bio*psy; and recent coinages like *bio*nic, *bio*rhythms. Note that **bio-** also appears within certain words: anti*bio*tics, sym*bio*tic

by- from Old English 'by', giving compounds like *by*stander, *by*pass

cardi-, cardio- from Greek 'heart', as in *cardi*ac, *cardio*logy, electro-*cardio*gram

cata- from Greek '(broken) down', as in *cata*logue, *cata*strophe, *cate*chism, *cath*artic, *cath*edral (from Greek *kata*, 'down', and *hed*, 'sit', giving Latin *cathedra*, 'seat' or bishop's 'throne')

cent-, centi- from Latin 'hundred', as in *cent*enary, *centi*grade, *centi*metre, *centi*pede, *cent*ury, per*cent*(age)

chron-, chrono- from Greek 'time', as in *chron*ology, *chrono*meter, *chron*icle, ana*chron*ism, syn*chron*ise

cine- from Greek 'movement', which gave '*cine*ma' (moving pictures) and hence *cine*-camera, *cine*-film, *cine*matography

circum-, circu- from Latin 'round', as in *circum*stance, *circum*navigate, *circum*ference, *circum*vent, *circu*late, *circu*it, *circum*cise

con-, com- from Latin *com*-, 'together with', as in *com*pound, *com*pact, *com*pare, *con*sonant, *con*tend, *con*duct, *con*nect. This prefix often combines with other consonants, as in *col*lide, *col*lect, *cor*rect, *cor*rupt, *co*erce. Compounds such as *co*operate, *co*-star, *co*-publish, etc. are also formed from this prefix.

contra-, contro-, counter- from Latin 'counter', 'opposite' or 'against', as in *contra*ry, *contra*dict, *contra*vene, *contra*ceptive, *contra*flow, *contra*distinction, *contro*versy, *contra*band, *counter*attack, *counter*balance, *counter*weight, *counter*feit

de- from Latin 'down' or 'from', yielding (1) verbs indicating an opposite or reverse action, as in *de*activate, *de*classify, *de*congestion, *de*militarise, *de*mystify; (2) verbs indicating the removal of something, as in *de*-ice, *de*coke, *de*capitate, *de*frost, *de*scale, *de*skill; and (3) a reduction, as in *de*grade, *de*value, *de*fuse. There is also a wide range of other verbs: *de*press, *de*scend, *de*part, *de*pend, *de*note, *de*scribe, *de*vise, *de*mure, *de*legate, including recent creations like *de*criminalise, *de*segregate, *de*-escalate.

deca- from Greek 'ten', as in *deca*thlon, *deca*de, *deca*hedron

deci- from Latin 'tenth', as in *deci*bel, *deci*mal, *deci*mate

demi- from Old French 'half', as in *demi*john, *demi*god. See also **half-** and **semi-**, below

demo-, dema- from Greek for 'town', as in *demo*crat, *dema*gogue, *demo*tic, *demo*graphy

derm- from Greek 'skin' or 'hide', giving *derm*al, *derm*atology, (suffix) epi*dermis*

di-, dis- from Greek 'two', as in *di*phthong, *di*lemma, *di*saster (from Latin, 'two stars' in conflict), *di*syllable

dia- from Greek 'through' or 'apart', as in *dia*logue, *dia*meter, *dia*phanous, *dia*phragm, *dia*lectic

dis-, dif-, di- from Latin 'apart' or 'asunder'. This prefix can elide or combine with other consonants, giving words like *di*ffuse, *di*vide, *di*ffer. More importantly, it also combines with many existing verbs to give their opposites: *dis*agree, *dis*appear, *dis*approve, *dis*sociate (*dis*associate), *dis*connect, *dis*embark, *dis*infect, *dis*inherit, *dis*integrate, *dis*like, *dis*lodge, *dis*obey, *dis*organise, *dis*qualify, etc.

double- from Old French meaning 'two', as with *double*-glazing, *double*-locked, *double*-sided, *double*-jointed, *double* Dutch, etc. There is also a connotation of deception with compounds such as *double*-talk, *double*-dealing, *double*-cross.

down- from Old English, giving compounds such as *down*fall, *down*cast, *down*beat, *down*grade, *down*trodden, *down*turn, as well as vogue terms like *down*side, *down*sizing

dys- from Greek 'bad', usually with the sense 'abnormal', as in *dys*function, *dys*lexic, *dys*pepsia, *dys*entery, *dys*trophy

eco-, ec- from Greek 'house', now with the sense of 'habitat' or 'environment', giving words like *eco*logy, *eco*species, *eco*sphere, *eco*system, *eco*-freak, *eco*-nut, *eco*-disaster

en-, em-, el- from Greek 'in', as in *en*ergy, *en*thusiasm, *en*demic, *em*phasis, *em*porium, *em*blem, *el*lipse. The prefix also functions as a sort of intensifier in words like *en*rich, *en*able, *en*close, *en*courage, *en*danger, *en*dear, *en*force, *en*rage, *en*rapture, *en*slave, *en*tangle, *en*trance, *en*twine.

endo- from Greek 'within', as in *endo*gamy ('inbreeding'), *endo*crine, *endo*thelium

epi- from Greek, 'on', 'upon', 'for', as in *epi*gram, *epi*logue, *epi*stle, *epi*phany, *epi*taph

equi- from Latin 'equal', giving *equi*valent, *equi*vocal, *equi*lateral, *equi*distant, *equi*librium

Euro- a prefix now synonymous with the European Community (EC) and related activities, spawning items such as *Euro*sceptic, *Euro*bond, *Euro*vision, *Euro*crat, *Euro*currency, *Euro*bank, *Euro*market

ex-, ef-, e- from Latin 'out of', as in *ex*hale, *ex*tol, *ex*ceed, *ex*haust, *ex*hume, *ex*patriate, *ex*pire, *ex*onerate. The prefix forms **ef-** and **e-** before certain consonants, as in *ef*fusive, *e*merge, *e*lapse, *e*rase, *e*vade, *e*scape, *e*duce, *e*ducate. Words such as *ex*-husband, *ex*-boxer, *ex*-king, *ex*-president, indicating people who 'used to be' something, are also from this prefix.

exo- from Greek for 'outside', as in *exo*tic, *exo*gamy

extra- from Latin for 'beyond', as in *extra*ordinary ('beyond the ordinary'), *extra*-special, *extra*-marital, *extra*-curricular, *extra*vagant, *extra*neous. In many of its hyphenated constructions popular with advertising scriptwriters, the prefix means 'very' and functions as an intensifier: *extra*-large, *extra*-bright.

for- from an Old English preposition usually indicating prohibition (*for*bid, *for*fend), abstention (*for*bear, *for*go, *for*swear), or neglect (*for*sake, *for*get, *for*lorn)

fore- from Old English 'before' or 'in front', giving compounds such as *fore*tell, *fore*cast, *fore*father, *fore*warn, *fore*going, *fore*noon, *fore*stall, *fore*legs, *fore*head. Not to be confused with **for-**, or vice versa.

gain- from the same source as Old English 'again' and 'against', giving *gain*say

hand- from Old English, giving compounds with the meaning 'made or operated by the hands' or 'for the use of the hands', such as *hand*-made, *hand*-stitched, *hand*writing, *hand*bag, *hand*kerchief, *hand*cuff, *hand*shake, *hand*stand

hetero- from Greek 'other' or 'different', giving words like *hetero*sexual (sexual relationship between people of different sexes), *hetero*geneous, *hetero*dox

hom-, homo- from Greek 'same', giving *homo*geneous, *home*opathy, *homo*phobe, *homo*sexual, *homo*nym, *homo*phone

hyper- from Greek for 'over' or 'above', in the sense of 'excessively', as in *hyper*active, *hyper*critical, *hyper*inflation, *hyper*market, *hyper*sensitive, *hyper*bole. A prefix functioning as an intensifier, **hyper-** also functions nowadays as an independent noun, meaning 'agitated' or 'keyed up', and appears in the words *hype* and *hyped*-up.

hyph-, hypo- from Greek for 'under' (therefore the opposite of **hyper-**), as in *hypo*crite, *hypo*dermic, *hypo*tenuse, *hypo*thermia, *hypoth*esis, *hyph*en (two words 'under one', or 'into one')

in- from Latin for 'into', as in *in*born, *in*come, *in*side, *in*vade, *in*cite, *in*duce, *in*nate, *in*trude. The prefix also forms **im-, en-, em-, il-, ir-** before certain consonants, as with *il*lusion, *im*mense, *im*prove, *im*pulse, *im*pel, *em*brace, *em*broil, *en*courage, *en*dure, *ir*radiate.

in- from Latin for 'not', as with *in*advertent, *in*capable, *in*curable, *in*convenient, *in*nocent. The prefix also forms **ig-, il, im-, ir-** with certain consonants, as with *ig*noble, *il*logical, *il*legitimate, *il*literate, *im*mortal, *im*proper, *ir*regular, *ir*rational.

in- from an Old English preposition, giving compound items such as *in*sight, *in*bred, *in*let, *in*come, *in*hale, as well as *en*dear, *en*thral, *en*grave, *em*bed/*im*bed

infra- from Latin 'beneath' or 'lower', giving *infra*structure, *infra*sonic, *infra*-red, *infra* dig ('beneath one's dignity')

inter-, intel-, enter- from Latin for 'between', as in *inter*act, *inter*continental, *inter*marriage, *inter*view, *inter*rupt, *inter*course, *inter*com, *inter*-city. The prefix also forms **intel-** and **enter-**, giving *intel*ligent, *enter*prise, *enter*tain.

intra- from Latin 'within', now used as an opposite of **extra-**, as in *intra*-European, *intra*venous, *intra*muscular, *intra*-uterine. Not to be confused with **inter-**, or vice versa.

intro- from Latin 'to or towards' or 'within', giving *intro*duce, *intro*vert, *intro*spection

low- productive contemporary compound, giving *low*-key (restrained), *low*-profile (unsensational), *low*-budget (cheap), *low*-grade (inferior)

macro- from Greek 'large' or 'long', the opposite of **micro-**. Most words formed with this prefix are technical: *macro*economics, *macro*biotic, *macro*structure, *macro*cosm

mal- from Old French 'bad', used in words describing imperfection, such as *mal*formation, *mal*nutrition, *mal*adjusted, *mal*practice, *mal*function

mega- from Greek 'large', a buzz prefix of the 1980s, nowadays giving *mega*buck, *mega*star, *mega*rock, *mega*bid, *mega*thon, *mega*trend, as well as the independent adjective *mega* (equivalent to the 'cool' of an earlier generation). This prefix has suited the spirit of an age ever in search of the new superlative. Earlier constructions were *mega*phone, *mega*lithic, *mega*lomania, *mega*lopolis. The prefix also has the technical meaning of a unit of measurement one million times bigger than the unit referred to: *mega*hertz, *mega*watt, *mega*ton, *mega*cycle, *mega*byte.

meta- from Greek 'change' or 'transformation', as with *meta*morphosis, *meta*phor, *meta*physics, *meto*nymy, *met*hod

micro- from Greek 'small', as in *micro*scope, *micro*cosm, *micro*biology, *micro*film, *micro*processor, *micro*computer, *micro*electronics, *micro*wave

mid- from Old English 'middle', giving *mid*most, *mid*night, *mid*day, *mid*summer, *mid*-term

milli- from Latin 'thousand', as in *milli*metre, *milli*bar, *milli*micron, *milli*pede

mini- from Latin 'lesser' and 'least', as in *mini*mum, *minim*, *mini*bus, *mini*cab, *mini*skirt

mis- partly from Old English for 'wrongly' or 'badly', and partly from Latin *minus* via Old French *mes*, which came to have a similar meaning, giving *mis*behave, *mis*judge, *mis*apply, *mis*construe, *mis*manage, *mis*place, *mis*truth, *mis*deed, *mis*hap, *mis*chief

mono- from Greek 'one alone', giving *mono*logue, *mono*chrome, *mono*tonous, *mono*xide, *mono*gamy, *mono*cle

multi- from Latin 'many', as in *multi*tude, *multi*farious, *multi*form, *multi*ply, *multi*plicity, *multi*dimensional, *multi*purpose

neo- from Greek 'new' or 'recent', akin to Latin *novus*, giving *neo*logism ('new wordism'), *neo*lithic, *neo*-natal (recently born, i.e. less than a month old). The prefix also means a follower of a person or school of thought: *neo*-classical, *neo*-Marxist, *neo*-Nazi, *neo*-Freudian.

neur-, neuro- from Greek for 'nerve', giving *neur*ology, *neur*asthenia, *neuro*surgery, *neur*on, *neur*algia

news- an example of an English noun which readily combines with others to form new compounds: *news*agent, *news*cast, *news*desk, *news*paper, *news*worthy, *news*print, *news*flash, *news*letter

non- from Old French 'not', giving *non*sense, *non*entity, *non*committal, *non*conformist, *non*flowering, *non*involvement, *non*resistant, *non*smoking. There is a contemporary tendency to overuse this prefix, creating words (nonwords?) like *non*presence (for absence), *non*permanent (for temporary), *non*success (for failure), *non*obligatory (for optional).

ob- from Latin 'towards' or 'facing against', as in *ob*ject, *ob*verse, *ob*fuscate, *ob*durate. The prefix assimilates before certain consonants as **oc-, of-, op-, os-**, giving also *op*pose, *oc*cur, *of*fer, *oc*cult, *os*tentation.

off- from Old English, giving compounds such as *off*set, *off*cut, *off*spring, *off*shoot, *off*hand, *off*al ('off-fall')

omni- from Latin 'all', as in *omni*potent, *omni*present, *omni*vorous

out- from Old English, giving compounds with the meaning 'do better than', and where the root is stressed, such as *out*strip, *out*wit, *out*do, *out*run, *out*smart, *out*manoeuvre; others such as *out*fall, *out*rage, *out*law, where the prefix is stressed; and Americanisms such as *out*asight, *out*front

over- from Old English, giving compounds such as *over*come, *over*take, *over*do, *over*see, *over*eat, *over*reach

para-, par- from Greek for (1) 'beside', as in *para*military ('beside the military'), *para*medic, *para*normal, *para*typhoid; (2) '(defence) against', giving *para*pet, *para*sol; (3) other meanings such as *para*graph, *para*phrase, *para*noia, *para*digm, *para*dise, *para*plegic, *para*dox; and (4) actions involving *para*chutes, such as *para*gliding, *para*scending, *para*trooper

pene- from Latin 'almost', as in *pen*insula, *pene*plain

per-, pel- from Latin 'through', as in *per*ambulate, *per*secute, *per*turb, *per*vert, *per*mit, *per*form, *per*tain, *pel*lucid, *pil*grim (from *per* + *ager*, a person travelling 'through the country')

peri- from Greek 'round', as with *peri*meter, *peri*scope, *peri*phery, *peri*od

poly- from Greek 'many', denoting plurality and diversity, as in *poly*andry, *poly*anthus, *poly*chromatic, *poly*gamy, *poly*glot, *poly*gon, *poly*syllabic, *poly*technic

post- from Latin 'after', as in *post*pone, *post*humous, *post*script, *post*date, *post*-war, *post*-Gorbachev

pre-, prae- from Latin 'before', as in *pre*face, *pre*cede, *pre*decease, *pre*judge, *pre*vent, *pre*mature, *pre*dict, *pre*destination, *pre*text, *pre*-Christian, *pre*-war, *pre*monition

pro- from Greek 'before', as in *pro*boscis, *pro*scenium, *pro*logue, *pro*phet, *pro*gramme, *pro*blem

pro-, por-, pur-, pol- from Latin 'on', 'forth' or 'before', and akin to the Greek prefix, giving *pro*ceed, *pro*gress, *pro*ject, *pro*noun, *por*tend, *por*tray, *pur*loin, *pur*chase, *pol*lute. Also in the sense of an agent 'holding the line', in titles such as *pro*consul, *pro*-vice-chancellor, *pro*curator. Finally, and very productively, in the sense of 'in favour of' or 'on behalf of', there is the wide range of compounds like *pro*-British, *pro*-communist, *pro*-feminist, *pro*-life, etc.

pros- from Greek 'towards' or 'in addition to', as in *pros*ody, *pros*elytise

pseud- from Greek 'false' or 'spurious', used pejoratively to suggest bogus or sham or pretentious qualities, as in *pseudo*-friend, *pseudo*-literary, and yielding in the 1960s the independent noun *pseud*, 'a bogus intellectual'. *Pseuds' Corner* in the magazine *Private Eye* popularised this use. Earlier derivatives of this prefix were *pseudo*nym ('fictitious name') and *pseudo*pregnancy ('false pregnancy').

psych-, psyche-, psycho-, from Greek 'soul' or 'mind', giving *psyche*, *psycho*logy, *psychi*atry, *psycho*dynamic, *psycho*somatic, and more recent flowerings of the Beat generation such as *psyche*delic, and phrasal verbs *psych* up and *psych* out

re-, red- (1) from Latin 'back', as in *re*turn, *re*tract, *re*cant, *re*fute, *re*deem, *re*duce, *re*nounce, *re*sound, *re*sign, *re*veal; (2) the prefix can also be used for 'again', and requires a hyphen where the meaning might otherwise be ambiguous, as in *re*-sign, *re*-bound, *re*-cover

retro- from Latin 'backwards', as in *retro*grade, *retro*spect, *retro*rocket

se-, sed- from Latin 'aside' or 'apart', as in *se*cede, *se*lect, *se*clude, *se*dition, *se*duce, *se*crete

semi- from Latin 'half', as in *semi*circle, *semi*-acid, *semi*-detached, *semi*-liquid, etc. By extension, the prefix can be used as a more general qualifier meaning 'partly', as in *semi*-dark, *semi*-literate, *semi*-invalid, *semi*-official, *semi*-permanent, *semi*-skilled.

sub-, suc-, suf-, sug-, sup-, sur-, sus-, su- from Latin 'under' or 'up from below', as in *sub*marine, *sub*terranean, *sub*merge, *sub*due, *sub*ject, *sub*vert, *sub*conscious. **Sub** also assimilates variously before consonants, as with *su*spect, *suc*ceed, *suf*fer, *sug*gest, *sup*pose, *su*spend, *su*spect, *suc*cinct, *sup*press, *sur*rogate, *su*sceptible, *suf*fuse, *sup*plant.

subter- from Latin 'beneath', as in *subter*fuge

super-, sur- from Latin 'over', as in *super*intend, *super*structure, *super*-natural, *super*cilious, *super*fluous, *super*lative, *super*stition, *super*vene, *sur*plus, *sur*vive, *sur*feit, *sur*charge, *sur*name, *sur*face

syn-, sy-, syl-, sym- from Greek 'together with', as in *syn*thesis, *syn*tax, *syn*onym, *syn*agogue, *syl*lable, *sy*stem, *sym*ptom, *sym*pathy

techn- from Greek 'craft' or 'skill', giving *techn*ical, *techn*ology, *techn*ocrat, *techn*ique, pyro*techn*ic ('skill with fire'), hi-*tech*, as well as pejoratives like *techno*freak, *techno*babble

tele- from Greek 'distance', giving *tele*vision, *tele*graph, *tele*printer, *tele*pathy, *tele*scope, *tele*phone, *tele*

thorough-, through- from the Old English preposition with variant spellings, giving *thorough*going, *thorough*fare, *thorough*bred, *through*out

to- from the Old English intensive meaning 'this', giving *to*day, *to*morrow, *to*night

trans-, tran-, tra-, tres- from Latin 'across', suggesting 'movement' or 'change', giving *trans*atlantic, *trans*action, *trans*late, *tran*scend, *tran*scribe, *trans*fusion, *trans*port, *trans*plant. Prefix assimilations give *tra*dition, *tres*pass, *tra*duce, *tra*jectory, *tra*verse.

ultra- from Latin 'beyond', giving *ultra*marine, *ultra*montane, *ultra*modern, *ultra*violet

un- from Old English meaning (1) 'not', as in *un*clean, *un*wise, *un*true, *un*fair, *un*tidy; or (2) 'back', with the connotation of reversal, as in *un*tie, *un*fold, *un*bend, *un*do

under- from Old English, giving compounds such as *under*stand, *under*growth, *under*wear, *under*hand, *under*cover

uni- from Latin 'one', giving *uni*form, *uni*fy, *uni*ty, *uni*te, *uni*on, *uni*lateral, *uni*sex, *uni*cycle, *uni*verse

up- from Old English, yielding compounds such as *up*roar, *up*land, *up*set, *up*right, *up*river, *up*stage, *up*stream, *up*thrust, *up*tight, *up*wind, *up*front, *up*chuck

vice- from Latin for 'in place of', as in *vice*-chancellor, *vice*-president, *vice* versa

wel-, well- from the Old English adverb, giving *wel*come, *wel*fare, *well*-bred, *well*-trained, *well*-tried, *well*-to-do

with- from the Old English preposition, giving *with*stand, *with*hold, *with*draw (*with*drawing room = drawing room)

Suffixes

Before listing the suffixes alphabetically, it is perhaps appropriate to draw attention to certain rules of spelling. If the suffix begins with a vowel, it is necessary to double the final single consonant for:

- monosyllables, as in drop/dro*pp*ing, pat/pa*tt*ing, sit/si*tt*ing
- stressed last syllables, as in admit/admi*tt*ance, repel/repe*ll*ent, regret/regre*tt*able
- a consonant following a single stressed vowel, as in grit/gri*tt*er, refer/refe*rr*al, infer/infe*rr*ing (but refer/reference, infer/inference, because here the second syllable is not stressed)

These are called the **gemination** ('twinning') **rules**, because they govern the doubling of consonants before a suffix.

Another simple rule governs words ending with -*e*. If they add a suffix beginning with a vowel, the -*e* is usually dropped. If they add a suffix beginning with a consonant, the -*e* is usually retained. Thus:

Drop the -e	Retain the -e
sense + ory = sens**ory**	shame + ful = sham**eful**
creative + ity = creativ**ity**	care + free = car**efree**
cube + oid = cub**oid**	gentle + ness = gentl**eness**

Exceptions include: mil*eage*, acr*eage*, aw*ful*.

Note that the -*able*/-*ible* dilemma is one of the commonest causes of spelling error. Some of the -*ible* spellings that worry people are:

access*ible*	aud*ible*	collaps*ible*
combust*ible*	compat*ible*	comprehens*ible*
convert*ible*	corrupt*ible*	cred*ible*
deduct*ible*	defens*ible*	destruct*ible*
digest*ible*	discern*ible*	divis*ible*
ed*ible*	elig*ible*	fall*ible*
feas*ible*	flex*ible*	forc*ible*
horr*ible*	incorrig*ible*	indel*ible*

intang*ible*	intellig*ible*	leg*ible*
neglig*ible*	percept*ible*	permiss*ible*
plaus*ible*	poss*ible*	resist*ible*
respons*ible*	revers*ible*	sens*ible*
terr*ible*	vis*ible*	

Some of the *-able* spellings that worry people are:

advis*able*	adapt*able*	ador*able*
ami*able*	approach*able*	avail*able*
believ*able*	calcul*able*	cap*able*
change*able*	conceiv*able*	cur*able*
defin*able*	demonstr*able*	depend*able*
desir*able*	despic*able*	dissolv*able*
dur*able*	excit*able*	excus*able*
expend*able*	foresee*able*	forget*table*
forgiv*able*	immov*able*	impass*able*
impecc*able*	implac*able*	impression*able*
indescrib*able*	inimit*able*	insuffer*able*
manage*able*	measur*able*	pleasur*able*
prefer*able*	read*able*	recognis*able*
reconcil*able*	regret*table*	remov*able*
reput*able*	transfer*able*	understand*able*
unmistak*able*	us*able*	wash*able*

(Several of these words are also listed in the list of **common spelling errors**, on pp. 191–99.)

-able, -ible, -ble Latin adjective suffixes, as in admir*able*, ami*able*, cap*able*, culp*able*, ed*ible*, drink*able*, flex*ible*, horr*ible*, indigest*ible*, permiss*ible*, predict*able*, prob*able*, sol*uble*, wash*able*

-acious Latin adjective suffix, denoting a tendency, sometimes excessive, as in loqu*acious*, vor*acious*, viv*acious*, ver*acious*, ten*acious*, fall*acious*, sag*acious*

-age Latin abstract noun suffix, as in break*age*, bond*age*, cour*age*, drain*age*, herit*age*, hom*age*, leak*age*, marri*age*, measur*age*, person*age*, sav*age*, shrink*age*, till*age*, verbi*age*, voy*age*, umbr*age*. The suffix also gives a place, as anchor*age*, cott*age*, orphan*age*, hermit*age*, vicar*age*; and a reference of measure, as in acre*age*, foot*age*, mile*age*, tonn*age*, volt*age*.

-aholic suffix of the 1970s blended from the latter part of *alcoholic* (NB NOT alc*aholic*), with the meaning 'addicted to', and forming adjectives by analogy, as work*aholic*, choc*aholic*, shop*aholic*, writ*aholic*, golf*aholic*

-al, -ar Latin suffix giving (1) adjectives, as in comic*al*, equ*al*, gener*al*, leg*al*, loy*al*, norm*al*, or*al*, politic*al*, regul*ar*, secul*ar*, singul*ar*; (2) nouns denoting action, as in buri*al*, betray*al*, dismiss*al*, renew*al*, rent*al*, withdraw*al*

-an, -ian, -ane, -ain, -on Latin suffixes giving (1) nouns denoting a person, as in artis*an*, grammar*ian*, vill*ain*, surge*on*, sext*on*; (2) adjectives such as pag*an*, urb*an*, urb*ane*, hum*an*, hum*ane*, mund*ane*, cert*ain*, sylv*an*; (3) adjectives from places, as in Americ*an*, Australi*an*, Brazil*ian*, Ethiopi*an*, Nigeri*an*

-ance, -ancy, -ence, -ency Latin abstract noun suffixes, as in dist*ance*, resist*ance*, cad*ence*, const*ancy*, dec*ency*, inf*ancy*, persist*ence*. Many of these nouns are formed from a corresponding verb, as in admitt*ance*, observ*ance*, accept*ance*, disturb*ance*, disappear*ance*, entr*ance*, guid*ance*, insur*ance*, mainten*ance*, perform*ance*, resist*ance*; or from an adjective, as in arrog*ance*, brilli*ance*, fragr*ance*, ignor*ance*, irrelev*ance*, reluct*ance*, repugn*ance*, vigil*ance*

-ant, -ent Latin suffixes giving (1) nouns denoting a person, as in assist*ant*, attend*ant*, claim*ant*, combat*ant*, depend*ant*, ten*ant*, ag*ent*, assail*ant*, serv*ant*, stud*ent*; (2) adjectives such as arrog*ant*, const*ant*, depend*ent*, ignor*ant*, pleas*ant*, pregn*ant*, pat*ent*, innoc*ent*, flu*ent*

-arch, -archy from Greek 'chief', giving mon*archy*, hier*archy*, matri*archy*, patri*archy*, olig*archy*, squir*earchy*

-ary, -arian, -arious Latin suffixes giving (1) adjectives as in contr*ary*, exempl*ary*, mercen*ary*, milit*ary*, necess*ary*, sedent*ary*, station*ary*, antiqu*arian*, agr*arian*, veget*arian*, sect*arian*, parliament*arian*, utilit*arian*, octogen*arian*, greg*arious* – with several forms becomin? independent nouns, words like libr*arian*, gramm*arian*, formed by analogy in this category; (2) nouns with the connotation 'belonging to', as in libr*ary*, infirm*ary*, penitenti*ary*, gran*ary*, avi*ary*; or agent nouns, as in actu*ary*, mission*ary*, advers*ary*, secret*ary*, lumin*ary*, emiss*ary*; or nouns with other meanings, as annivers*ary*, bound*ary*, diction*ary*, gloss*ary*, obitu*ary*, sal*ary*, summ*ary*, vocabul*ary*

-ate, -ee, -ey, -y Latin suffixes denoting (1) nouns indicating a person or agent, as in advoc*ate*, cur*ate*, episcop*ate*, magistr*ate*, nitr*ate*, leg*atee*, nomin*ee*, trust*ee*, committ*ee*, attorn*ey*, cov*ey*, all*y*, deput*y*, jur*y*; (2) verbs, as advoc*ate*, anticip*ate*, complic*ate*, concentr*ate*, eradic*ate*, fascin*ate*, incapacit*ate*, supplic*ate*, vener*ate*

-ate, -ete, -eet, -ite, -ute, -te Latin adjective suffixes, as in deliber*ate*, desol*ate*, emascul*ate*, fortun*ate*, concr*ete*, eff*ete*, discr*eet*, erud*ite*, min*ute*

-ation see **-ion**

-bound English adjective suffix, as in house*bound*, duty-*bound*, earth*bound*, snow*bound*, out*bound*, hide*bound*, spell*bound*

-centric Greek adjective suffix, relating to 'a centre', as in con*centric*, ego*centric*, ec*centric*, anthropo*centric*

-cide Latin noun suffix from 'kill', as in infanti*cide*, geno*cide*, parri*cide*, pesti*cide*, sui*cide*, fungi*cide*, insecti*cide*, herbi*cide*, spermi*cide*

-craft English noun suffix, giving (1) words to do with transport, formed by analogy with air*craft*, as in hover*craft*, space*craft*, landing-*craft*; and (2) words to do with particular skills, as in handi*craft*(s), needle*craft*, wood*craft*, bush*craft*, stage*craft*, film*craft*, witch*craft*

-cred a contemporary suffix meaning 'acceptability among young people' and formed from an abbreviation of *street credibility*, now giving street *cred*, and by analogy star *cred*, stage *cred*, force *cred*

-cy Old French noun suffix indicating (1) a state or quality, as in accura*cy*, buoyan*cy*, decen*cy*, deficien*cy*, diploma*cy*, discrepan*cy*, in-fan*cy*, litera*cy*, pregnan*cy*, transparen*cy*; (2) a trade or rank, as in accountan*cy*, baronet*cy*, captain*cy*, pira*cy*, consultan*cy*, presiden*cy*; and (3) a wider range of words formed by analogy – agen*cy*, constituen*cy*, falla*cy*, lega*cy*, pharma*cy*, prophe*cy*, tenden*cy*

-dom English abstract noun suffix, indicating (1) a state or condition, as in bore*dom*, free*dom*, hippie*dom*, official*dom*, martyr*dom*, star*dom*; and (2) a territory, as in king*dom*, earl*dom*, Christen*dom*, heathen*dom*

-down English suffix giving (1) compound adjectives, as in head-*down*, face-*down*, top-*down*, nose-*down*; and (2) a range of nouns as in break*down*, crack*down*, shut*down*, splash*down*, show*down*, touch*down*, tumble*down*, sun*down*

-ed, -t English suffixes forming (1) the regular past tense and past participles of verbs, as in start*ed*, stop*ped*, talk*ed*, wait*ed*; with some of these verbs, both the -*ed* or the -*t* ending are possible, as burn*t*/ burn*ed*, knel*t*/kneel*ed*, lean*t*/lean*ed*, leap*ed*/leap*t*, learn*ed*/learn*t*, smell*ed*/smel*t*, spell*ed*/spel*t*, spill*ed*/spil*t*, spoil*ed*/spoil*t*; (2) past participles used as adjectives, as in cook*ed* meat, excit*ed* children, escap*ed* convicts; (3) compound adjectives, as in magenta-colour*ed*, brown-eye*d*, three-legg*ed*

-ee from the French ending, giving nouns describing persons affected by an action, as in amput*ee*, deport*ee*, employ*ee*, franchis*ee*, interview*ee*, licens*ee*, train*ee*, trust*ee*; or performers of an action, as in absent*ee*, divorc*ee*, refer*ee*. Also gives matin*ée*, soir*ée*, néglig*ée*, toup*ee*.

-eer Latin suffix giving verbs and nouns, as in car*eer*, domin*eer*, volunt*eer*, gazett*eer*, mulet*eer*, privat*eer*, pion*eer*

-el, -le English suffix (1) producing nouns that denote an object or instrument, as in shov*el*, shutt*le*. There is also a diminutive connota-tion, as in thimb*le* (from 'thumb'), sett*le* (a small seat, from 'sit', from which also comes sadd*le*), rid*dle* (a small reading problem, from 'read'); (2) adjective suffix, as in britt*le*, fick*le*, id*le*, litt*le*; (3) verb suffix, giving a **frequentative** meaning (expressive of the repetition of an action), as in dazz*le* (from 'daze'), wad*dle* (from 'wade'), drib*ble* (from 'drip'), knee*l* (from 'knee'), swad*dle* (from 'swathe'), spark*le*, start*le*, strug*gle*, crumb*le*, gob*ble*, ming*le*, hurt*le*

-el, -le Latin diminutive suffix, as in citad*el*, chap*el*, dams*el*, mongr*el*

-en English suffix giving (1) diminutive nouns, as in chick*en*, kitt*en*, maid*en*; (2) verbs denoting making or doing, as in broad*en*, deep*en*, fatt*en*, soft*en*, op*en* (from 'up'), fright*en*, gladd*en*, light*en*, length*en*, sweet*en*; (3) adjectives to indicate what something is made of, as in wood*en*, wooll*en*, silk*en*, wax*en*, earth*en*, gold*en*, lead*en*

-ence Latin suffix that combines with verbs to give abstract nouns, as in coher*ence*, correspond*ence*, depend*ence*, insist*ence*, pret*ence*, refer*ence*, reminisc*ence*, resid*ence*, rever*ence*, subsist*ence*. See also **-ance**.

-ent Latin suffix, which combines with verbs to form nouns and adjectives, as in correspond*ent*, insist*ent*, persist*ent*, stud*ent*, differ*ent*, depend*ent*

-er highly productive English suffix giving (1) the standard form of the comparative adjective, as in old*er*, young*er*, bigg*er*, small*er*, fatt*er*, thinn*er*; (2) nouns denoting a person or do*er* of an action, often indicating a job or a pastime, as in sing*er*, bak*er*, employ*er*, lawy*er*, sail*or*, speak*er*, mill*er*, manag*er*, photograph*er*, report*er*, farm*er*, teach*er*; sometimes spelt **-ar**, as in begg*ar*, li*ar*; see also **-or**; (3) nouns denoting equipment or machinery, as in blend*er*, cook*er*, mix*er*, comput*er*, record*er*, print*er*, slic*er*, strain*er*, wip*er*, cutt*er*, mow*er*; (4) frequentative verbs, as in batt*er*, flutt*er*, glimm*er*, spatt*er*, stagg*er*, stutt*er*, wand*er*

-ery Latin noun suffix, giving (1) words suggesting actions or behaviour, as in discov*ery*, deliv*ery*, cook*ery*, forg*ery*, mock*ery*, recov*ery*, flatt*ery*, buffoon*ery*, snobb*ery*; (2) places, as in bak*ery*, brew*ery*, cream*ery*, distill*ery*, nurs*ery*, refin*ery*, shrubb*ery*, tann*ery*; (3) collections of items, as in crock*ery*, drap*ery*, artill*ery*, machin*ery*, pott*ery*, iron-mong*ery*, scen*ery*

-esce Latin verb suffix, suggesting the start of an action, as in coal*esce*, efferv*esce*

-ese Latin suffix 'belonging to', giving place of origin/language, as in Japan*ese*, Chin*ese*, Portugu*ese*, Vietnam*ese*; by extension, it has given words indicating various sorts of jargon and dialect, as in journal*ese*, computer*ese*, official*ese*, American*ese*, Pentagon*ese*

-esque adjective suffix adopted from Old French, giving pictur*esque*, statu*esque*; added to certain proper names, it means 'derivative' or 'after the fashion of', as in Pinter*esque*, Swinburn*esque*, Runyon*esque*

-ess Latin noun suffix denoting a female agent, as in actr*ess*, empr*ess*, duch*ess*, govern*ess*, heir*ess*, host*ess*, steward*ess*, mistr*ess*. There is a current tendency to avoid some of these nouns, female writers favouring the neutral term author rather than author*ess*, for example. Other redundant nouns in this category are poet*ess*, sculptr*ess*, manager*ess*.

-est English suffix giving the standard form of the superlative adjective, as in bigg*est*, small*est*, old*est*, young*est*, dark*est*, fair*est*

-et, -ete, -ate Greek noun suffix denoting an agent, as po*et*, proph*et*, athl*ete*, com*et*, plan*et*, apost*ate*

-ette, -et Latin diminutive noun suffix via Old French, as in cigar*ette*, co*quette*, eti*quette*, nymph*ette*, ros*ette*, servi*ette*, flor*et*, isl*et*, pock*et*

-fold English adjective suffix meaning 'multiplied by', as in two*fold*, three*fold*, hundred*fold*, mani*fold*

-folk English noun suffix, as in towns*folk*, country*folk*, kins*folk*, men*folk*, women*folk*. These words were old-fashioned until the 1980s, when they were thrown a lifeline by writers keen to avoid sexist language and words like townsmen, countrymen, kinsmen, etc.

-free English adjective combining with nouns to form new adjectives, as in care*free*, duty-*free*, interest-*free*, rent-*free*, stress-*free*, tax-*free*, trouble*free*, additive-*free*, pollution-*free*

-friendly contemporary compound adjective, on the model of user-*friendly*, now giving customer-*friendly*, ozone-*friendly*, environment-*friendly*

-ful English adjective suffix, showing (1) quantity, as in bag*ful*, hand*ful*, pocket*ful*, spoon*ful*; (2) characteristics, as in aw*ful*, beauti*ful*, dread-*ful*, scorn*ful*, shame*ful*, tear*ful*, truth*ful*, wil*ful*, youth*ful*. There is some debate about pluralising (1), and bags*ful*/bag*fuls*, hands*ful*/hand*fuls*, etc. are both found; the latter form is commoner.

-gate suffix coinage of the 1970s and 1980s denoting some sort of political or financial scandal, formed by analogy from the Water*gate* affair (which brought down the Nixon presidency in the USA in 1972), as in Iran*gate*/Contra*gate*, Mulder*gate*, Westland*gate*, Maxwell-*gate*, sleeze*gate*

-gon Greek 'angle', giving poly*gon*, octo*gon*, penta*gon*

-gram Greek 'writing' or 'drawing', as in tele*gram*, ana*gram*, dia*gram*, holo*gram*, picto*gram*

-graph Greek 'written', as in mono*graph*, tele*graph*, auto*graph*, photo-*graph*

-hand English noun affixed to other nouns giving (1) a job, as deck*hand*, farm*hand*, field*hand*, cow*hand*; (2) position, as right-*hand*, left-*hand*

-head English noun affixed to other nouns giving (1) a range of mainly pejorative nouns, as egg*head*, hot*head*, muddle*head*, fat*head*, sleepy*head*, thick*head*, dick*head*; (2) the top or front of something, as in mast*head*, pin*head*, spear*head*, letter*head*, pit*head*, stair*head*, beach*head*, figure*head*

-headed adjective formed from **-head**, suggesting characteristics or appearance, as in cool-*headed*, hard-*headed*, muddle-*headed*, bare*headed*, bald-*headed*, shock-*headed*, curly-*headed*

-hood English abstract noun suffix, often suggesting a state or condition, as in boy*hood*, child*hood*, man*hood*, widow*hood*, neighbour*hood*, brother*hood*, priest*hood*

-ian, -an, -ean Latin suffix which gives (1) nouns indicating a job or pastime, as in comed*ian*, electric*ian*, histor*ian*, magic*ian*, music*ian*, optic*ian*, physic*ian*, politic*ian*, technic*ian*; (2) nouns and adjectives based on proper names of famous people, as in Elizabeth*an*, Shake-spear*ean*, Dickens*ian*, Victor*ian*, Wagner*ian*

-iana Latin noun suffix, which combines with famous names to describe memorabilia or collections of items relating to these people, as in Victori*ana*, Churchill*iana*, Wordsworth*iana*

ible, -ibility Latin adjective and noun suffixes, giving digest*ible*/digest*ibility*, corrupt*ible*/corrupt*ibility*, resist*ible*/resist*ibility*. See also **-able**, which is more frequent and is the currently productive suffix.

-ic, -ical Latin adjective suffixes meaning (1) 'like', as in angel*ic*, barbar*ic*, bucol*ic*, class*ic*, enthusiast*ic*, histor*ic* (or histor*ical*), moron*ic*, meteor*ic*, rhythm*ic*, vitriol*ic*, volcan*ic*, uni*que*, Byron*ic*, Milton*ic*; (2) philosoph*ical*, geograph*ical*, scept*ical*, metr*ical*, satir*ical*

-ice, -ise Latin abstract noun suffix, as in avar*ice*, just*ice*, serv*ice*, exerc*ise*, merchand*ise*

-ics Greek suffix, originally for the study of a scientific subject, as economi*cs*, acousti*cs*, electroni*cs*, linguisti*cs*, obstetri*cs*, geneti*cs*, athleti*cs*, politi*cs* (all singular nouns); and tacti*cs*, statisti*cs*, ethi*cs*, heroi*cs*, hysteri*cs* (all plural nouns)

-id Latin adjective suffix, as ac*id*, cand*id*, ferv*id*, morb*id*, plac*id*, rab*id*, sol*id*, splend*id*, turb*id*, tep*id*, vap*id*

-ide suffix from Old French, for scientific compounds, as in ox*ide*, sulph*ide*, cyan*ide*, fluor*ide*, brom*ide*

-ie, -y English diminutive noun suffix, as in Ann*ie*, Charl*ie*, Jimm*y*, Bobb*y*, lass*ie*, bab*y*, dogg*y*

-ify Latin verb suffix descriptive of processes, as in ampl*ify*, beaut*ify*, clar*ify*, dign*ify*, ident*ify*, not*ify*, pur*ify*, sat*isfy*, simpl*ify*

-ile, -il, -eel, -le Latin adjective suffixes, as in frag*ile*, mob*ile*, serv*ile*, sen*ile*, civ*il*, fra*il*, gent*eel*, gent*le*, humb*le*, ab*le*

-ine Latin adjective suffix, denoting 'belonging to', as in can*ine*, div*ine*, equ*ine*, fel*ine*, femin*ine*, sal*ine*, lacustr*ine*

-ing standard suffix of the English verb when forming the present participle or gerund, as in runn*ing*, jump*ing*, stand*ing*, used also as nouns and adjectives

-ion, -tion, -ition, -sion, -som, -son Latin abstract noun suffixes which originally denoted the action of the verb from which they were formed, as in act*ion*, decis*ion*, direct*ion*, exhibit*ion*, ignit*ion*, operat*ion*, react*ion*, reduct*ion*, situat*ion*; as well as pot*ion*, opin*ion*, rans*om*, reas*on*, seas*on*, posit*ion*, nat*ion*, occas*ion*, tens*ion*, fus*ion*

-ise, -ize Greek verb suffix signifying action, as bapt*ise*, critic*ise*, eulog*ise*, final*ise*, hospital*ise*, paral*yse*. **-ize** is an alternative spelling favoured by Americans (and also by growing numbers of British dictionaries with an eye for sales into US markets). But note that some verbs must be spelled **-ise**; these include adver*tise*, ad*vise*, a*rise*, comp*rise*, compro*mise*, des*pise*, de*vise*, dis*guise*, exer*cise*, impro*vise*, prac*tise*, pro*mise*, re*vise*, super*vise*, sur*mise*, sur*prise*, tele*vise*

-ish English adjective suffix, indicating (1) characteristics diluted in quantity from those indicated by the original adjective, as in big*gish*, small*ish*, old*ish*, young*ish*, boy*ish*, brut*ish*, child*ish*, fool*ish*, girl*ish*, good*ish*, green*ish*, slav*ish*, swin*ish*, wasp*ish*; (2) nationality, as in Brit*ish*, Ir*ish*, Scott*ish*, Pol*ish*, Turk*ish*, Kurd*ish*, Span*ish*; (3) age or time, as in thirty*ish*, eight-*ish*

-ish Latin verb suffix, as in abol*ish*, ban*ish*, cher*ish*, establ*ish*, fin*ish*, flour*ish*, nour*ish*, per*ish*, pol*ish*, pun*ish*. English fam*ish* is formed by analogy.

-isk Greek noun suffix signifying a diminutive, as in aster*isk* (originally a 'little star'), obel*isk*, basil*isk*, tamar*isk*

-ism Greek noun suffix denoting (1) the result of an action, as in barbar*ism*, critic*ism*, de*ism*, despot*ism*, ego(t)*ism*, fatal*ism*, hero*ism*, alcohol*ism*, plagiar*ism*; (2) a following or a school of thought, as in Gaull*ism*, Marx*ism*, Hitler*ism*, Thatcher*ism*, Catholic*ism*, Presbyterian*ism*, sex*ism*, age*ism*

-ist Greek noun suffix denoting (1) a person with certain beliefs or behaviour, as in athe*ist*, fasc*ist*, femin*ist*, pessim*ist*, ideal*ist*, Method*ist*, terror*ist*; (2) certain occupations, as in botan*ist*, cartoon*ist*, dent*ist*, physic*ist*, psychiatr*ist*, guitar*ist*, trombon*ist*, cell*ist*

-ite, -ete Latin suffix forming (1) verbs, as in exped*ite*, un*ite*, del*ete*; (2) nouns indicating a committed follower of someone/something, sometimes carrying a derogatory inference, as in Trotsky*ite*, Thatcher*ite*, aesth*ete*

-ition see **-ion**

-itis Latin suffix indicating an illness, as in arthr*itis*, appendic*itis*, hepat*itis*, mening*itis*; or – informally – any general obsession, as in election*itis*, consumer*itis*

-ity Latin suffix combining with adjectives to form abstract nouns, as in absurd*ity*, complex*ity*, creativ*ity*, curios*ity*, familiar*ity*, hostil*ity*, popular*ity*, productiv*ity*, simplic*ity*; also nouns like local*ity*, minor*ity*, personal*ity*, public*ity*, univers*ity*

-ive, -iff Latin suffixes forming (1) nouns denoting persons and things, as in capt*ive*, fugit*ive*, plaint*iff*, detect*ive*, representat*ive*, addit*ive*, contracept*ive*, locomot*ive*, sedat*ive*; (2) adjectives originally denoting inclination, as in act*ive*, pass*ive*, rest*ive*, plaint*ive*, mass*ive*, capt*ive*, fugit*ive*, nat*ive*, conclus*ive*

-ize see **-ise**

-k English frequentative verb suffix, as in har*k* (from hear), stal*k* (from steal)

-kin English diminutive noun suffix, as in cat*kin*, lamb*kin*, manni*kin*

-less English adjective suffix, indicating (1) a lack or absence of something, as in fear*less*, heed*less*, hope*less*, god*less*, law*less*, tooth*less*, worth*less*; (2) an infinity of something, as in count*less*, age*less*, number*less*, price*less*, time*less*

-let Old French diminutive noun ending, as in drop*let*, pig*let*, stream*let*, star*let*, book*let*, flat*let*, cut*let*; also items of jewellery, as in arm*let*, wrist*let*, brace*let*, ank*let*, circle*t*

-like, -ly English adjective suffix, as in bird*like*, child*like*, dream*like*, war*like*, life*like*, business*like*, heaven*ly*, man*ly*, ghast*ly*, like*ly*, father*ly*, love*ly*, order*ly*, saint*ly*

-ling English diminutive noun suffix, as in duck*ling*, gos*ling*, nest*ling*, suck*ling*, dar*ling* (from dear)

-ly (1) the standard and most productive English adverbial suffix, denoting manner, as in clean*ly*, sad*ly*, sweet*ly*, cheap*ly*, frequent*ly*, quick*ly*, and very many more; (2) a suffix indicating frequency, as in week*ly*, dai*ly*, night*ly*, hour*ly*, year*ly*, quarter*ly*

-ma Greek ending connoting 'the product or result of' the relevant verb, giving aro*ma*, asth*ma*, diplo*ma*, dog*ma*, dra*ma*, ene*ma*, enig*ma*, panora*ma*, stig*ma*

-man English noun combining with others to form new nouns indicating (1) a man's job, as in bar*man*, business*man*, camera*man*, clergy*man*, fire*man*, fisher*man*, frog*man*, milk*man*, ombuds*man*, post*man*, states*man*, tax*man*, trades*man*; (2) a man's origins, as in Cornish*man*, English*man*, French*man*, Scots*man*, Ulster*man*. In the past, the term applied to both men and women. Nowadays, words like chair*man*, spokes*man*, lay*man*, sales*man*, yes-*man* are often substituted by chair*person* (or chair), spokes*person*, lay*person*, sales*person*, yes-*person*.

-mate from Old English noun for 'a person who shared your meat', now giving compounds like bed*mate*, class*mate*, in*mate*, mess*mate*, play*mate*, ship*mate*, work*mate*

-ment Latin suffix which combines with verbs to form nouns, as in abandon*ment*, achieve*ment*, arrange*ment*, commit*ment*, develop*ment*, entertain*ment*, excite*ment*, manage*ment*, punish*ment*, retire*ment*

-meter from Greek 'measure', giving an instrument for measuring things, as in gas *meter*, baro*meter*, speedo*meter*, thermo*meter*. Often confused with **-metre**.

-metre from Greek 'measure', giving units of length, as in kilo*metre*, milli*metre*, centi*metre*. Often confused with **-meter**.

-monger from Old English word for a 'dealer', gives compound nouns for (1) occupations, as in fish*monger*, iron*monger*; (2) certain petty or discreditable people, as in gossip*monger*, scare*monger*, rumour*monger*, war*monger*

-most English adjective suffix, used as an intensifier, as in inner*most*, hind*most*, top*most*, upper*most*, fore*most*, ut*most*

-n, -en English adjective suffix (1) from the participle ending, as in drunk*en*, shak*en*, molt*en*, tor*n*; (2) denoting the material or coloration of an object, as in gold*en*, lin*en*, wood*en*, flex*en*, hemp*en*, leather*n*

-naut from Greek 'sailor', giving various kinds of navigator, as in cosmo*naut*, astro*naut*, aero*naut*, argo*naut*. (Note that jugger*naut*, a heavy lorry, is from a Hindu word for a massive object.)

-ness English abstract noun suffix, as in sad*ness*, happi*ness*, good*ness*, bad*ness*, gentle*ness*, weak*ness*, wilder*ness*, dark*ness*, wit*ness* (= one who wits)

-nik Russian or Yiddish suffix first used in the 1950s to describe a person connected with the word that precedes it, as beat*nik*, refuse*nik*, peace*nik*, kibbutz*nik*

-ock English diminutive noun suffix, as in bull*ock*, hill*ock*, padd*ock*

-ocracy Greek suffix for 'form of government', as in dem*ocracy*, the*ocracy*, aut*ocracy*, arist*ocracy*, bureau*cracy*, techn*ocracy*, plut*ocracy*. Supporters of these forms take the suffix **-ocrat**.

-oholic see **-aholic**

-oid Greek noun or adjective suffix, indicating 'something resembling', as spher*oid*, glob*oid*, petal*oid*, cub*oid*, tabl*oid*, ster*oid*

-ology Greek noun suffix for 'word' meaning 'study of', as in techn*ology*, ge*ology*, archae*ology*, meteor*ology*, gynaec*ology*. The adjective is **-ological**.

-or Latin agent noun suffix, as in act*or*, collect*or*, competit*or*, conduct*or*, direct*or*, edit*or*, govern*or*, inspect*or*, narrat*or*, prosecut*or*, spectat*or*, visit*or*; also forms certain objects, as calculat*or*, refrigerat*or*, escalat*or*, react*or*. See also **-er** (3).

-ory Latin adjective suffix, as in audit*ory*, sens*ory*, amat*ory*, admonit*ory*, illus*ory*

-osis Greek suffix used to indicate (1) illness or disease, as in cirrh*osis*, psych*osis*, thromb*osis*, tubercul*osis*; (2) a state or process, as hypn*osis*, diagn*osis*, progn*osis*, metamorph*osis*, osm*osis*

-our, -or Latin abstract noun suffix, as in lab*our*, hon*our*, clam*our*, ard*our*, sav*our*. Americans have reverted to the **-or** of the original Latin spelling of these words.

-ous, -ose Latin adjective suffix denoting a particular quality, often 'full of', as in fam*ous*, glori*ous*, graci*ous*, copi*ous*, assidu*ous*, querul*ous*, anxi*ous*, grandi*ose*, joc*ose*, ingenu*ous*, danger*ous*

-person English agent word preferred nowadays by many writers to **-man** as a general suffix, as chair*person*, spokes*person*, ombuds*person*, news*person*

-phile from Greek 'love', giving a person who likes a particular place or thing very much, as in Franco*phile*, Euro*phile*, Germano*phile*, biblio*phile*

-phobe, -phobic from Greek 'fear', giving a person who dislikes or fears a particular place or thing very much, as in Anglo*phobe*, Russo*phobe*, agora*phobe*, claustro*phobe*, arachno*phobe*. The condition itself has the suffix **-phobia**.

-phone from Greek 'sound' or 'voice', giving (1) names of instruments which produce or transmit sound, as in dicta*phone*, mega*phone*, hispano*phone*, tele*phone*, saxo*phone*, xylo*phone*; (2) names for people who understand a particular language, as anglo*phone*, franco*phone*, germano*phone*

-piece English noun which combines with others, as in mouth*piece*, centre*piece*, frontis*piece*, master*piece*, show*piece*, mantel*piece*

-proof English noun which combines with others to produce adjectives describing certain qualities, as in heat*proof*, weather*proof*, water*proof*, sound*proof*, bullet-*proof*

-red English abstract noun suffix, as in hat*red*, kind*red*

-ridden English verb, past participle of *ride*, which combines with nouns to form an adjective suggesting harassment and oppression, as in guilt-*ridden*, bullet-*ridden*, class-*ridden*, disease-*ridden*, maggot-*ridden*, priest-*ridden*, scandal-*ridden*, debt-*ridden*. A similar construction is **-stricken**.

-scape suffix thought to be from Dutch 'to shape (a picture)', giving land*scape*, and by analogy sea*scape*, sky*scape*, moon*scape*, city*scape*

-ship English abstract noun suffix, suggesting (1) personal qualities and skills, as in friend*ship*, hard*ship*, wor*ship* (from worth*ship*), fellow*ship*, leader*ship*; (2) craft qualities, as in craftsman*ship*, oarsman*ship*, musician*ship*, seaman*ship*, workman*ship*; (3) various types of ship, as in air*ship*, battle*ship*, flag*ship*, war*ship*

-side English noun combining with others to suggest the edge of something, as in bed*side*, grave*side*, ring*side*, river*side*, track*side*; or more generally, a part of something, as in far*side*, hill*side*, country*side*, under*side*, top*side*, back*side*, in*side*, off*side*

-sis Greek noun suffix denoting 'state', as in analy*sis*, cataly*sis*, empha*sis*, gene*sis*, paraly*sis*

-some English adjective suffix denoting a quality, as in quarrel*some*, tire*some*, win*some*, whole*some*, lis*som* (from lithe), bux*om*, hand*some*

-speak English verb which combines with nouns to form new nouns referring to the particular language or jargon of a group, derived from George Orwell's 'new*speak*' in the novel *Nineteen Eighty-Four* (1949), and now by analogy in nuke*speak*, legal*speak*, media*speak*, computer*speak*, double*speak*, Thatcher*speak*, Euro*speak*

-ster English noun suffix to denote a person, originally a feminine ending, as in spin*ster* (= an unmarried woman, whose occupation was to spin), song*ster*, young*ster*, bax*ter* (from bake*ster*), fo*ster* (from food*ster*)

-stricken past participle of English verb *strike*, which combines with nouns to form adjectives that refer to unpleasant emotions, as in grief-*stricken*, terror-*stricken*, guilt-*stricken*, horror-*stricken*, poverty-*stricken*. See also **-ridden**, which is a similar construction.

-style English noun which combines with others to form new words, as in life*style*, free*style*, hair*style*, Indian-*style*, old-*style*, 1980s-*style*

-ther English adverbial suffix, indicating direction towards, as in hi*ther*, thi*ther*, whi*ther*

-tor, -sor, -or, -our, -er, -eer, -ier, -ar Latin noun suffixes denoting persons, as in act*or*, audit*or*, auth*or*, doct*or*, chancell*or*, emper*or*, jur*or*, monit*or*, spons*or*, success*or*, vict*or*, savi*our*, arch*er*, found*er*, enchant*er*, preach*er*, ush*er*, auction*eer*, engin*eer*, brigad*ier*, grenad*ier*, vic*ar*, regis-tr*ar*, prem*ier*, farr*ier*

-trix Latin noun suffix denoting a female agent, as in execu*trix*, proprie*trix* (now old-fashioned)

-tude Latin abstract noun suffix, as in alti*tude*, forti*tude*, lati*tude*, magni*tude*, servi*tude*

-ular Latin adjective suffix, giving qualities, as in musc*ular*, gran*ular*, mod*ular*; and shapes, as in ang*ular*, circ*ular*, rectang*ular*, tub*ular*

-und Latin adjective suffix, as in joc*und*, rot*und*, mori*bund*

-ure Latin abstract noun suffix formed from verbs, as in clos*ure*, depart*ure*, expos*ure*, expendit*ure*, fail*ure*, mixt*ure*, pleas*ure*, sculpt*ure*, seiz*ure*; as well as a wider range of words, as cens*ure*, cult*ure*, gest*ure*, junct*ure*, meas*ure*, pict*ure*, literat*ure*, legislat*ure*

-ward(s) English suffix originally denoting adjectives and adverbs of direction, as in home*ward*, sea*ward*, north*ward*, to*ward*, awk*ward* (from awk, 'turned the wrong way'). The adverbs favour a final **-s**, as in home*wards*, heaven*wards*, in*wards*.

-ware English word for 'manufactured articles', which combines with others to form more specific nouns, as tin*ware*, brass*ware*, earthen*ware*, glass*ware*, stone*ware*, silver*ware*

-wise, -ways (1) English adverbial suffix, denoting manner or fashion, as in clock*wise*, any*wise*, no*wise*, other*wise*, al*ways*, side*ways*, length-*ways*, straight*way*; (2) the English noun meaning 'clever' also functions as a compound, as in street*wise*, worldly-*wise*, penny-*wise*

-woman English noun which combines with others to indicate a particular job or nationality, as in horse*woman*, needle*woman*, spokes-*woman*, yachts*woman*, English*woman*, Dutch*woman*

-work English word which combines with nouns to indicate (1) the material from which objects are made, as in brass*work*, iron*work*, wood*work*, scroll*work*, pastry*work*; (2) particular types of job or activity, as in brain*work*, needle*work*, case*work*, house*work*, farm-*work*, shift*work*

-worthy English word which combines with nouns to form adjectives, as news*worthy*, note*worthy*, credit*worthy*, trust*worthy*, sea*worthy*

-wright English noun for a person who has 'worked' or 'wrought', as in ship*wright*, wheel*wright*, play*wright*

-y adjective suffix (1) with English derivatives suggesting a quality, as in health*y*, hair*y*, might*y*, mood*y*, greed*y*, bush*y*, stick*y*, sorr*y* (from sore), guilt*y*, blood*y*; (2) with more general Latin derivatives, as in famil*y*, fanc*y*, cop*y*, memor*y*, miser*y*, stor*y*, victor*y*, aristocrac*y*; (3) used as an ending in familiar names, as Jimm*y*, Ronn*y*, Bett*y*, Lizz*y*.

four
Punctuation

I cannot take seriously the criticism of someone who doesn't know how to use a semicolon.

Shirley Conran,
in the *Observer*, 29/3/92

I know there are some *Persons* who affect to *despise* it, and treat this whole Subject with the utmost *Contempt*, as a Trifle far below their Notice, and a Formality unworthy of their Regard: They do not hold it difficult, but despicable; and neglect it, as being above it.

Yet many learned Men have been highly sensible of its Use; and some ingenious and elegant Writers have condescended to point their Works with Care; and very eminent Scholars have not disdained to teach the Method of doing it with Propriety.

James Burrow,.
*Essay on the Use of Pointing,** 1771
*pointing = putting in points, or stops
(an old word for punctuation)

[Punctuation] is a large subject. Taste and common sense are more important than any rules; you put in stops to help your reader to understand you, not to please grammarians. And you should try so to write that he will understand you with a minimum of help of that sort.

Sir Ernest Gowers,
The Complete Plain Words, 1954

Punctuation

Punctuation is used to mark off units of grammar and clarify a writer's meaning. In speech, emphasis and pauses are used to help get the spoken message across. In written English, punctuation has to serve the same purpose. Here the conventions are – for example – to mark off **sentences** by a combination of full stop + space; **words** are marked off by the insertion of spaces between them; **paragraphs** are marked off by indenting text on a new line, etc. Punctuation also indicates specific points of grammar. For example, an apostrophe indicates the possessive or the omission of a letter.

Lack of punctuation or incorrect punctuation often causes ambiguity and misunderstanding. Look at these pairs of sentences. The words are the same, but the meanings are different – because of the punctuation:

He has a noisy class of ten year-old children.
He has a noisy class of ten-year-old children.

Gypsies who live in caravans are seldom seen nowadays.
Gypsies, who live in caravans, are seldom seen nowadays.

Apostrophe [']

The **apostrophe** has two functions in punctuation. It marks the possessive or genitive case, and it indicates contractions or the omission of letters in spelling certain words.

Possession

the horse's mouth (singular)
the horses' mouths (plural)
the Women's Institute and the Mothers' Union
Monday's child
a life of one's own

Unlike possessive nouns such as the above, possessive pronouns (apart from *one's*) do not require an apostrophe:

She took hers, we took ours, and they took theirs.

Some units of measure also show a form of possession with an apostrophe:

in a week's time . . .
a six months' trip to Australia
twenty years' service

The 'group genitive', in which more than one subject or object is involved, is marked only on the last noun:

Gilbert and Sullivan'*s* operas
William and Mary'*s* reign

Contractions

I don'*t*, I can'*t*, and I won'*t* do it.
It'*s* a nice day, is*n*'*t* it?
Here'*s* something for you, and there'*s* something for John.

Omissions

A man'*s* a man for *a*' that. (*a*' = all; non-standard English)
Yo'*a*ll (= you all; non-standard English)
Class of '*86* / Harvest of '*63* / The '*45* Rebellion (omitting the century)
One *o*'clock / Ne'*e*r do well / Will *o*' the wisp

Brackets ( )

Brackets always come in pairs. There are several kinds, including round brackets ( ), square brackets [ ], angle brackets < >, and brace brackets { }. For normal purposes of punctuation in UK English, only round brackets need concern us in any detail. In US English, they are called parentheses.

Round brackets (parentheses)

These are used to cordon off and enclose supplementary or explanatory information which would otherwise interrupt the basic drift of a sentence or of a longer piece of writing. (The Greek word *parenthesis* means 'an insertion beside'.) The bracketed (or cordoned-off) material may be removed without changing the overall meaning or completeness of the text:

Robert Louis Stevenson (1850–94) is still a well-loved children's author.
If you are late again (which heaven forbid!), you will not be allowed to go forward to the exam.
See separate order form (yellow cover) for more information.
It costs 10 marks (roughly £5).

Brackets are also usually used to mark off alternatives, abbreviations and – in certain contexts – numerals from the main text:

Any volunteer(s) will be welcome.
The syllabus is devised by the National Curriculum Council (NCC).
Thirty (30) days' settlement is required.

He has to (1) write the essay, (2) deliver the talk, (3) prepare to defend his arguments.

Square brackets

These have two functions. Firstly, they are sometimes used for parentheses within parentheses. Secondly, they indicate an editorial comment:

Stevenson's stepson (Lloyd Osbourne [1868–1947]) collaborated in some of the master's later work.
The book was called *Paris, Pee Wee* [sic] *and Big Dog*.

Angle brackets

In scholarly work, these indicate that a piece of text is missing or defective.

Brace brackets

These are sometimes also called curly brackets, and they are used in mathematics and in tabular material.

Capital letters

Capital letters are used for two purposes in English punctuation. Firstly, they mark the beginning of a new sentence. Secondly, they indicate a proper noun. The main conventions are summarised below.

Capitals at the beginning of a sentence

Capital letters follow full stops. Capital letters invariably signal the beginning of a sentence, just as full stops (or equivalents) invariably signal the end of a sentence:

*T*he king was working in the garden. *H*e seemed very glad to see me. *W*e walked through the garden. *I*t was very jolly. *W*e talked for a long time. *L*ike all Greeks he wanted to go to America. (Ernest Hemingway)

Capitals at the beginning of direct speech

This rule is an extension of the rule regarding capitals at the beginning of sentences. Capitals are not always required following interruptions to direct speech:

The Prime Minister said to her colleagues, '*There* is no alternative.'
'There is no alternative,' *said* the Prime Minister to her colleagues, '*to* fighting our corner.'

Capitals after other punctuation marks

Sometimes – but not usually – capitals are found after other punctuation marks, including commas and colons. This unusual use of capitals signals a specific purpose, for instance introducing a quotation or a semi-quotation:

As the poet Burns said: *A* man's a man for a' that.
She was thinking, *By* this time tomorrow the die will be cast.

Capitals at the beginning of lines of poetry

Traditionally, the first word of a line of poetry was capitalised, whether the punctuation of the poem required it or not:

*W*ine comes in at the mouth,
*A*nd love comes in at the eye;
*T*hat's all we shall know of truth
*B*efore we grow old and die . . . (W.B. Yeats)

In much modern poetry, this rule no longer applies. Today the typesetter follows the requirements of the individual poet in the layout of a poem.

Capitals for proper nouns and proper names

With the exception of quirky writers like E.E. Cummings (who liked to style himself e e cummings), the rule for capitalising proper nouns is invariable. It covers people (*E*lla *S*mith, *J*ohn *D*os *P*assos, *M*argaret *T*hatcher, *F*rançois *M*itterrand), days of the week (*T*uesday, *S*aturday), months of the year (*J*anuary, *M*ay), other special calendar days (*E*aster, *R*amadan, *H*anukkah, *T*hanksgiving), countries of the world and their nationals (*C*anada, *L*ithuania, *S*paniards, *B*razilians), historical periods and events (the *T*hirty *Y*ears *W*ar, the *D*epression, the *R*enaissance, *but* the *e*ighteenth *c*entury, the *n*ineteen *n*ineties). Capitals are usually also used to refer to *G*od, the *P*rophet *M*uhammad, *B*uddha, and to the various scriptural books – the *B*ible and its individual books, the *T*almud, the *H*oly *K*oran, etc.

Occasional confusion arises over whether a reference is general or specific. Only specific proper names are capitalised:

the *O*rkney *I*slands *but* the *i*slands of the Mediterranean

the *River Thames but* the *river systems* of the Home Counties
Berkeley *Square but* the *squares* of London
the *Ritz Hotel but* the *best hotels*

Compass points are capitalised if they are part of a specific geographical region or entity, not if they are part of a general direction:

Northern *Ireland*   South Africa
a *westerly* gale   the *east* coast of Sweden

Honorific titles joined to proper names require a capital letter if they precede the names, not always if they follow the names:

Her *Royal Highness* the *Princess* of Wales
President Bush and *Chancellor* Kohl
President of the National Union of Journalists
Colonel Davitt of the US Marines *but* Jim Davitt, a *colonel* in the US Marines

Capitals are used for the titles of books, poems, movies and plays:

Roget's Thesaurus   the *Oxford Companion* to *English Literature*
For *Whom* the *Bell Tolls*   Gone *with* the *Wind*

In titles, note that it is only the main words – the first word of the title and the nouns and verbs – that are capitalised. The 'small' words – determiners and prepositions – don't usually take a capital:

The *Old Man* and the *Sea*
Across the *River* and *into* the *Trees*

The names of specific trains, ships, spacecraft and aircraft are spelt with an initial capital letter:

the *Orient Express*
the *Brighton Belle*   } They are also usually italicised
the *Spirit* of *St Louis*
Apollo 8

Capitals are used for trademark names and often for local names:

Martini   Apple *Macintosh*
Xerox machine   Kodak camera
Yorkshire pudding   Welsh rarebit

This area sometimes causes confusion, however, because some terms have so completely entered general circulation that the capital letter has now been dropped:

biro   *brussels* sprouts
venetian blinds   *cashmere*
wellington boots

Capitals are used to abbreviate the names of organisations, institutions, political groupings, countries, etc. Nowadays we tend to write these initial letters without stops:

UNESCO	USA
UNICEF	UCLA
UN	BP
ECOWAS	IBM
EC	

Capitals for pronouns

The only pronoun to take a capital letter is normally the first-person singular *I*:

I am the master of my fate, *I* am the captain of my soul.

Sometimes in religious writing, pronouns and determiners referring to God are capitalised:

God in *H*is mercy will comfort us.

Colon [:]

The **colon** as a punctuation mark within the sentence is used to explain, interpret or amplify what has preceded it. It is also used to introduce lists or series, and lengthy quotations. And thirdly it is used to separate elements such as numerals in ratios and time references, and the subtitles from the titles of books.

Colons introducing explanations and amplifications

The rescue services have been alerted: weather conditions on the mountain are atrocious and the party has been gone for ten hours.

His essay was very poor: the spelling and handwriting were quite childish.

There was only one thing to do: jump.

I have news for you: your father has arrived.

This use of the colon indicates a fairly close interdependence between the units that it separates. Normally, a capital letter is not used after the colon in this context.

Colons introducing lists, series, quotations

The competition was between three countries: Holland, Belgium and Denmark.

The following items are required: minced beef, onions, garlic, mushrooms, tomatoes and seasoning.

Please send the items listed: (i) passport, (ii) visa application, (iii) the correct fee.
The poet Pope expressed it nicely: 'To err is human, to forgive, divine.'

Only the last example here takes a capital letter after the colon, in order
to make the quotation stand out.

Colons in numerals, book references and titles

The bus leaves at 6:30 p.m. sharp.
Her date of birth is 04:09:1956.
Girls outnumbered boys in the ratio 11:9.
His text was Isaiah 65:13–25.
Goethe's Faust: A New Translation

Other uses of the colon

Colons are also used for purposes of punctuating memos and reports, as
in *To: From: Reference:* They are also preferred by Americans following
the opening salutation in formal correspondence, as in *Dear Sir:, Dear
Mr President:* (British office practice is to use a comma or no punctuation
at all.)

Comma [,]

After the full stop, the **comma** is the second key punctuation mark. It is
the commonest and most versatile mark *inside* the sentence. It may be
used to separate words, phrases, and some clauses. Some commas are
considered essential, while others are considered to be optional aids to
clarity.

The main uses of the comma are listed below. If the comma is
optional in any of the examples, it is shown in brackets thus: [,].

Commas in lists

The comma breaks up items in a list of three or more. The items to be
broken up may be words, phrases, or clauses – the rules are similar:

It was a cold, wet, windy afternoon.
We played soccer, baseball, rounders[,] and tennis.
He doesn't eat eggs, cheese[,] or butter.
He works constantly, travels frequently, has no private life to speak of, and no
obvious outside interests.

The main problem with this rule is whether to use a comma before the
last item in the list, which is frequently signalled by the use of a

conjunction like *and*. The rule here is not to omit this final comma (as in the sentences below) if that is likely to cause any confusion:

In one morning's shopping spree, she went to Harrods, John Lewis, Waterstone's, and Fortnum and Mason's. In the afternoon, she took in Hatchard's, Selfridges, and Hamley's.

A minor problem with this rule involves expressions like 'the grand old duke [of York]' or 'the pretty little girl'. The adjectives here would normally be used in a single, semi-affectionate sense, with *grand* modifying *old*, and *pretty* modifying *little*. They are not therefore lists of adjectives, and no commas are required.

Another minor problem is caused by lists like the following:

He works in an old, tumble-down, post-war municipal building.
He makes a small, monthly cash payment to his son.

No comma is necessary between *post-war* and *municipal*, unless *municipal* is parsed as the last adjective in a list and not as part of the compound noun *municipal building*. Similarly, *cash payment* is used here as a compound noun.

Commas separating main clauses

Commas are usually used to mark off main clauses, whether or not joined by a coordinating conjunction such as *and, but, or*. The longer the sentence, the more helpful the comma is:

They came, they saw, they conquered.
I looked for the book[,] but it was not to be seen.
I looked high and low for my homework book and my class notes, but I'm sorry to say that they were nowhere to be seen.

Commas separating relative and subordinate clauses

Commas often mark off relative and subordinate clauses from the main clauses of the sentence:

The London train, which departs from platform 5, is half an hour late.
We arrived at my son's house[,] where we were made welcome.
The man[,] who was in the process of making good his escape from justice[,] is thought to have been a terrorist.

Commas separating adverbs and adverbials

Adverbials that precede, follow, or interrupt the main clause are usually marked off by commas:

Finally[,] he came to the point[,] after much humming and hawing.
Meanwhile[,] across Europe[,] the storm clouds were gathering.
The army, after crossing the Tigris, fanned out across the plain.
He will be welcome[,] if he decides to come.

Commas for balance

Commas are often used to balance contrasting or opposing phrases and clauses within a sentence:

She's a lovely girl[,] but not very bright.
He will change his shirt, not his opinions.
The time is half past six, not half past seven.

Commas to mark off direct speech

Commas are used to introduce a direct quotation, or to terminate it. They are also used to split quotations:

The children said, 'Tell us a story.'
'Tell us a story,' said the children.
'Tell us a story,' said the children, 'before we go to sleep.'

Commas are not necessary if the quoted material doesn't represent dialogue:

He told her he would go 'straight to the hospital' and then I think he said he was
going to telephone her.

Commas to mark off parentheses

Modifiers and words in apposition are usually set off by commas from the main part of the sentence:

We visited the Tay Bridge, site of the famous disaster.
The Queen, a keen horsewoman, presented the cup.
His latest novel[,] *No Other Life*[,] has been very well received.

Sometimes the presence or absence of appositional commas can tell us quite a lot:

My brother John is a lawyer. (= I have several brothers.)
My brother, John, is a lawyer. (= I have one brother.)
Snakes which are poisonous are to be avoided. (Some snakes)
Snakes, which are poisonous, are to be avoided. (All snakes)

It is important to remember that if the parenthesis or apposition falls in the middle of the sentence, you need to use a pair of commas – one at the start and the other at the end.

Commas to mark off vocatives and interjections

We usually comma off these minor parenthetical elements from the main part of the sentence:

Ah, now I get the picture.
You, *Mary*, must leave at once.
Now, *sir*, what can I do for you?
I put it to you, *ladies and gentlemen*, we need your support.

As a kind of parenthesis, vocatives and interjections need to be marked off with a pair of commas if they fall within the sentence rather than at the beginning or end of it.

Commas to mark off question tags

Commas separate question tags from the rest of the sentence. This usage is straightforward and more or less invariable:

It's a terrible day, isn't it?
You've missed your bus, haven't you?
She'll be able to come, won't she?

Commas to show omission

A comma is sometimes used to show that a grammatical ellipsis has been admitted to the sentence, and certain words must be supplied to make the construction grammatically correct:

Jones gave a negative, but Bloggs a positive response.
A Riesling is preferred by some experts; by others, a Hock.

But the comma is required only if the meaning of the sentence is unclear without it. The following sentence does not require a comma:

She was in love with him and he with her.

Commas to avoid ambiguity

We need commas to mark off chunks of text, if without them the reader is tempted to miss the separation:

Outside, the car park had been full for hours.
In the morning, rolls are delivered to the house.
I want you to meet my friend Mary, Jane.
I am sick, and tired of studying punctuation.

Without the commas, we will read:

Outside the car park . . .
. . . morning rolls . . .
. . . Mary Jane . . .
. . . sick and tired . . .

Commas with *however, meanwhile, nevertheless*

However, meanwhile and *nevertheless* are three adverbs which are particularly prone to attract gratuitous commas. The following pairs of sentences should remind us not to comma off these words unthinkingly:

However you look at it, theft is not really justifiable.
However, lots of people try to justify it.

But meanwhile a number of steps will have to be taken.
Meanwhile[,] back at the ranch[,] . . .

He slept badly. Nevertheless, he spoke well at the rally.
He slept badly, but nevertheless spoke well at the rally.

Commas with inverted word order

Commas are helpful to the reader if the word order of the sentence has been inverted. They assist the text's readability:

Until the fighting stopped, the UN was helpless to act.
Because of the continuing fighting, the relief operation has had to be postponed.
The Allied Command having discussed strategic aims until well into the night, a
declaration of intent was released to the press this morning.

Commas to set off titles, dates, geographical references

Commas usually mark off precise titles, dates, or geographical references from the main part of a text:

M. François Mitterrand, President of France, took the salute.
On Saturday[,] 16 September[,] 1949, they were married.
He teaches in Lafayette, Indiana, seat of a large American university.

Commas in numbers

Commas are used with numbers above 10,000. They are not generally used in numbers between 1000 and 10,000:

The population of Ireland is around 5,000,000. (5 million)
Melrose (population 2000) is a picturesque village in the Scottish Borders.
His personal fortune was put at $10,000,000.

Commas misplaced

It is quite common to find commas in the wrong place:

He locked the door, and running across the hall, bumped into the intruders.
A brutal, and on the face of it, a motiveless crime.

These should of course be:

He locked the door and, running across the hall,
A brutal and, on the face of it,

Another common error is the comma in place of the full stop:

I visited her in Suffolk, she was not at home.

These are two sentences, with two different subjects and no conjunction, so they should be separated by a full stop.

Commas missing

We have seen above how the presence of commas can make all the difference to the meaning of a sentence:

They thought of taking a house in Brittany perhaps with the Kellys.

What is the function of *perhaps* here? As it stands, the sentence is ambiguous and could take two interpretations:

They thought of taking a house in Brittany, perhaps with the Kellys.
They thought of taking a house in Brittany perhaps, with the Kellys.

Dash [–]

A dash is used to indicate a break in the continuity of a sentence, often informally. Generally, it is better to avoid using a dash in formal or academic writing, where a comma or brackets is usually more appropriate. Try imagining sentence 1 below with a comma instead of the dash, and sentence 2 with brackets around the second part:

Hello, it's me – Twinkletoes.
I've arrived – and to prove it, I'm here.

Without the dashes, the impression of colloquial and slightly breathless informality would be lost completely.

The dash to break the continuity of the sentence

Fancy meeting you here – I thought you were in America!
I don't believe it – champagne!

The dash to introduce an afterthought

I'm Charley's aunt from Brazil – where the nuts come from. (Brandon Thomas)
We're none of us infallible – not even the youngest among us. (W. H. Thompson)

These examples are based on spoken and not written English, the first being from a playscript and the second from a speech.

The dash instead of commas or brackets

I am in earnest – I will not equivocate – I will not excuse – I will not retreat a single inch – and I will be heard. (Wm Lloyd Garrison)

No sun – no moon!
No morn – no noon –
No dawn – no dusk – no proper time of day. (Thomas Hood)

Again, the writers are contriving to simulate spoken English.

The dash introducing a summary statement

Poor old Daddy – just one of those sturdy old plants left over from the Edwardian Wilderness, that can't understand why the sun isn't shining any more. (John Osborne)
Wine, women, and song – it's not a lot to ask for once in a while.

The comments after the dash provide a summary on the words or phrases which preceded it.

The dash in broken sentences

There are nine and sixty ways of constructing tribal lays,
And – every – single – one – of – them – is – right! (Rudyard Kipling)
Can't you understand? You – are – on – the – wrong – train!

This particular use of dashes conveys emphasis. Alternatively, this use of dashes can also convey hesitation or uncertainty in speech accompanied by lots of pregnant pauses:

Oh – um, erm – well, I don't – erm – I don't know what – erm, to say.

The dash for balance or amplification

It takes two to speak the truth – one to speak and another to hear. (H. D. Thoreau)
The most powerful weapon against ignorance – the diffusion of printed material. (Lev Tolstoy)
I am not arguing with you – I am telling you. (J. McN. Whistler)

You should study the Peerage, Gerald – it is the best thing in fiction the English have ever done. (Oscar Wilde)

Take it from me – he's got the goods. (O. Henry)

More formal writers might prefer to use colons here.

The dash for parentheses, repetition or emphasis

It was – on balance – a successful operation. (parenthetical dashes)

Kent, sir – everybody knows Kent – apples, cherries, hops, and women. (Dickens; dashes for emphasis)

She is come at last – at last – and all is gas and gaiters. (Dickens; dashes for repetition)

The parenthetic use of dashes – in pairs – marks a break in very much the same way as brackets. Brackets, however, would look rather strong in the above.

'What's the water in French, sir?' 'L'eau,' replied Nicholas. 'Ah!' said Mr Lillywick shaking his head mournfully. 'I thought as much. Lo, eh? I don't think anything of that language – nothing at all.' (Dickens)

Here the dash is used to introduce a lugubrious repetition. Dickens was a writer who rather liked dashes, and used them to great effect.

Dashes to indicate incompleteness

All summer, he conducted a discreet affair with Miss C –.

Mind your own – business!

'Well, I'll be – !' he exclaimed.

This use of dashes indicates that part of a name has been omitted, or that an expletive has been deliberately deleted.

Dashes to indicate a series of ranges

In the following examples, the dash is equivalent to the word *to*:

1939–1945	volumes I–VI
pages 77–141	A–Z

Ellipsis [. . .]

Ellipses (plural) are series of full stops (usually three or four), and sometimes they are referred to as **omission marks**. An ellipsis is used to suggest that something is missing or omitted or withheld from a text, within or at the end of a sentence:

Who the . . . does he think he is?

An ellipsis sometimes also indicates that a sentence is tailing off in an incomplete way – perhaps because it is becoming inaudible to the listener, or because the rest of the sentence is left to the listener's imagination (to indicate a more dramatic break, a dash is used):

> An eerie silence hung over the bay, and we waited and waited . . .
> We shall leave them there, Dear Reader, whispering sweet nothings under an autumn moon . . .

An ellipsis is also often used to indicate an incomplete quotation:

> How does it go? 'Cowards die many times before their deaths . . .' I'm afraid I forget the next line.
> Do you promise to tell the truth, the whole truth and nothing but . . .

If an ellipsis occurs at the end of a sentence, and you are representing it by three dots, it is not necessary to add a fourth dot to indicate the full stop.

Exclamation mark [!]

Like the question mark, the **exclamation mark** is a specialised version of the full stop. It signals strong feelings or urgency, and is used at the end of an emphatic utterance or phrase:

> Get out of my house! And don't come back!
> How lovely she looked!

An exclamation mark is also usually found after an interjection:

Sh!	Hey!
Be quiet!	Ugh!
Cheers!	Ow!
Encore!	

Multiple exclamation marks are to be avoided in print. They usually indicate a rather desperate attempt to pep up a tired piece of text and are much loved by writers of comic strips and tabloid press headlines:

> NUDE PRINCESS SCANDAL – EXCLUSIVE ! ! !
> Eeeeeek!!!!!!!!!!! Kerplonk!!!!!!!!!!!

Full stop [.]

The **full stop** – or **period** (in American English) – is the first and the basic punctuation mark. It ends all sentences and sentence fragments that are not direct questions or exclamations:

> We arrived home late. Very late. We had just got into bed when we heard the milkman on his rounds.
> I love you. Honestly. Truly.

Full stops following abbreviations and contractions were also in general use until very recently. The tendency now is to omit full stops here. So you may find either:

Wm. Wordsworth	*or*	Wm Wordsworth
C.S. Lewis	*or*	C S Lewis
Bloggs & Co. Ltd.	*or*	Bloggs & Co Ltd
U.K. and U.S.A.	*or*	UK and USA
N.A.T.O. and U.N.E.S.C.O.	*or*	NATO and UNESCO
Dr. and Mrs. Smith	*or*	Dr and Mrs Smith
A.D. and B.C.	*or*	AD and BC
i.e. and e.g. and etc.	*or*	ie and eg and etc

Full stops are not used for decimal currency (£ and p) or for metric measurements (km, m, cm, kg, g, l, etc.).

Hyphen [-]

Hyphens have two main uses: they join certain words together (*father-in-law, X-ray, self-control*), and they divide words at the end of a line of print.

Hyphens at the end of a line of print

Nowadays, when everyone seems to use a word-processor, the subject of word breaks has a renewed importance. Traditional typesetters and compositors were trained in the proper division of words, and followed certain rules. One-syllable words were not broken. Words were never broken immediately before the last letter or after the first letter. Words were not broken in such a way as to mislead the reader: for example, words broken by a hyphen into *leg-ends, reap-pear, screwd-river, the-rapist, mans-laughter, not-able, rein-stall, un-ionised,* etc. were considered highly confusing for rapid readers, because the meanings of their components (words in their own right) bear no relation to the meanings of the unbroken words. Words were always split at a syllable, or at a prefix or suffix – these were considered to be the 'natural' breaks. This rule should still be applied, as far as possible, although the 'natural' breaks are now thought to be phonetic rather than etymological. So: *photog-rapher* not *photo-grapher, biolo-gist* not *bio-logist.*

Hyphens between some prefixes and root words

Hyphens are used when the prefixed element is a proper noun (*pre-Renaissance, anti-Hitler*), a number (*pre-1066*), or an abbreviation (non-EC countries).

It is also necessary to use hyphens to make meanings clear:

re-form ('constitute again')	reform ('turn over a new leaf')
re-bound ('given a new binding')	rebound ('bounce back')
re-cover (a chair)	recover (from an illness)

Hyphens also still tend to be used – in British if not in American English – to avoid sequences of the same vowel or other awkward results:

anti-inflationary	semi-independent
infra-red	time-exposure
co-opt	co-ordinate

Hyphens with certain compound nouns

Most compound nouns have now been run together into single words:

bedroom	toothbrush
horsepower	doorkeeper
handmaid	stepfather
wheelbarrow	bricklayer

A few compound words tend to 'look' too long for comfort, and are still commonly spelt with a hyphen:

engine-driver	stomach-pump

It is best to consult a dictionary for these.

The following noun compounds take hyphens:

- noun/adjective compounds:

president-elect	secretary-general
brigadier-general	half-term

- nouns in apposition:

actor-manager	king-emperor

- nouns preceded by a letter:

U-turn	X-ray
S-bend	T-junction

- reduplicating nouns (where words are repeated; see p. 90):

clip-clop	tick-tock
topsy-turvy	hush-hush

- compound nouns containing prepositions:

sister-in-law	good-for-nothing
jack-of-all-trades	

- double-barrel family names:

Armstrong-Jones   Bowes-Lyon
Sackville-West   Douglas-Home

- placenames containing prepositions:

Newcastle-upon-Tyne   Stratford-on-Avon
Southend-on-Sea   Weston-super-Mare

Hyphens with certain compound adjectives

Hyphenation in compound adjectives is normally only necessary preceding a noun. Compare:

an *oil-based* mixture
a mixture that is *oil based*

Hyphens are used for compound adjectives comprising

- noun/adjective + present participle:

a *wheat-growing* programme
a *short-lasting* impact

- noun + past participle:

a *chocolate-coated* cake
a *rice-based* diet
a *disease-ridden* beast

- adjective + noun:

a *used-car* salesman
a *common-sense* suggestion
a *high-frequency* occurrence

- phrases:

a *once-in-a-lifetime* opportunity
a *never-to-be-forgotten* trip
a *couldn't-care-less* attitude

Adjectival compounds are also hyphenated if they begin with:

- self-:

a *self-evident* truth   a *self-sufficient* economy

- well-/ill-:

a *well-known* opera   a *well-defined* proposal
an *ill-judged* investment   an *ill-contrived* strategy

- a numeral:

a *nine-man* junta   *eighteenth-century* architecture
a *thirty-gallon* tank   a *twenty-year* lease

a *third-year* student   a *ten-year* jail sentence
a *three-year* contract

Finally, it is worth noting the results of omitting the hyphen from adjectival compounds such as:

a *little expected* conclusion
egg laying hens
a *long standing* Member of Parliament
a *fair skinned* English gentleman
a magic *walking stick*
a *high handed* autocrat

and pondering the ambiguities of:

a *light housekeeper* as against a *lighthouse-keeper*

Trailing hyphens

Occasionally two compound adjectives with the same second element are used conjunctively to modify a noun, e.g.:

Long-haired varieties and short-haired varieties . . .

This would normally be contracted, with a trailing hyphen on the first word, to:

Long- and short-haired varieties . . .

Hyphens with compound numbers

All the compound numbers between 21 and 99 take a hyphen: thus *twenty-seven, thirty-one, forty-four,* etc. Compound numbers such as *two hundred, three thousand,* etc. are not hyphenated.

Hyphens in fractions

Words like *three-quarters, seven-eighths, nine-tenths* are normally hyphenated.

Hyphens for special effects

'Please s-p-e-a-k u-p c-l-e-a-r-l-y. I'm rather deaf.'
'I'll b-b-b-break your b-b-b-bloody neck!'

In the first example, the speaker is spelling it out. In the second, he is stuttering.

Paragraph

Paragraphing is one of the important conventions of written English, and was devised as a visual aid for drawing the reader's attention to the organisation of a piece of extended text. Commas and colons and dashes are punctuation marks inside the sentence. Full stops are punctuation marks signalling the ends of sentences. Paragraphs are punctuation marks showing how sentences are grouped together. The sentences within a paragraph usually deal with one specific theme or topic or idea which can stand alone. A new paragraph indicates that a new theme or topic or idea has been broached. Paragraphs may be long or short; they represent a unit of thought not a unit of length. Paragraphs should also be sequenced; they should offer a series of steps towards a conclusion.

A well-paragraphed text is a well-planned text, and user-friendly. It shows its organisation beyond the sentence in clearly demarcated chunks of meaning.

A new paragraph is marked in two ways: firstly, by a new line; and secondly, by indenting the first word from the left-hand margin. Instead of indenting, a recent alternative has been to leave a line space between paragraphs. (If you follow this alternative, you do not also need to indent.)

In an essay, the opening and closing paragraphs are of special importance. The opening paragraph is used to introduce the subject or to state the problem, perhaps with some brief comments about how it will be treated in the body of the essay. The closing paragraph sums up the points covered, offers a conclusion, and perhaps expresses the writer's own opinions on the matter.

Paragraphing dialogue in fiction

In fiction, each speaker's dialogue usually starts a new paragraph. Paragraphing in dialogue may therefore be viewed as representing new speakers (and, by implication, new perspectives and points of view), rather than the new themes or ideas or topics of the essay or non-fictional text. An example follows:

Something about him made her leap into *non sequiturs*. 'I'm so worried about Nick,' she said. 'Suppose his ankle is broken, like he said?'

'Suppose it is; another hour won't make any difference. He's on his second drink and feeling no pain. What about you?'

'Me?' Her thoughts were still aimed at wiping those [wet marks on the tabletop].

'All summer my wife's been raving to me about what a terrific figure this woman has down at the beach.'

'If you're looking for your wife, she's in the dining room talking to somebody.'

'Don't I know it. What can I get you, Katie?'

'Get me?' He was one of those men whose chest hair comes up very high; above the neck of his sweatshirt there was a froth the colour of pencil shavings.

'G-and-t, whiskey, Bloody Mary . . .'

'Just a white-wine spritzer,' she said. 'Very weak.'

'I might have guessed,' he said, with cheerful disgust, and did not follow her into the dining room . . .

(from 'Getting into the Set', in *Trust Me*, by John Updike, 1987)

There is more information on setting out dialogue under **quotation marks** (p. 135).

Question mark [?]

This is a specialised version of the full stop. It is used to end an interrogative sentence or sentence fragment:

Who is Sylvia? What is she?

Have you paid your poll tax?

He looks tired, doesn't he?

The last sentence, however, may also be viewed as a statement, and appear without a question mark.

When a direct question is being reported, the question mark is not required:

Where are you going? (direct question)

She asked me where I was going. (reported speech)

Question marks sometimes punctuate a list of question elements:

By Friday morning, can you give me a list of key customers? tell me their current level of debt? and indicate the dates when their payments become due?

Only the punctuation marks at the end of the following sentences tell you which sentence is a statement, which a question, and which an exclamation:

There is a body in the library. (Fetch a doctor at once.)

There is a body in the library? (I don't believe it – you must be joking.)

There is a body in the library! (Help! Murder! Police!)

Sometimes a question mark is used to indicate that a fact is unverified.

She lectures on the poetry of William Dunbar (?1460–?1520) and the Scottish Chaucerians.

Sometimes multiple question marks are found in print to indicate strong feelings, but these, like multiple exclamation marks, are not to be encouraged in formal writing.

What the hell do you think you're doing???

Quotation marks [single: ' ' double: " "]

Quotation marks are sometimes called **quotes** or **inverted commas**. They come in pairs, one to open and one to close the quotation. They may be single or double, with British usage favouring single quotation marks, and American usage favouring double. They are used to mark off direct speech; to show that a word or phrase has been highlighted; and to indicate the title of a short story, an article, or a short poem.

Direct speech

Direct speech is always enclosed within quotation marks:

'Where are you going?' he asked the child. 'And where is your coat?'
'I'm going to the circus,' was the reply, 'to see the clowns. I don't need a coat — I'm not cold.'

Highlighting

Quotation marks are used to highlight particular words and phrases:

When we were children, we called the verb a 'doing word'.
She called herself a 'psychometrist', whatever that is.
He loved the puppy dearly, even though he called it his 'daft wee dug'.
The word *polycentric* means 'having more than one centre', according to my dictionary.
Schools used to talk about certain children as being 'slow learners'; nowadays we define them as having 'special needs' and we provide them with 'positive discrimination' in the allocation of funds.

In the second example, there is a suggestion that the writer disagrees with the use of the highlighted word. In the third example, the use of dialect is effectively quarantined. In the final example, educational jargon is brought under the spotlight. Although highlighting is a useful device, it becomes invalid when it is abused, as when some writers use it instead of seeking out the right word or phrase:

She's 'no oil painting', it is true, but then she has a 'heart of gold'.

Here the quotation marks are saying: I know these are clichés, but I can't be bothered to find my own words.

Titles

Titles of short stories, shorter poems, chapters, articles, essays, lectures, etc. are usually enclosed in quotation marks. This is in contrast to titles of books, long poems that have been published in their own right, plays, newspapers and movies, which in print are usually set in italics:

He read the poem called 'Anthem for Doomed Youth'.

He studied Milton's *Paradise Lost* for the exam.

Chapter XXI of R. L. Stevenson's novel *St Ives* is called 'I Become the Owner of a Claret-Coloured Chaise'.

The title of this year's Dimbleby Lecture is 'The Monarchy – What Price?'

Quotes within quotes

As stated earlier, British preference is for single quotes, while American usage favours double. For quotes within quotes, the preferences are reversed – double quotes for UK and single quotes for US usage:

'The key witness said, "I saw the whole thing," and looked at the judge for encouragement.'

'Kindly refrain from calling me your "sweetie pie",' she remarked.

Semicolon [;]

The **semicolon** has two main punctuational uses within the sentence: it is used in complex lists, and it is used as an alternative to the overuse of conjunctions.

Especially in long or complex sentences, some lists may already use lots of commas, so the semicolon is brought into use as a refinement:

She sent a fax to their branches in Toronto, Canada; Tokyo, Japan; and Wiesbaden, Germany.

Candidates require a good degree, preferably in Spanish; a knowledge of current events in Argentina, Chile and Uruguay; and the ability to work long hours, travel long distances, and keep colleagues at head office briefed on relevant developments.

Semicolons are also useful in sentences with two (or more) main clauses not joined by a coordinating conjunction:

Some people are excellent public speakers; others are not.

She may have been brought up in America; she may have had a strong New York accent; she may have told us kids to 'keep to the sidewalk'; yet she considered herself as British as John Bull.

Sometimes – but by no means invariably – phrases such as *however, nevertheless, hence, furthermore, moreover, also, that is to say*, are preceded by a semicolon:

The Japanese are an ingenious and industrious people; hence the powerful development of their economy.

These exercises are recommended; however, they are not obligatory.

Slash [/]

The **slash** is sometimes called the **oblique mark**, and – by the Americans – the **virgule**. It has become common in recent years, and has acquired several punctuational uses.

Slashes to show alternatives

Dear Sir/Madam
You will need a passport and/or visa.
Dinner jacket/lounge suit to be worn.

Modifications of this use are common in advertisements:

advanced/proficiency courses in Russian
two-room flat in the Islington/King's Cross/Clerkenwell area

and in 'politically correct' non-sexist language constructions:

s/he
Everyone must do his/her best.

Slashes to indicate periods of time

These are particularly common in fiscal and academic contexts:

Costs for 1993/4 are not yet fixed.
He's claimed the new allowance in his 1992/3 tax form.
She spent the academic year 1991/2 at the University of Leeds.

Slashes in itineraries

This use is now quite common in the travel trade:

Lufthansa flight 321 Frankfurt/Nairobi/Johannesburg
The New York/Memphis/New Orleans bus leaves at noon.

Slashes marking off lines of verse

When for reasons of space a poem is not properly laid out line for line, the line breaks are shown by a slash.

Up the airy mountain,/Down the rushy glen,/We daren't go a-hunting/For fear of little men.

Slashes for abbreviation

Several abbreviations commonly incorporate a slash:

I'm staying c/o Beattie, 49 Bentinck Drive. (c/o = care of)
Charge to my a/c. (a/c = account)
Major Macmillan is the officer i/c this unit. (i/c = in charge of)

Per is generally shown by a slash:

60 ft/sec   100km/hr

five
Figures of speech and literary devices

He understood . . . Walt Whitman who laid end to end words never seen in each other's company before outside of a dictionary, and Herman Melville who split the atom of the traditional novel in the effort to make whaling a universal metaphor.

David Lodge, *Changing Places*, 1975

Oft on the dappled turf at ease
I sit, and play with similes,
Loose types of things through all
　　degrees . . .
　　Wordsworth, 'To the Daisy', 1802

One simile, that solitary shines
In a dry desert of a thousand lines.
　　Pope, 'Satires and Epistles of Horace
　　　　　　　Imitated', 1738

Figures of speech and literary devices

Few people nowadays seem able to identify **figurative language**, although of course we all use it as much as ever. In classical times, various types of figurative language were identified by grammarians, and many of the terms they coined remain extant to this day. There is not complete agreement on the definition of the various figures of speech, but the following list gives the main devices with examples and comments.

Allegory

An **allegory** is a form of story which operates on more than one level – it has a surface significance, and a deeper significance below the surface. The characters in an allegory usually personify or represent a vice or virtue (see **personification**, pp. 156–7), with common nouns capitalised to give characters' names – *Sloth, Lust*. Allegory was popular in the Middle Ages, and the best-known English allegories are *The Faerie Queene*, by Edmund Spenser (1552?–99), and *Pilgrim's Progress*, by John Bunyan (1628–88). More modern allegorists include authors such as Nathaniel Hawthorne (1804–64), C.S. Lewis (1898–1963), and George Orwell (1903–50).

Alliteration

Alliteration is the repetition of initial sounds or letters in a sequence of words; or, in verse, of stressed syllables:

Round and *round* the *rugged rocks*, the *ragged rascal ran.*

Peter Piper picked a *peck* of *pickled peppers.*

sing a *song* of *sixpence*

the *wild* and *woolly west*

I hear *lake* water *lapping* with *low sounds* by the *shore* . . . (Yeats)

In poetry, alliteration is often used as a phonetic device to unify the passage in which it occurs, so in that context it may be regarded as a form of **rhyme**. Much medieval English poetry was written according to a variety of alliterative schemes:

In a *somer season* when *soft* was the *sonne* . . . (*Piers Plowman*)

A *fair field full* of *folk found* I between

Of all *manere men*, the rich and *meane*

Working and *wandering* as the *world* asketh . . . (*Piers Plowman*)

A more modern poet much given to alliteration was Swinburne:

When the *hounds* of spring are on winter's traces,

The *m*other of *m*onths in *m*eadow or plain
Fills the shadows and windy places
With *l*isp of *l*eaves and *r*ipple of *r*ain. (*Atalanta in Calydon*)

Now all strange hours and all strange loves are over,
*D*reams and *d*esires and *s*ombre *s*ongs and *s*weet. ('Ave atque Vale')

Alliteration is much loved by modern advertisers:

*G*raded *g*rains make *f*iner *f*lour.
*T*etley *t*ea *t*otally *t*antalises *t*astebuds.
*P-p-p-p*ick up a *P*enguin.

Anacoluthon

This is a figure of speech, often inadvertent, in a sentence where a fresh construction is adopted before the original is complete. The Greek word means 'lacking sequence':

You really ought – well, do it your own way.
I'd like to introduce – I don't think you are listening to me.

Analogy

An analogy is a kind of **simile** (see pp. 158–60) in which there is an inference of resemblance between two items which are equated or compared:

Time is like the tide – it waits for no man.
The child is the analogy of a people at the dawn of history.

Anticlimax

An anticlimax is a figure of speech consisting of a sudden descent from the lofty or sublime to the trivial or ridiculous. Deliberate anticlimax has a comic or satiric effect in good writing. (See also **bathos**, pp. 142–3.)

A better cavalier ne'er mounted horse,
Or, being mounted, *e'er got down again*. (Byron)

Not louder shrieks to pitying heaven are cast,
When husbands *or when lapdogs* breathe their last. (Pope)

A man, a master, a marvel . . . *a mouse*.

Antithesis

A figure of speech in which there is a striking opposition or contrast of ideas. Although the words are opposed, they are balanced. **An antithesis** may be quite succinct – *Action, not words* – or it may be longer:

My words fly up, my thoughts remain below. (Marlowe)
Better to reign in hell than serve in heaven. (Milton)
To err is human, to forgive, divine. (Pope)
Marry in haste; repent at leisure.
Hair today, bald tomorrow!
One small step for man; one giant leap for mankind. (Neil Armstrong)

Apostrophe

In addition to being a punctuation mark (see pp. 114–15), the **apostrophe** is a figure of speech. It is a kind of rhetorical address or speech to an absent listener:

O Liberty, what things are done in thy name! (Carlyle)
O Romeo, Romeo! wherefore art thou Romeo? (Shakespeare)

In the sense that no answer is expected, the apostrophe is a form of **rhetorical question** (see p. 158).

Assonance

Assonance is a repetition of two or more identical vowel sounds, as in feet/steer/steam; spin/skip/grid; or red/hen/held. It is always involved in rhyme, as in see/flee; or red/dead. Poetic examples of assonance are found in:

Rend with tremendous sound your ears asunder
With gun, drum, trumpet, blunderbuss, and thunder.

We shall see, while above us
The waves roar and whirl,
A ceiling of amber,
A pavement of pearl. (Arnold)

Fair daffodils we weep to see
You haste away so soon. (Wordsworth)

And a grey mist on the sea's face and a grey dawn breaking. (Masefield)

Bathos

The term for a passage that is meant to be solemn and impressive, but which fails to live up to its intention because of some textual incongruity. The result is often a ludicrous **anticlimax** (see p. 141).

The piteous news, so much it shocked her

She quite forgot to send the doctor. (Wordsworth)

Along the wire the electric message came:
He is no better, *he is much the same.*
> (Alfred Austin, on the illness of the Prince of Wales)

Catch phrase

A term for a slogan or quotation (often a misquotation), usually from an actor or politician or an advertisement, and popularised by much use. Popular catch phrases of their day were:

You've never had it so good. (Harold Macmillan)
A week is a long time in politics. (Harold Wilson)
There is no alternative. (Margaret Thatcher)
Guinness is good for you. (advertisement)
Come up and see me some time. (Mae West)

Clerihew

A **clerihew** is a humorous, four-line, light verse form that rhymes AABB. It was popularised in the late 1920s by Edmund Clerihew Bentley (1875–1956) and is named after him. The distinctive feature of the clerihew is that it usually deals with a person named in the first line, and then goes on to describe that person in a fanciful way.

Sir Christopher *Wren*   A
Said, 'I am going to dine with some *men*.   A
If anyone *calls*   B
Say I am designing St *Paul's.*'   B

Sir Humphrey Davy
Abominated gravy.
He lived in the odium
Of having discovered sodium.

John Stuart Mill
By a mighty effort of will
Overcame his natural bonhomie
And wrote 'Principles of Political Economy'.

Cliché

A **cliché** is a stereotyped, or hackneyed, or trite phrase or expression. Clichés often serve as courtesy fillers or formulas in polite, unrehearsed conversation. In a harsh judgment, George Orwell attributed clichés to speakers making appropriate noises in the larynx, but whose brains were not involved in choosing their words for themselves.

Clichés may be words (*nice* used to be held up as a cliché adjective), or phrases (*at this point in time, part and parcel, intents and purposes, conspicuous by its absence, tender mercies, from time immemorial*), or figures of speech (*come hell or high water, at death's door, swing of the pendulum, thin end of the wedge, white elephant, as old as the hills*), or formulas (*have a nice day, how do you do?*). They are often confusing to non-native English speakers.

One of the most fertile fields for the creation of British clichés is politics: *the war against inflation, stand on our own feet, light at the end of the tunnel, the green shoots of economic recovery* may be among the current crop, but each parliament spawns its own.

It is pointless to draw up a list of clichés with some sort of health warning: cliché – keep off. Context determines whether the word or phrase is used merely as a cliché or because it is the best way of expressing a meaning. See also **dead metaphor** (p. 145).

Part of the appeal of Oscar Wilde was his knack of reversing clichés:

Nothing succeeds like excess.
Work is the curse of the drinking classes.
Her hair has gone quite gold with grief.

Colloquialism

A **colloquialism** is a figurative expression used in informal everyday speech, including slang. Examples include:

at a loose end nothing to do
at the double very quickly
chew the fat with someone chat with someone
come a cropper fail
dead beat exhausted
down in the mouth dejected, in poor spirits
face the music confront the worst
get cracking hurry up
have a heart be reasonable
hold your horses wait a minute
keep one's powder dry be ready to cope with surprises

lead up the garden path fool someone
play the game act fairly
put the cart before the horse start at the wrong end
smell a rat suspect something
take forty winks take a short sleep
take the bull by the horns confront an adversary
under a cloud in trouble or disfavour
a wet blanket a discouraging person

Idioms trawl the language of colloquialism for some of their most memorable lines (see pp. 148–9).

Dead metaphor

There are two types of *dead metaphor*. Firstly, there are the figurative expressions that are no longer recognised as such. They have entered the language as literal terms. Examples are everyday items like *the arm of a chair, the leg of a table, to foot the bill, break of day, nightfall, blueprint,* etc. In a more specialist context – in this case the world of economics – terms like *targets, ceilings, backlogs,* and *bottlenecks* tend no longer to be used with any awareness of their metaphoric origin; so they too are dead metaphors.

The other kind of dead metaphor is perhaps better termed an overworked metaphor. Like a **cliché** (see pp. 143–4), it is an overused expression which has lost all freshness, and is used mainly for convenience. It is often a form of jargon. Examples from equestrianism are terms like *he has taken the bit between his teeth, she's flogging a dead horse,* and the very widespread *the situation is in hand.* Other metaphors one might like to see dead include *the lower income bracket, exploring every avenue,* and *leaving no stone unturned.*

Doubles

Doubles are pairs of words that habitually go together. They are sometimes called dyads, from Greek *dyo*, 'two'. They are formed in various ways:

- Repetition of the word:

  again and again
  by and by
  neck and neck
  over and over

  out and out
  so and so
  such and such

- Repetition of the meaning:

  goods and chattels
  hale and hearty
  stuff and nonsense
  fast and furious

  rant and rave
  hue and cry
  bawl and shout
  aided and abetted

- Alliteration:

  kith and kin
  humming and hawing
  might and main
  part and parcel

  alas and alack
  rough and ready
  rack and ruin
  time and tide

- Opposites:

  this and that
  on and off

  ancient and modern
  here and there

great and small
give and take

come and go
ups and downs

- Rhyme or assonance:

high and dry
fair and square

wear and tear
out and about

Epigram

Originally, an **epigram** was a short inscription (often on a tomb). Nowadays, it is a pithy saying, effective by its wit, ingenuity, brevity and balance. In true epigrammatic form, Coleridge defined it thus:

What is an epigram? a dwarfish whole,
Its body brevity, and wit its soul.

The French writer François de La Rochefoucauld (1613–80), in his *Maximes*, was a source of many epigrams based on Roman and Greek writers:

The glory of great men must always be measured by the means they have used to obtain it.
Hypocrisy is the homage that vice pays to virtue.
We are almost always bored by the very people whom we must not find boring.
Everyone complains of his memory; no one of his judgment.

More modern attempts at epigrams include:

A self-made man is forever praising his creator.
We learn from history that we do not learn from history.
A life of idleness is hard work.
When a man kills a tiger, he calls it sport; when a tiger kills a man, he calls it vicious.
A lawyer is a wise man who rescues your estate from your enemies and keeps much of it for himself.
Poor folk want food for their stomachs; rich folk want stomachs for their food.

Oscar Wilde (1854–1900) was a master of the epigram:

A cynic is a man who knows the price of everything and the value of nothing.
Men can be analysed, women merely adored.

Euphemism

In **euphemism**, an accurate but explicit word is substituted with a gentler and less distasteful term. Its use is justified when the cold truth is inappropriate, e.g. to avoid giving offence or causing distress. It is not the same thing as **meiosis** or **litotes** (see pp. 151 and 150–1).

For example, many people avoid direct reference to death, preferring terms like *the departed, pass on, pass away, terminally ill*. Rather than say *When I die . . .*, they prefer, *If anything should happen to me . . .* Other contexts prone to euphemism include illness, mental handicap, old age, obesity, poverty, dishonesty, and sex. Hence:

She's a little confused. (= She's mentally disturbed.)
He's a senior citizen/getting on in years. (= He's old.)
She has a full figure. (= She's fat.)
Terminological inexactitude. (= a lie)
He's been economical with the truth. (= He lied.)
They're sleeping together. (= They're having sexual intercourse.)
His clothes have seen better days. (= They're shabby.)
A Third World country (= a poor country)

Euphemism sometimes goes to ludicrous or even to wicked lengths, as in:

A terminal episode (= death, in American jargon)
Schedule overrun (= late/overdue, in business jargon)
Ethnic cleansing (= mass displacements of populations)
The final solution (= Nazi term for the extermination of the Jews)

A special variety of euphemism is 'nukespeak', where acronyms are cunningly deployed to gloss over the obscenities to which they refer – an ICBM or a MIRV looks so much friendlier than an Inter-Continental Ballistic Missile or a Multiple Independently-Targetable Re-entry Vehicle; and carefully devised positive-sounding terms like 'clean strike', 'surgical strike', and 'collateral damage' are dreamt up by the official thought police of Western capitalism to make the unthinkable thinkable. Here euphemism melts into George Orwell's 'mind control'.

Another set of euphemisms derive from the current notion of 'political correctness'. Nowadays we are told not to call someone 'small' (even if he is): he is 'vertically challenged'. Similarly, sex-change operations have become 'gender realignment'.

Haiku

The **haiku** is a short Japanese poetic form, in three unrhymed lines, with an exact number of syllables per line. The syllable pattern is 5–7–5. The traditional subject matter is usually something out of nature. Haiku are often thoughtful and rather haunting word-pictures:

Cat stretching slowly
Pads outside to the garden.
Shiver, small creatures!

O fan of white silk,
Clear as frost on the grass-blade,
You also are laid aside. (Ezra Pound)

Hyperbole

Hyperbole is overstatement. As a figure of speech, it consists of an extravagant statement or exaggeration. It is used to emphasise the importance or extent of something. It is in use when Lady Macbeth says: 'Here's the smell of blood still: *all the perfumes of Arabia* will not sweeten this little hand.' Or when the deposed Richard II says: '*Not all the water in the rough rude sea* can wash the balm from an anointed king'.

More prosaically, we employ hyperbole if we say we are *dying of hunger* if we merely wish to go for lunch; or if we say there were *millions of people* on the train this morning merely to indicate that it was very busy. Other colloquial examples:

He ran like lightning.
He ran me off my feet.
She was boiling hot.
He embraced her a thousand times.
He snapped my head off.

From hyperbole comes the sales/marketing term **hype**, a form of extravagant promotion designed to publicise a product or event.

Idiom

An **idiom** is an expression whose meaning cannot easily be worked out from the words it contains. For example, the expression *to let the cat out of the bag* has nothing to do with cats or bags in the usual sense of those words. It is an idiom, meaning 'to reveal a secret'. Idioms have the potential to cause foreign learners of a language some difficulty. If you say to a native speaker visiting a place for the first time, 'How did you *find* Stratford?' you will get the response, 'Great – I loved it,' or, 'I didn't like the place at all.' But if you ask a non-native speaker the same question, the response may be blank puzzlement. 'How did I *find* Stratford? The train took me there.' Here, *find* is used idiomatically.

Where there is no resemblance between the meaning of the individual words and the meaning of the idiom, it is called **opaque**. If part of the phrase retains a literal meaning, the idiom is **semi-opaque**. Where the meaning of the whole can be guessed from the meaning of the parts, the idiom is **transparent**.

● Opaque idioms:

sacred cow
straw that breaks the camel's back
to jump the gun
to give the show away

to pull the wool over someone's eyes
to score a hat trick
to pass the buck
to lead someone up the garden path
a shot in the arm

- Semi-opaque idioms:

to come down on someone like a ton of bricks
to lay down the law
to force someone's hand
keen as mustard
to leave someone to his own devices

- Transparent idioms:

to keep a straight face
to stand shoulder to shoulder
to be a devil/angel

Many idioms are used in only colloquial English. Some are acceptable in formal English: for example, *to be the life and soul of the party*.

The form of many idioms is fixed, while others permit slight rearrangement of their component parts. It is possible to 'cut a *sorry/ fine/handsome* figure'. But you can only '*bite* the *dust*' (= die); idiomatically you cannot '*chew/suck/lick* the *earth/soil/ground*'.

Innuendo

Innuendo is a type of **irony** (see below), where something is hinted at, but not stated openly. It works by implication rather than by direct statement. It often involves a veiled allusion, sometimes malicious or equivocal, reflecting on a person's character:

Frank Harris is invited to all the great houses of England – once. (attr. Oscar Wilde)

Irony

Irony is a figure of speech where the speaker says one thing but implies the opposite. Compare the following:

That will fetch a good price.
A good price *that* will fetch!

The words may be the same, but the second sentence means the opposite of the first. It is an ironical way of saying, 'That will not fetch a good price.' Similarly, with suitable emphasis, for these expressions:

That's a great help (I don't think)!

Much good that will do!
You're a fine cook/A fine cook *you* are!

Dramatic irony is a literary device which occurs when a character (of a novel, play, etc.) says something which is meaningful to him/herself on one level, but has a different meaning on a different level for the reader/ audience. Tragic irony is a refinement of this.

When Mark Antony says: 'For Brutus is an honourable man; so are they all, all honourable men,' the audience is more aware of their recent and *dis*honourable deed – the assassination of Julius Caesar – than of anything honourable about them. Thus Shakespeare builds irony into a dramatic scene.

Had Queen Marie Antoinette of France said in 1789, 'The King and I have not the slightest intention of losing our heads over these silly popular revolutions!' she would have uttered an ironic statement.

Limerick

The **limerick** is a humorous, five-line, light verse form rhyming AABBA. There are usually three stressed beats in the A lines and two stressed beats in the B lines. The form became popular after the 1846 publication of *The Book of Nonsense*, by Edward Lear (1812–88):

There was an old man of Darjeeling	A
Who got on a train bound for Ealing.	A
It said on the door,	B
'Please don't spit on the floor.'	B
So he got up and spat on the ceiling.	A

There was a young lady from Twickenham
Whose boots were too tight to walk quick in 'em.
So after a while
She sat down on a stile,
And took off her boots and was sick in 'em.

There was a young bard of Japan
Whose limericks never would scan.
When they said it was so,
He replied, 'Yes, I know,
But I make a rule of always trying to get just as many words into the last line as I
    possibly can.'

Litotes

Litotes is a special kind of understatement, in which a positive statement is achieved by denying something negative – i.e. something is expressed by denying its opposite:

He's *not a bad* swimmer. (= He's quite a good swimmer.)
This is *no easy* task. (= It's a difficult task.)
Her life was *no bed of roses*. (= She had a hard life.)
no mean city (= a great city, in St Paul's remark about Rome)

Other common expressions involving litotes:

by no means negligible
in no small measure

Malapropism

This term denotes the incorrect use of a word, often a scholarly word. It derives from Mrs Malaprop, an amusing character in *The Rivals* (1775), the classic comedy by R.B. Sheridan (1751–1816). Mrs Malaprop's name is from the French *mal à propos* (= 'not apt or apposite, inappropriate'), and she is much given to the sorts of utterances for which the term was coined – the misapplication of long words. She confuses words such as *alligator* and *allegory*, *allusion* and *illusion*, *hydrostatics* and *hysterics*. Some of her memorable throwaway lines include:

She's as headstrong as an *allegory* on the banks of the Nile.
An aspersion upon my parts of speech . . . Sure, if I *reprehend* anything in this
    world, it is the use of my *oracular* tongue, and a nice *derangement* of *epitaphs*.

Meiosis

Meiosis is deliberate understatement, for the sake of effect. The aim of meiosis is to emphasise the size, importance, etc. of what is apparently belittled. It is a colloquial and quintessentially English figure of speech, indicated by the use of words like *rather*. **Litotes** (see pp. 150–1) is a form of meiosis:

She's *rather* nice. (= I like her very much.)
He made a *decent* contribution. (a generous one)
This is *some* game. (It's an epic game.)

Metaphor

Metaphorical language is not the same as the classical view of language, according to which words are thought of as 'labelling' things in the 'real' world. **Metaphors** express a way of conceptualising, a way of seeing and understanding one's surroundings. We often forget how pervasive metaphorical language is. But as C.S. Lewis said, 'Human beings are incurably metaphorical'; and I.A. Richards has called metaphor 'the omnipresent principle of language'.

Metaphor is a way of wording the world. It reminds us that language constructs as well as reflects, and that it is not always a transparent vehicle. It is a figure of speech in which A is identified with B. It is based on substitution and comparison. The process of comparison yields a **simile** (see pp. 158–60), while the process of substitution yields a metaphor. So:

The law is an *ass*. (Dickens)

The waves were *soldiers* moving. (Wallace Stevens)

These utterances are not to be understood literally – they are to be taken as pictures of the author's (or speaker's) meaning.

Metaphors come in all shapes and sizes. They can be examined from the point of view of their grammatical construction. We may identify:

- **appositional metaphors**:

  My wife, a *rose* among *thorns*.

- **vocative**, or **apostrophic metaphors**:

  My *flower*, my darling!

- **verbal metaphors**:

  The minutes *crept by* slowly.

  She *was rooted* to the spot in terror.

  Their blows *rained down* on the innocent victim.

- **prepositional metaphors**:

  The *apple of* my eye

  The *knife of* pain and betrayal

- **adjectival metaphors**:

  With *leaden* feet

  A *flaming* temper

  A *stony* silence

- **adverbial metaphors**:

  He was caught *red-handed*.

  A *grief ago*. (Dylan Thomas)

Metaphors can also be analysed for the kind of work they do. So we can identify:

- **animistic metaphors**, in which inanimate nouns receive animate qualities:

  A good book is the *best of friends*.

- **concretive metaphors**, in which abstractions are given substance:

  Music is the *brandy* of the damned! (G.B. Shaw)
  Liberty's a glorious *feast*! (Burns)

- **humanising metaphors**, in which non-human nouns are given human attributes:

  A *babbling* brook
  An *angry* sky
  April is the *cruellest* month . . . (T.S. Eliot)

(See also **personification**, pp. 156–7)

- **dehumanising metaphors**, in which people are given non-human characteristics:

  Christ the *tiger* (Blake)

- **deifying metaphors**, in which divine qualities are attributed to people or things:

  The *almighty* dollar
  The *eternal* triangle

- more broadly – **paradoxical metaphors**, in which qualities associated with one thing are attributed to another:

  To a *green* thought in a green shade. (Andrew Marvell)
  Thoughts of a *dry* brain in a dry season. (T.S. Eliot)

(See also **paradox**, p. 156.)

Metonymy

Metonymy is a figure of speech which refers to someone or something via an associated item. For example, *the Crown* and *Downing Street* are terms often used in the UK when speaking about the monarchy and the Prime Minister. Other metonymic expressions are:

King of the *ring* (= boxing)
He has taken to the *bottle*. (= alcoholic liquor)
She was called to the *bar*. (= the profession of a barrister)

Metre

Metre means 'measure', and may be defined as any form of measured, or regulated, rhythm. All language has stressed and unstressed syllables, and in English poetry metre is the technical term for the rhythmic arrangement of those syllables. Just as English grammar was based on Latin grammar, so too English poetic metre was based on Latin. The basic measure of Latin verse was the **foot**, and four popular types of poetic foot in regular English verse are:

- **iambic** (unstressed + stressed, shown as x/):

God gives all men all earth to love,	x/x/x/x/ (= 4 iambic feet)
But, since man's heart is small,	x/x/x/
Ordains for each one spot shall prove	x/x/x/x/
Belovèd over all. (Kipling)	x/x/x/

- **trochaic** (stressed + unstressed, shown as /x):

Beauty, midnight, vision dies:	/x/x/x/ (= 3.5 trochaic feet)
Let the winds of dawn that blow	/x/x/x/
Softly round your dreaming head	/x/x/x/
Such a day of sweetness show . . . (Auden)	/x/x/x/

- **anapaestic** (2 unstressed + 1 stressed, shown as xx/):

At the corner of Wood Street, when daylight appears,	xx/xx/xx/xx/ (= 4 anapaestic feet)
Hangs a thrush that sings loud, it has sung for three years . . . (Wordsworth)	xx/xx/xx/xx/

- **dactylic** (1 stressed + 2 unstressed, shown as /xx):

Fast they come, fast they come;	/xx/xx (= 2 dactylic feet)
See how they gather!	/xx/x
Wide waves the eagle plume,	/xx/xx
Blended with heather . . . (Scott)	/xx/x

Particular names were given to lines with a certain number of feet. So a line with five feet is a **pentameter**, a **hexameter** has six feet, a **heptameter** has seven, etc. An **iambic pentameter** has five iambic feet.

Onomatopoeia

Onomatopoeia is a kind of sound symbolism. Words are onomatopoeic if the sound of the word suggests its sense. They are sometimes called **mimic words**, and obvious examples are:

babble, bubble, burble, buzz
crack, click, clack, clatter, crunch, clang, croak
fizzle, flutter
gurgle, grate, grunt, gleam, glow, glisten
hiss, hush, hum, hurly-burly
lullaby
plop, plonk, patter
rustle

shush, slush, slap, slime, slink, slither
twang, tinkle, twinkle, twitter

From the above list, it can be deduced that in English certain sounds particularly lend themselves to onomatopoeia. Many words beginning with *sl-* seem to have unpleasant connotations, while various words beginning with *gl-* are associated with light.

A form of writing that has created its own range of onomatopoeic terms is the comic strip with its special effects: *wham, zap, kerplonk, splat!*

Sometimes onomatopoeic words imitate a person or an animal's sound: *yum yum, yuk, bow wow, cock-a-doodle-doo, cuckoo, peewit.*

There was much poetic use of onomatopoeia, often with alliteration thrown in for good measure:

Over the *c*obbles he *c*lattered and *c*lashed . . . (Browning)

There was never a sound beside the wood but one,
And that was my long scythe whispering to the ground. (Robert Frost)

Then I heard the boom of the blood-lust song
And a thigh-bone beating on a tin-pan gong. (Vachel Lindsay)

Keeping time, time, time,
In a sort of Runic rhyme,
To the tintinnabulation that so musically wells
From the bells, bells, bells, bells. (Edgar Allan Poe)

Oxymoron

The **oxymoron** is a kind of **paradox** (see p. 156) – a combination of contradictory or incongruous words, like *deafening silence, bitter-sweet, sublimely bad, cruel kindness,* or *devoted enemies.* It is a figure of speech mainly employed to make a special impact, either in poetry or for humorous effect:

His *honour* rooted in *dishonour* stood,
And *faith unfaithful* kept him *falsely true.* (Tennyson)

Evil, be thou my *good.* (Milton)
There's no *success* like *failure.* (Bob Dylan)
Include me *out.* (Sam Goldwyn)
A *verbal contract* isn't worth the *paper it's written on.* (Sam Goldwyn)
I'll give you a *definite maybe.* (Sam Goldwyn)
Silence is wonderful to *listen to.* (Sam Goldwyn)

Oxymorons may be used cynically, as when *military intelligence* or the *Yugoslavian state* are called contradictions in terms.

Palindrome

The arrangement of numbers, words, or lines of text to give the same message backwards as forwards is called a **palindrome**. The word is from Greek *palin dromo*, 'to run back again'. They have also been called **Sotadics**, after their reputed inventor, Sotades, a Greek poet of the 3rd century BC. Examples of palindromic words are *madam*, *level*, and *noon* and numerals like 1991 or 2002. Longer examples are:

Madam, I'm Adam.
Was it a cat I saw?
Lewd did I live, and evil I did dwel. (Philips, 1706)
Able was I ere I saw Elba. (attr. Napoleon)
A man, a plan, a canal — Panama!

One of the longest palindromes in English is:

Dog as a devil deified/Deified lived as a god.

A **word palindrome** is one in which only the words are reversed:

What? So he is dead, is he? So what?

Paradox

A **paradox** is a statement that appears contradictory or contrary to common sense, and yet is true in some other sense:

The child is father of the man. (Wordsworth)
He who would save his life must lose it. (Bible)

Personification

Personification is a special kind of metaphor. It is a figure of speech in which some abstraction or inanimate thing is represented as a person, or is given human qualities. **Allegory** (see p. 140) makes special use of personification. *Giant Despair*, in Bunyan's *Pilgrim's Progress*, is an example of a personification: the abstract concept of despair represented as a person. Other examples:

Truth sits upon the lips of dying men. (Arnold)
Riches are a good handmaid, but the worst mistress. (Bacon)
Prudence is a rich ugly old maid, courted by incapacity. (Blake)
Time, the great healer . . .
Can Honour's voice provoke the silent dust,/Or Flatt'ry soothe the dull
  cold ear of Death? (Gray)
Slowly, silently, now the moon/ Walks the night in her silver shoon.
  (De la Mare)
Ol' man river, he just keeps rolling along . . .

Other 'humanising' **metaphors** (see p. 153), by giving an adjective normally associated with a person to a non-human noun, are also a sort of personification:

a *babbling* brook
Come, *friendly* bombs, and fall on Slough . . . (Betjeman)

Proverb

A **proverb** is a popular saying memorably expressed:

Once bitten, twice shy.
Easy come, easy go.

Proverbs tend to encapsulate traditional or accepted wisdom, and to be anonymous or unattributable. Common stylistic devices used in proverbs include:

● Rhyme or assonance:

Early to bed, early to rise,
Makes a man healthy, wealthy and wise.

Birds of a feather flock together.

A stitch in time saves nine.

Red sky at night – shepherds' delight.
Red sky in the morning – shepherds' warning.

● Alliteration:

Love laughs at locksmiths.
A cat may look at a king.
A miss is as good as a mile.
Every dog has his day.

Some proverbs betray their age by retaining linguistic archaisms:

Pride goeth before a fall.
He goes a-sorrowing who goes a-borrowing.
Shoemakers' wives are worst shod.

Proverbs is the name of a book of the Old Testament, containing, as the name indicates, quantities of proverbial utterances. Many of them were originally attributed to King Solomon.

The fear of the Lord is the beginning of knowledge.
Hope deferred makes the heart sick.
He that has knowledge spares his words.
A good name is rather to be chosen than great riches.
A fool utters all his mind.
Where there is no vision, the people perish.

Pun

A **pun** is a figure of speech that uses words in such a way as to convey – and make a play on – their double meaning. Puns were popular in the nineteenth century and in earlier periods, but are nowadays regarded by many as rather childish:

> Ask for me tomorrow, and you shall find me a *grave* man. (= dead, Shakespeare, *Romeo and Juliet*)
> When is a door not a door? When it's *ajar*. (= a jar)
> Drilling holes is *boring*.
> King Kong was the orginal urban *guerrilla*. (= gorilla)
> 'His sins were scarlet but his books were *read*.' (= red, Belloc, 'On His Books')
> The Egyptians received a *check* on the bank of the Red Sea which was *crossed* by Moses. (cheque)
> Marriage isn't a word – it's a *sentence*! (King Vidor)

Examples appearing on notices in, respectively, a chemist's shop window, a photographer's shop window, a gents' toilet, and the back window of a bridal limousine:

> WE DISPENSE WITH ACCURACY
> OUR BUSINESS IS DEVELOPING
> WE AIM TO PLEASE – YOU AIM TOO, PLEASE
> AISLE ALTAR HYMN

Then there was the unfortunately ambiguous newspaper headline:

> TRAIN ON FIRE – PASSENGERS ALIGHT

and the old favourite school report-card comment:

> Your son is *trying*. (making an effort/exasperating)

Rhetorical question

A **rhetorical question** is asked for effect, and requires no answer. Often it is the equivalent of an emphatic statement:

> Was I hungry? (i.e. I was extremely hungry.)
> Do you take me for an imbecile? (i.e. I'm an intelligent person.)

Sometimes it is intended as a passing observation:

> What are things coming to?

Simile

A **simile** is a figure of speech in which one thing or person is explicitly compared with another, and is said to be *like* another. It is used for explanatory, illustrative, or ornamental purpose. The word is from Latin *similis*, 'like', and the words *like* or *as* are usually used in similes:

I wandered lonely *as* a cloud . . . (Wordsworth)
My love is *like* a red, red rose . . . (Burns)
Money is *like* muck, not good except it be spread. (Bacon)
Float *like* a butterfly, sting *like* a bee. (Muhammad Ali)
Squat *like* a toad he sat . . . (Milton)

Poetic simile is often extended over several lines:

Thick *as* autumnal leaves that strow the brooks
In Vallombrosa, where th' Etrurian shades
High over-arched embow'r . . . (Milton, *Paradise Lost*)

And we are here *as* on a darkling plain
Swept with confused alarms of struggle and flight,
Where ignorant armies clash by night. (Arnold, 'Dover Beach')

Some similes or comparisons are very well established and widely used. Others have almost become clichés and are to be used with care:

as agile as a cat	as grim as death
as ambitious as the devil	as happy as a lark
as bald as a coot	as hard as nails
as big as a whale	as heavy as lead
as black as soot/a boot	as helpless as a baby
as blind as a bat	as hideous as the witch of Endor
as bold as brass	as hollow as a drum
as brown as a berry	as hungry/ravenous as a wolf
as cheap as dirt	as innocent as a lamb/baby
as cheerful as the day is long	as keen as mustard
as cool as a cucumber	as mad as a March hair
as crafty/cunning as a fox	as mean as a miser
as dead as a doornail	as naked as the day (one) was born
as deaf as a post	as obstinate as a mule
as deep as the sea	as pale as death/Banquo's ghost
as dry as dust	as plain as a pikestaff
as dull as ditch water	as playful as a kitten
as false as Judas	as pleased as Punch
as fast as light	as poor as a church mouse
as fidgety as an old maid	as pretty as a picture
as fit as a fiddle	as proud as a peacock
as flat as a pancake	as quiet as a mouse
as frisky as a colt/lamb	as restless/ruthless as the sea
as game as a fighting cock	as sharp as a razor
as good as gold	as sick as a dog

as simple/easy as ABC
as slow as a snail
as sly as a fox
as sober as a judge on circuit
as stealthy as a cat
as stiff as a ramrod
as stubborn as a mule
as sure as fate/death
as swift as an arrow/lightning
as thick as thieves

as tough as nails
as ugly as sin
as uncertain as the weather
as vast as the ocean
as warm as toast
as weak as water
as wet as a drowned rat
as wise as Solomon
as young as the morning

Spoonerism

A **spoonerism** is an accidental transposition of initial sounds in two or more words, as in *sons of toil* for *tons of soil*. It is named after the Rev. W.A. Spooner (1844–1930) of Oxford University, who was said to be given to this form of linguistic confusion. To a student, he is reputed to have said: 'You have *hissed* all my *mystery* lectures,' instead of 'You have *missed* all my *history* lectures.' Other often-quoted spoonerisms:

Let us drink to the *queer* old *Dean*. (proposing the loyal toast)
Kinkering kongs their titles take. (announcing hymn in chapel)

A popular, latter-day dilution of the spoonerism is the transposition of two words:

Take that silly *face* off your *expression*!
Did you get a nice *flight* on the *meal* out?
Excuse my *pig* – he's a *friend*!

Syllepsis

Syllepsis is a stylistic device in which a number of words depend on, or relate to, one word, but this word does not agree with all of them in number or in gender:

I don't think Mrs Brown or the children *know*.
James and Alice *each have their* duties.

Sometimes syllepsis is used as a synonym for **zeugma** (see p. 161).

Synecdoche

Synecdoche is the figure of speech that puts the part for the whole (as 'fifty *sail*' for 'fifty *ships*', or 'ninth *bat*' for 'ninth *batsman*'); or the whole for the part (as in '*Parliament* voted to . . .' for '*A majority of the members of Parliament* . . .'). Other examples:

Britannia rules *the waves* (= the sea)
an estate belonging to *the Crown*
Such matters need the authorisation of *the Foreign Office*.
He made his career on *the boards*.
Hampshire won the toss and opened the batting.
Two heads are better than one.

It is common for the term 'England' to be used as a synecdoche for the 'United Kingdom', giving offence to Scots, Welsh and Northern Irish; and for Canadians and Mexicans to be called 'Americans'.

Zeugma

Zeugma is a stylistic device in which a word, usually a verb, is followed by two words which in conventional language would not be found together. The result is an unexpected coming together of constituents, often deployed for humorous effect. It is a form of **ellipsis** (see p. 76)

Mr Pickwick *took* his hat and his leave.
See Pan with flocks, with fruits Pomona crowned.
She *arrived* in a bikini and a flood of tears.
He *plays* with verve and with Sheffield Wednesday.
John *left* Mary in the library and in a hurry.
Her mother and the fish stew *upset* Alice.
She *filed* the papers and her nails.
They *opened* their door and their hearts to the orphan boy.

six
Common errors and confusibles

The English Language
Some words have different meanings
   and yet they're spelled the same.
A cricket is an insect,
   to play it – it's a game.
On every hand, in every land,
   it's thoroughly agreed,
The English language to explain,
   is very hard indeed.

Some people say that you're a dear,
   yet dear is far from cheap.
A jumper is a thing you wear,
   yet a jumper has to leap.
It's very clear, it's very queer,
   and, pray, who is to blame
For different meanings to some words
   pronounced and spelled the same?

A little journey is a trip,
   a trip is when you fall.
It doesn't mean you have to dance
   whene'er you hold a ball.
Now here's a thing that puzzles me:
   musicians of good taste
Will very often form a band –
   I've one around my waist!

You spin a top, go for a spin,
   or spin a yarn maybe –
Yet every spin's a different spin,
   as you can plainly see.
Now here's a most peculiar thing,
   'twas told me as a joke –

A dumb man wouldn't speak a word,
  yet seized a wheel and spoke!

A door may often be ajar,
  but give the door a slam
And then your nerves receive a jar –
  and then there's jars of jam.
You've heard, of course, of traffic jams,
  and jams you give your thumbs.
And adders, too, one is a snake,
  the other adds up sums.

A policeman is a copper,
  it's a nickname (impolite!)
Yet a copper in the kitchen
  is an article you light.
On every hand, in every land,
  it's thoroughly agreed,
The English language to explain
  is very hard indeed!
    Harry Hemsley, in *Verse That Is Fun*,
        ed. Ireson (Faber, 1962)

Hints on Pronunciation for Foreigners
I take it you already know
Of tough and bough and cough and
  dough?
Others may stumble, but not you
On hiccough, thorough, laugh and
  through,
Well done, and now you wish perhaps
To learn of less familiar traps?

Beware of heard, a dreadful word
That looks like beard and sounds like
  bird.
And dead: it's said like bed, not bead –
And only Scotsmen call it deed!
Watch out for meat and great and
  threat.
They rhyme with suite and straight and
  debt.

A moth is not a moth in mother,
Nor both in bother, broth in brother,

And here is not a match for there
Nor dear and fear for bear and pear,
And then there's dose and rose and
   lose –
Just look them up – and goose and
   choose.
And cork and work and card and ward,
And font and front and word and sword,
And do and go, and thwart and cart –
Come, come, I've hardly made a start!
A dreadful language? Man alive –
I'd mastered it when I was five.

Herbert Farjeon

Common errors and confusibles

There are two A–Z listings in this section of the book – neither of which is exhaustive. The first list is a selection of words which writers commonly confuse, for one reason or another. Sometimes the words are **homonyms** (i.e. they sound the same, as *alter* and *altar*, *meter* and *metre*, *serial* and *cereal*). Generally, the entry shows the two (or more) words in the contexts in which they frequently appear, by means of example sentences or phrases. The confusible word is usually then explained by a synonym.

The second list is of commonly misspelled words. If there is a word that is almost invariably misspelled, that is highlighted in bold type to bring the problem to the reader's attention. The words are arranged in groups of ten, in the hope that bad spellers will work their way through this section, group by group, practising their spelling.

The best way to practise spelling is to follow the **look/cover/write/ check** procedure. That is to say: **look** at the shape of the word and how it is formed; **cover** it over; **write** it down on a sheet of paper; and finally **check** your written version with the version in the book.

Speaking more generally, the best way actively to develop your spelling and to guard against misspellings and confusibles is to make a regular and routine habit of checking words (spellings, etymologies, usage) in a good dictionary. This habit is no longer very widespread, and does not seem to be very actively encouraged and developed by schools.

A list of confusibles

abdicate, abrogate, arrogate

King Edward VIII *abdicated* the British throne in 1936. (= relinquished)

He *abrogated* his traditional responsibilities. (= formally annulled)

The prime minister has *arrogated* to herself numerous responsibilities which were traditionally the responsibility of the Cabinet. (= assumed)

abuse, misuse

Patients were sometimes physically *abused*. (= improperly used, mistreated)

The crowd shrieked *abuse* at the prime minister. (= insults)

Misuse of one's time, *misuse* of a word (= incorrect use)

accede, exceed

To *accede* to this request would set a dangerous precedent. (= agree, submit)

It is dangerous to *exceed* the speed limit. (= go over)

accept, except

She *accepted* a gift of food and clothes. (= took)

Everyone was sick *except* me. (= apart from)

acerbic: see **acid**

acetic, ascetic

Acetic acid is the main substance in vinegar. (Latin *acetum*, 'vinegar')

His face was pale, thin, *ascetic*. (= austere)

acid, acrid, acerbic

He spilled a solution of weak *acid*. (= chemical substance)

The room was filled with an *acrid* smoky smell. (= pungent)

There was an *acerbic* sharpness in her voice. (= bitter)

acknowledgement, acknowledgment

Either spelling is acceptable.

acrid: see **acid**

activate, actuate

He quickly *activated* the spacecraft's retro-rockets. (= set in motion)

Most of his work is *actuated* by selfish motives. (= motivated)

adherence, adhesion

This country's *adherence* to a treaty, *adherence* to communism/democracy (= attachment/obedience to)

This glue gives a very strong *adhesion*. (= sticking power)

adjacent, adjoining

A bedroom with bathroom *adjacent* (= nearby, but not with direct access)

A bedroom with bathroom *adjoining* (= with direct access)

adverse, averse

He received an *adverse* report on the proposed takeover. (= unfavourable)

I am not *averse* to the occasional whisky. (= disinclined)

advice, advise

He needs some paternal *advice*. (noun)

I *advise* you to see a doctor. (verb)

aesthetic, ascetic

Aesthetic means appreciative of, or relating to beauty. *Ascetic* means austere or monastic, practising self-denial.

affect, effect

What is the *effect* of putting acid on wood? (= result)

He *effected* his getaway under cover of darkness. (= made)

His death has badly *affected* us all. (= distressed)

afflict, inflict

He is *afflicted* with Parkinson's disease. (= suffers from)

Rangers *inflicted* a 6:nil defeat on the visiting team. (= imposed)

He has an *affected*, lisping accent. (= unspontaneous, artificial)

ageing, aging

Either spelling is acceptable.

aggravate, exacerbate, exasperate

Aggravate means to annoy or irritate, and *exasperate* also means to annoy, while *exacerbate* means to make matters worse. The original meaning of *aggravate* too was to make something worse: scratching would *aggravate* a chilblain; *exacerbate* is used more of a moral dilemma than of a physical problem.

all ready, already

We were *all ready* for the visitors long before they arrived. (= prepared)

I've *already* had some tea. (= previously)

all right, alright

All right is still felt to be more correct, though *alright* is now widely accepted in a sentence such as 'Are you feeling *alright*?' On the other hand, a sentence such as 'Are your test answers *all right*?' (meaning all correct) would not run these two words together.

allusive, elusive

He made an *allusive* speech, with numerous echoes from the writings of his favourite Classical authors. (= full of references)

The owl is an *elusive* nocturnal bird. (= difficult to find or see)

altar, alter

The minister stood before the church *altar*. (= communion table)

The ship *altered* course to avoid the iceberg. (= changed)

alternately, alternatively

Alternately means one after another; *alternatively* means one instead of another.

altogether, all together
He didn't *altogether* trust his boss. (= entirely)
The prisoners assembled *all together* in the yard.
ambiguous, ambivalent
The words 'light house keeper' are *ambiguous*. (= have more than one meaning)
Most people are *ambivalent* about the value of antiquated institutions such as the Royal Family. (= in two minds)
amend, emend
Amend means to improve; *emend* means to correct.
amiable, amicable
He had an *amiable*, chatty manner. (= friendly)
They made an *amicable* decision to separate. (= in a spirit of friendliness and goodwill)
among, amongst
Among is preferable; *amongst* is old-fashioned. Similarly, *amid* is better than *amidst*, *while* than *whilst*.
among, between
The cash was divided *among* the members of the gang. (many people)
The votes were divided evenly *between* Mr Black and Mr White. (two people)
amoral: see **immoral**
annex, annexe
There was a short war when Iraq tried to *annex* Kuwait. (verb)
John works in the science *annexe*. (noun)
antagonist, protagonist
Hitler was a formidable *antagonist*. (= enemy)
He was the leading *protagonist* in the anti-abortion lobby. (= champion)
arbiter, arbitrator
Arbiter is the more general term, and includes *arbiters* of taste and fashion as well as people with the general power to mediate in or control a situation. An *arbitrator* is a more specific term for a person who is appointed to settle a dispute.
Arctic, Antarctic
The *Arctic* is the region around the North Pole, the *Antarctic* being the region around the South Pole.
arrogate: see **abdicate**
artist, artiste
An *artist* is a person who draws, paints, sculpts, etc. as a job or as a hobby; or who is very skilled at something. A music-hall or circus *artiste* is a popular professional entertainer.
ascetic: see **acetic** and **aesthetic**

assure, ensure, insure

She was not *assured* till she saw him safe and unhurt. (= persuaded that all was well)

The state's duty is to *ensure* the safety of its citizens. (= guarantee)

Is the house *insured* against fire? (= covered against loss)

astonished, astounded, dumbfounded

These words express various and increasing degrees of surprise, with *astounded* implying a temporary inability to react, and *dumbfounded* implying not only inability to act but also inability to speak – because struck dumb.

astronomy, astrology

Astronomy is the scientific study of the stars and planets in the galaxy. *Astrology* is the non-scientific study of the same subject, in the belief that it can foretell things about your future.

atheist, agnostic

An *atheist* denies the existence of God or of divine things. An *agnostic* takes the view that God's existence cannot be proved or disproved, and is therefore sceptical on the subject.

averse: see **adverse**

aural, oral

Aural concerns the ear, while *oral* concerns the mouth. An *oral* exam is therefore a spoken exam (for example in French), while an *aural* exam tests listening (for example in music).

authoritative, authoritarian

To make an *authoritative* comment implies that the speaker is a genuine authority on the subject. An *authoritarian* person, on the other hand, is dictatorial – the father in a Victorian family was said to be *authoritarian*, for example.

backward, backwards

The adjective is *backward*, as in 'a rather *backward* pupil'. The adverb can be spelled either way: 'The train started going *backwards/backward*.'

bail, bale

They *bailed* out the leaking dinghy. (= empty of water)

The court set his *bail* at $20,000. (= security)

The barn was full of *bales* of hay. (= stacks)

baited, bated

The bears were cruelly *baited*. (= teased)

He stood with *bated* breath. (= held, from 'abated')

bale: see **bail**

bath, bathe

She gave the baby its evening *bath*. (= noun, wash)

The sea was too stormy for a *bathe*. (= noun, swim)

He was advised to *bathe* the wound daily. (= verb, cleanse)

bereaved, bereft

She has recently been *bereaved*. (= lost a member of her family through death)

The trees are now *bereft* of leaves. (= devoid)

beside, besides

Oh, I do like to be *beside* the seaside. (= near)

Besides us, only John is here. (= in addition to)

between: see **among**

biannual, biennial

Biannual means twice yearly. *Biennial* has two meanings: (1) every two years; (2) used of plants, means lasting for two years, flowering in the second year.

biased, biassed

Either spelling is acceptable.

born, borne

She was *born* in Edinburgh in 1943. (= had her birth)

She has *borne* five children. (= carried, given birth to)

She has *borne* her troubles with fortitude. (= put up with)

break, brake

Don't *break* the speed limit. (= exceed)

There was a squeal of *brakes* and a smell of burning rubber. (= device for slowing down a vehicle)

brothers, brethren

These are the two plurals of *brother*, and *brothers* is the one generally used. *Brethren* is archaic and biblical, and now limited to religious uses.

burned, burnt

The adjective is usually *burnt*, as in '*burnt* toast', '*burnt* ochre'. For the verb, *burned* is usually preferable, as in 'He *burned* his finger.'

burst, bust

The balloon *burst* with a loud pop. (= punctured)

The company went *bust* in the 1990s recession. (= collapsed)

She is a statuesque woman with a very large *bust*. (= chest)

callous, callused

A *callous*, heartless act (= cruel)

Hard, *callused* hands (= with thick, horny skin)

cannon, canon

The warship bristled with heavy *cannon*. (= big guns)

He is a *canon* of Westminster Cathedral. (= priest)

The *canon* of 20th-century classic fiction. (= authoritative list, corpus)

canvas, canvass

They were sleeping in the garden under *canvas*. (= in a tent)

A fine, oil on *canvas* painting (= on cloth)

The candidates have been *canvassing* support far and wide. (= soliciting)

capital punishment, corporal punishment

The former means 'removal of the head' (*caput*, in Latin), or execution. The latter is a physical punishment of the body (*corpus, -oris*, in Latin), such as beating, flogging, etc.

carat, carrot

A 200-*carat* diamond, 24-*carat* gold (= measurement of weight or purity)

A dish of boiled beef and *carrots* (= orange-coloured root vegetables)

censor, censure, censer

The mail of all prisoners is *censored*. (= officially inspected)

The Opposition has strongly *censured* the Government's handling of the issue. (= criticised)

Incense is burned in a *censer*. (= specially made container)

cereal, serial

Wheat, oats, and barley are *cereal* crops. (= grain producing)

He was watching an Australian TV *serial*. (= episode in a series)

ceremonial, ceremonious

Millions of viewers watched the Trooping the Colour *ceremonial*. (= traditional ritual)

He addressed us in a *ceremonious* and flamboyant manner. (= slightly theatrical)

childish, childlike

She decided to punish his *childish* tantrums. (= immature)

He never lost a somewhat *childlike* faith in human goodness. (= innocent)

chord: see **cord**

classic, classical, Classics

Traditionally, if you studied Latin and Greek you were called a student of *Classics*, and had received a *classical* education. Down the years, other writers (such as Milton and Scott and Dickens) have come to be described as *classic* writers of British literature. More recently and more narrowly, Agatha Christie or P.D. James could be said to have written *classics* of detective fiction, i.e. masterpieces of their genre. *Classical* architecture was inspired by the Ancients. *Classical* music is from the canon of great European music – Haydn, Mozart, Bach, Beethoven, etc.

clench, clinch

She muttered angrily through *clenched* teeth. (= tightly fixed)

A trade deal has at last been *clinched*. (= finalised, agreed)

climactic, climatic

The *climactic* finale was an operatic tour de force. (adjective of climax)

Favourable *climatic* conditions (= pertaining to the weather)

cloths, clothes

Factories make *cloth*, which tailors and dressmakers then make into *clothes*. We have dish*cloths*, floor*cloths*, table*cloths*, altar *cloths*, etc., but we go out each morning in our working *clothes*, cut the hedge in our gardening *clothes*, and sleep under bed*clothes*.

coarse: see **course**

commitment, committal

He has a strong *commitment* to the cause. (= loyalty)

The *committal* ceremony was private. (= burial, committing of the body to the ground)

complement, compliment

She prepared an excellent salmon dish *complemented* by a fine hock wine. (= enhanced)

May I *compliment* you on an excellent speech. (= congratulate)

contemptible, contemptuous

His lack of courage was *contemptible*. (= despicable)

He addressed us in haughty tones of *contemptuous* disdain. (= scornful)

continually, continuously

The former suggests a succession of occurrences, with the possibility of short breaks in the sequence. *Continuously* describes something that never stops; it does not admit of breaks in the sequence.

comic, comical

A *comic* actor's job is to make you laugh. (= deliberately funny)

His attempt to appear sober was *comical*. (= unintentionally or unexpectedly funny)

cord, chord

The term for a length of rope etc. is *cord*, as in 'dressing-gown *cord*', 'umbilical *cord*', 'spinal *cord*'. The musical or emotional term is *chord*, as in the '*chord* of C sharp', the 'lost *chord*', or 'His speech struck the right *chord*.'

corporal punishment: see **capital punishment**

correspondent, co-respondent

He is the Far East *correspondent* for the *Independent* (= journalist, writer)

He was cited as *co-respondent* in the Duchess of Argyll's divorce proceedings. (= adulterous lover)

council, counsel

There is a monthly meeting of the town *council*. (= elected body)

Never take *counsel* from such an unreliable person. (= advice)

They were well *counselled* by the Citizens' Advice Bureau. (= advised)

course, coarse

'An eighteen-hole *course*', 'a three-*course* meal', 'a difficult *course* of study'; here *course* means a 'sequence or progression'.

'*Coarse* cloth', '*coarse* language', and '*coarse* fishing' means 'rough or basic'.

credible, creditable, credulous

His story is not quite *credible*. (= believable)

His exam result was very *creditable*. (= worthy of credit)

It was a trick to convince only the most *credulous*. (= gullible)

crevice, crevasse

The rock face was full of little *crevices* for footholds. (= cracks, gaps)

The glacier is broken up by several deep *crevasses*. (= large fissures)

criterion, criteria

Criterion is singular, *criteria* is plural. So it is wrong to say, 'He has only one *criteria*.'

currant, current

The *currant* is a small dried grape, and the black*currant* and red*currant* are berries. *Current* means (1) a steady flow, as in 'Swimming against the *current*' or an 'electric *current*'; (2) the present time, as in '*current* affairs/events'.

deadly, deathly

His French classes are *deadly* dull. (= extremely)

Cyanide is a *deadly* poison. (= lethal)

Her face was *deathly* white. (= as white as in death)

decidedly, decisively

A person of *decidedly* anarchist opinions. (= emphatically)

The election results *decisively* settled the matter. (= conclusively)

deduce, deduct

What can we *deduce* from this evidence, Watson? (= conclude, infer)

Tax is *deducted* from your salary. (= taken away)

defective, deficient

The car's brake was found to be *defective*. (= faulty)

Old people are often *deficient* in vitamins. (= lacking, short of)

definite, definitive

I'll give you a *definite* answer tomorrow. (= certain, clear)

Richard Ellmann's is the *definitive* biography of James Joyce. (= ultimate, best)

defuse, diffuse

The bomb was *defused* by an army expert. (= neutralised)

A *diffused* glow of orange light hung over the darkened landscape. (= spread out)

delivery, deliverance

Delivery for a letter, a baby, a speech, etc. *Deliverance* from evil, danger, a fate worse than death, etc.

delusion: see **illusion**

dependent, dependant

In British English, in the days when spelling was drilled, these spellings used to cause endless heart-searching and dictionary-hunting. *Dependent* is the adjective and *dependant* the noun. Nowadays, there is a tendency to copy our American cousins, drop the heart-searching –

and use only the word *dependent*.

deprecate, depreciate

The whole village *deprecated* such a wanton act of hooliganism. (= deplored)

His investment is certain to *depreciate*. (= decline in value)

His comment was sensible. There is no need to *depreciate* it. (= disparage)

deprivation, depredation

It was an inner-city area suffering from multiple *deprivation*. (= poverty)

The *depredations* of the locusts have wiped out the crop. (= attacks)

derisive, derisory

'*Derisive* laughter' mocks something or someone. 'A *derisory* proposal' is one which deserves derision.

desert, dessert

They were lost in the Sahara *desert*. (= dry region)

He promised never to *desert* her. (= leave)

He took strawberries and cream for *dessert*. (= pudding)

despatch, dispatch

Either spelling is acceptable.

detract, distract

Poor weather *detracted* from the success of the holiday. (= diminished)

Don't *distract* the driver. (= take the attention of)

device, devise

His office is full of labour-saving *devices* and contraptions. (= gadgets)

We have *devised* a new method of sending urgent messages. (= invented)

diffuse: see **defuse**

disc, disk

He is suffering from a slipped *disc*. (= the cartilage between spinal vertebrae)

Musical tapes and compact *discs* (= records)

Computer *disk*, floppy *disk* (= information store)

discreet, discrete

She watched the proceedings from a *discreet* distance. (= safe, cautious)

The company operates world-wide as a number of small, *discrete* units. (= autonomous, not overlapping)

disinterested, uninterested

I try to be a *disinterested* observer. (= objective)

She was totally *uninterested* in current events. (= without interest)

disoriented, disorientated

More or less interchangeable, with British English favouring the longer version and American favouring the shorter.

dominate, domineer

A church spire may *dominate* a townscape, a loquacious person may *dominate* a conversation, and a brand leader will *dominate* a certain market. A *domineering* person is overbearing, and tries to control others at any price.

doubtful, dubious

The building's safety is *doubtful/dubious*. (= uncertain)

His business contacts are very *dubious*. (= shady, potentially dishonest)

draft, draught

A money *draft* (= order)

A *draft* outline/proposal (= preliminary)

A howling *draught* (= current of air)

Draught beer (= from the barrel)

A *draughts*man (= one who makes drawings)

dual, duel

Dual carriageway, *dual* purpose (= double)

A *duel* with swords, a verbal *duel* (= contest between two people)

dubious: see **doubtful**

dumbfounded: see **astonished**

dying, dyeing

Dying of hunger/old age, *dying* to see you, etc.

Indigo is used for *dyeing* cloth blue. (= colouring)

earthly, earthy

This *earthly* life (= worldly)

An *earthy* smell (= of the earth, unrefined)

eatable, edible

Eatable means merely fit to be eaten; while *edible* means suitable for eating, or able to be eaten.

These carrots are so dried up that they are hardly *eatable* – better buy some fresh ones. (= they won't contain much nourishment)

These mushrooms don't look *edible* to me. (= they might be poisonous)

effect: see **affect**

e.g., i.e.

Two common abbreviations which indicate that more information follows.

E.g. (Latin *exempli gratia*, 'for sake of an example') means 'for example'.

I.e. (Latin *id est*, 'that is') means that an explanation follows.

Reasonable expenses, *e.g.* train fares, meals away from home, will be reimbursed.

Crustaceans, *i.e.* sea creatures with legs and a hard shell, are the staple diet.

elder: see **older**

elusive: see **allusive**

emend: see **amend**

emigrant: see **immigrant**

eminent, imminent
An *eminent* physicist (= distinguished, famous)
An *imminent* attack (= about to happen)
emotional, emotive
She was in a state of physical and *emotional* exhaustion. (= psycho-
logical, mental)
Abortion is an *emotive* issue in Catholic countries. (= people are not
objective about it)
enquiry, inquiry
He made a polite *enquiry* about my health. (= he asked after . . .)
The police have set up an *inquiry*. (= formal investigation)
ensure: see **assure**
equable, equitable
Britain has an *equable* climate. (= not extreme, without great variation)
We are looking for an *equitable* court decision. (= just, well balanced)
exasperate, exacerbate: see **aggravate**
exceed: see **accede**
except: see **accept**
exceptional, exceptionable
She is an *exceptional* teacher. (= of rare quality)
His *exceptionable* behaviour has ostracised him from society. (= objec-
tionable)
exercise, exorcise
He's a fitness fanatic and takes lots of *exercise*. (= gymnastic movement)
The ghost of the former owner of the house was *exorcised* by means of a
special ceremony. (= expelled, eradicated)
exhausting, exhaustive
The climb to the summit was *exhausting*. (= very tiring)
The police conducted an *exhaustive* inquiry. (= comprehensive)
faint, feint
She fell down in a dead *faint*. (= collapse)
There was a *faint* smell of ether in the air. (= slight)
It was a contest of *feint* and counter-*feint*. (= dummy move)
farther: see **further**
fatal, fateful
Another *fatal* accident on the A74 (= deadly)
A *fateful* decision (= momentous)
fearful, fearsome
She is very *fearful* of the dark. (= frightened)
A *fearful* mess, a *fearful* argument (= very bad)
An angry bear is a *fearsome* beast. (= causes fear)
ferment: see **foment**

fiancé, fiancée

These words follow French spelling conventions, with *fiancé* the masculine and *fiancée* the feminine version.

fictional, fictitious

Sherlock Holmes and Dr Watson are a famous *fictional* pair. (= existing only in fiction)

He bought the weapon under a *fictitious* name. (= false, invented)

flare, flair

She has a really bad temper which *flares* up from time to time. (= erupts)

He has a *flair* for cooking. (= aptitude)

flaunt: see **flout**

fleshy, fleshly

A *fleshy* person, *fleshy* legs (= fat, plump)

Fleshly desires and pleasures (= carnal, of the flesh)

flounder, founder

The Government *flounders* from crisis to crisis. (= struggles)

The ship *foundered* on the rocky shore. (= broke up)

George Heriot, the *founder* of a famous school. (= person who founded)

flout, flaunt

Where the law is an ass, we must *flout* it. (= disregard)

She likes to *flaunt* her huge wedding ring. (= show off)

foment, ferment

She goes about *fomenting* distrust. (= stirring up)

The country is in a political *ferment*. (= upheaval)

forage, foray

He *foraged* in the kitchen for some food. (= rummaged about)

He went on a *foray* round the junk shops. (= excursion)

forceful, forcible

He was a *forceful,* competent leader. (= powerful)

There has been a *forcible* imposition of military control. (= by force)

forebear, forbear

His *forebears* are all from the west of Ireland. (= ancestors)

She will *forbear* to ask for financial support.(= forswear, abstain)

forever, for ever

She is *forever* interrupting the conversation. (= endlessly)

She has left him *for ever*. (= permanently)

foregone, forgone

The outcome of the election was said to be a *foregone* conclusion. (= obvious, inevitable)

She has *forgone* her holiday as a result of the fire. (= gone without)

formally, formerly

He was *formally* introduced to the Princess of Wales. (= officially)

He dressed *formally* for the occasion. (= smartly)

St Petersburg was *formerly* called Leningrad. (= previously)
fortuitous, fortunate
We met *fortuitously* in George Street. (= by chance)
He made a *fortunate* escape from his captors. (= lucky)
fulfil, fulfill
Fulfil is British spelling, *fulfill* is American. The past tense of both
versions is *fulfilled*.
further, farther
Further seems to be the norm nowadays, with *farther* confined to
sentences specifying physical distance, like 'Glasgow is *farther* from
London than it is from Dublin.' Thus: 'Until *further* notice' or '*Further*
to your recent letter . . .' or 'Any *further* questions?' or '*further*
education'.
gamble, gambol
He *gambled* all his savings on that horse. (= bet)
The lambs *gambolled* about in the spring sunshine. (= skipped and
jumped)
gaol: see **jail**
gipsy, gypsy
Both spellings are accepted.
gorilla, guerrilla
The *gorilla* is the largest of the apes.
The army was attacked by well-armed *guerrillas*. (= insurgents)
gourmand, gourmet
He was a famous *gourmand* and bon viveur. (= person who enjoys food
and drink)
He was a *gourmet* of good cheeses. (= person who knows a lot about food
and drink)
graceful, gracious
Graceful describes elegant physical movement, forms, shapes: as in 'a
graceful colonnade', 'a *graceful* pas de bas'. *Gracious* means kind,
courteous, well mannered: as in '*gracious* living', 'ladylike and
gracious', 'a *gracious* tribute'.
grey, gray
British spelling favours *grey*, while Americans prefer *gray*.
grisly, gristly, grizzly
A *grisly* murder (= nasty, gruesome)
A *gristly* lamb chop (= tough, full of gristle)
A *grizzly* infant (= crying, whingeing). Also a *grizzly* bear
gypsy: see **gipsy**
hale, hail
Hale and hearty (= healthy)
Sleet and *hail* (= frozen rain)

Hail a hackney (= call a taxi)

histrionics: see **hysterics**

handiwork, handwork

She stood back and admired her *handiwork*. (= skill, efforts)

Lace-making used to be a very labour-intensive form of *handwork*. (= work with the hands)

hanged, hung

The regular past tense of the verb *hang* is *hung*, as in 'He's *hung* up his coat and hat.' *Hanged* is used only in the context of an execution: 'You will be *hanged* by the neck until you are dead.'

hanger, hangar

Clothes are hung on a *hanger*. Planes are kept in a *hangar*.

hereditary, heredity

A *hereditary* illness, a *hereditary* title (= inherited; an adjective)

Your *heredity* is your genetic inheritance (= genetics; a noun)

holy, holey, wholly

Holy books, *holy* scripture, *holy* Jesus (= sacred)

Holey socks, *holey* cheese (= full of holes)

Wholly innocent, *wholly* convincing (= entirely)

hoofs, hooves

Either plural spelling is acceptable.

horde, hoard

She was surrounded by *hordes* of shrieking children. (= multitudes)

A *hoard* of Viking treasure has been uncovered. (= secret collection)

hull, hulk

A ship's *hull* is its body; a ship's *hulk* is its dismantled or sunken frame.

human, humane

Human beings, the *human* race, the *human* body (= concerning people)

We wish to see a more *humane* and civilised society. (= decent, considerate)

hung: see **hanged**

hysterics, histrionics

She went into a fit of sobbing *hysterics*. (= an uncontrolled fit, in this case, of crying)

He's full of *histrionic* gestures. (= over-dramatic)

idle, idol

He sits there, bone *idle*, watching others work. (= lazy, useless)

The shrine was full of statues of strange *idols*. (= gods)

illegal, illicit

He was jailed for *illegal* possession of marijuana. (= forbidden by law)

His *illicit* association with a certain actress was well known. (= not approved by society)

illegible: see **unreadable**

illusion, delusion

She had no *illusions* about his intentions. (= false ideas)

He suffers from *delusions* that the world is about to end. (= erroneous ideas)

immigrant, emigrant

An *immigrant* has come into a country, while an *emigrant* has gone out of it.

immoral, amoral

An *immoral* person has bad or low moral standards, while an *amoral* person has no moral standards.

imply, infer

Her comment *implied* that he was stupid rather than lazy. (= hinted)

It is fair to *infer* that the car will not go if the engine is not switched on. (= deduce)

impractical, impracticable

He may be a brilliant academic, but he's completely *impractical* about the house. (= useless, not handy)

The idea was quite *impracticable*. (= impossible to achieve)

incredible, incredulous

In its day, running the four-minute mile was an *incredible* achievement. (= not believable)

He stood there with an *incredulous* expression on his face. (= disbelieving)

inflict: see **afflict**

infringe, impinge, impugn

I have no wish to *infringe* the rules of the game. (= break)

His work *impinges* heavily on his family life. (= overlaps into)

He is *impugning* my professional reputation. (= challenging)

ingenious, ingenuous

The film's plot was extremely *ingenious*, and the final scene came as a surprise to everyone. (= clever)

He made a frank and *ingenuous* apology for the error. (= obviously honest)

inimitable, inimical

He spoke in his own *inimitable* manner. (= not to be imitated)

The desert is *inimical* to most forms of life. (= unfavourable, hostile)

inquiry: see **enquiry**

insure: see **assure**

intense, intensive

Intense heat, *intense* effort, *intense* pain, *intense* excitement (= acute)

Intensive care, *intensive* agriculture, *intensive* study, *intensive* training (= thorough, rigorous)

inveigle, inveigh

She was *inveigled* into donating £20 to the charity. (= cajoled, persuaded)

People like to *inveigh* against the taxman. (= attack, rail against)
its, it's
The dog licked *its* paws. (= belonging to it)
It's a long way to Tipperary! (= It is)
jail, gaol
The first spelling is commoner, though either is acceptable in British
 English. Americans do not use the second spelling.
judgment, judgement
Either spelling is acceptable.
judicial, judicious
There is usually a *judicial* enquiry into financial scandals. (= legal)
The *judicious* use of EC investment has stimulated the local economy.
 (= careful)
knit, knitted
When *knitting* needles and wool are involved, the past tense is *knitted*, e.g.
 'She *knitted* me a pair of socks.' In other contexts, *knit* is commoner,
 e.g. 'He *knit* his brows.' Past participles are similar, e.g. 'a *knitted* hat'
 but 'a close-*knit* community'.
leeward, windward
These words are opposites, *leeward* meaning in the lee of the wind, or
 sheltered from it; *windward* meaning exposed to the wind.
licence, license
Do you have an international driving *licence*? (noun)
A ship's captain is *licensed* to perform marriages and burials. (verb)
lie, lay
Three confusible verbs are *lie/lying/lay/lain* (intransitive), meaning to
 rest or stretch out in a horizontal position; *lie/lying/lied* (intransitive),
 meaning to tell untruths; and *lay/laying/laid* (transitive), meaning to
 put down, or prepare, or produce.
Come *lie* with me and be my love. (= sleep)
The body *lay* in state. (= was reposing)
The dog was *lying* stretched out on the hearth. (= resting)
Don't *lie* to me – I want the truth. (= tell untruths)
Please *lay* the table. (= set)
I wouldn't so much as *lay* a finger on you. (= put)
The shipyard is *laying off* a hundred riveters. (= sacking)
The goose that *laid* the golden eggs. (= produced)
lighted, lit
Both past tense/participle forms are used, but *lit* is commoner as a verb,
 lighted as a participle in use as an adjective, e.g. 'We *lit* the bonfire'; 'a
 lighted match'.
liquidate, liquidise
He has *liquidated* his assets. (= made them liquid, or saleable)

Al Capone *liquidated* his opponents. (= eliminated, killed)

Liquidise the mixture in a blender. (= make it into a liquid)

liquor, liqueur

Liquor is any alcoholic drink. A *liqueur* is a sweet alcoholic drink taken after a meal as a digestif. Popular *liqueurs* are Drambuie, Cointreau, Benedictine, and Kummel.

literal, literate, literary

I need a *literal* translation. (= word for word)

He was the first *literate* member of the family. (= able to read and write)

Paris in the 1920s was a base for many *literary* Americans. (= involved in literature)

livid, lurid

His expression was *livid* with rage. (= furious)

A *livid* bruise (= black and blue)

She wore a *lurid* pink and orange coat. (= garish)

He's full of *lurid* stories about his girlfriends. (= shocking)

loathe, loath, loth

He *loathes* the smell of cigarettes. (= hates)

He was *loath/loth* to sell his sports car. (= reluctant)

lose, loose

He tends to *lose* things rather easily. (= mislay)

She has gone to the dentist about a *loose* tooth. (= wobbly)

lurid: see **livid**

luxuriant, luxurious

He was sporting a *luxuriant* moustache. (= abundant, growing vigorously)

We dined in a *luxurious* restaurant. (= expensive, comfortable)

madam, madame

Madam is the English spelling of this French word. *Madame* is the French spelling. English stresses the first syllable, French the second.

magic, magical

A *magic* wand, a *magic* carpet (= with magic qualities)

A *magical* experience, a *magical* visit (= delightful, enchanting)

malevolent, malignant

He spoke in *malevolent* tones. (= wishing someone ill)

The cancer was *malignant*. (= fatal, not medically controllable)

A witch with a *malignant* power (= able to do evil)

masterly, masterful

A *masterly* analysis, a *masterly* performance (= brilliant, excellent)

There was a *masterful* tone to his voice. (= authoritative, determined)

maybe, may be

Maybe I will and *maybe* I won't. (= perhaps)

The bus *may be* late.

medieval, mediaeval
The first spelling is commoner. It is standard in American English.

medium, media
A *medium* (from Latin *medius*) was something 'in the middle'. It soon came to mean an 'intermediary' or 'means of communication' between the earthly world and the spirit world. Nowadays we talk about 'the *media*' (plural of *medium*) when referring to the various means of mass communication, including the press, radio, television, etc.

melted, molten
Melted is the general form, both as verb and adjective. *Molten* is used only as an adjective, and only of substances which melt at very high temperatures: thus '*molten* lava' or '*molten* iron', but '*melted* chocolate'.

metal, mettle
Brass is a good-looking *metal*. (= hard mineral substance)
The new recruit was on his *mettle*. (= on the alert)

meter, metre
A measuring instrument (e.g. for parking, water, gas, etc., as well as a speedometer, thermometer, etc.) is a *meter*. A unit of length is a *metre*, thus kilo*metre*, centi*metre*, etc. (unless you are American, in which case you spell it kilo*meter*, centi*meter*, etc.). The poetic measure is also spelled *metre*.

militate, mitigate
The drought is *militating* against effective self-help farming initiatives. (= hindering)
The Government is endeavouring to *mitigate* the people's distress. (= alleviate)

misuse: see **abuse**

molten: see **melted**

moral, morale
The *moral* is clear: don't marry for money. (= lesson)
The victory gave a great boost to *morale*. (= feelings of confidence)

motive, motif
I question the Government's *motives*. (= unarticulated intentions)
Her dress was blue with a white *motif*. (= pattern)

mucus, mucous
Mucus is the noun, *mucous* is the adjective.

naturist, naturalist
A *naturist* is a nudist, or a person who tries to go back to nature. A *naturalist* is a person who studies nature; zoologists, entomologists, ornithologists are all *naturalists*.

naval, navel
Hornblower was an eighteenth-century *naval* officer. (= in the Navy)

Some people are said to contemplate their *navels*. (= belly buttons)
nicety, niceness
Let's forget the *niceties* and get to the point. (= quibbles, finer details)
Her *niceness* smiled out of her face at you. (= pleasantness)
no one, no-one
The two-word version is preferable, but the hyphenated version is also
  common. The one-word version *noone* is to be avoided.
notable, noticeable
Robert the Bruce was a *notable* Scottish king. (= famous)
His right eye had a *noticeable* squint. (= conspicuous)
nutritional, nutritious
What is the *nutritional* value of peanut butter? (= dietary)
Honey is said to be highly *nutritious*. (= nourishing)
obsolete, obsolescent
The steam engine has long been *obsolete*. (= outmoded, out of use)
Nuclear weapons have reduced most other armaments to *obsolescence*.
  (= they are becoming obsolete)
of, off
The grand old Duke *of* York.
Keep *off* the grass.
official, officious
The prime minister's office will be putting out an *official* statement.
  (= formally authorised)
She's an *officious* old busybody. (= bossy, interfering)
older, elder
The adjective *old* has comparative and superlative *older/elder* and *oldest/*
  eldest, with *older* and *oldest* being the standard forms. *Elder* and *eldest*
  occur only within the family to describe seniority, e.g. 'an *elder*
  brother', and in certain specific usages, e.g. 'an *elder* statesman'.
onward, onwards
Onward is commoner nowadays. *Onwards* is almost confined to British
  English, and is used only as an adverb.
oral: see **aural**
ordinance, ordnance
There used to be various *ordinances* prohibiting Sunday trading.
  (= regulations)
Weapons and other *ordnance* were issued to soldiers. (= military
  supplies)
The *Ordnance* Survey is the British agency that is charged with the
  production of detailed maps of the country.
outdoor, outdoors
Outdoor is the adjective, *outdoors* is the adverb.

outward, outwards

Outward is the adjective, *outwards* is the adverb.

partly, partially, partiality

He is by background *partly* French, *partly* American. (= not completely)

A *partially* clothed body, a *partially* blind person (= semi-)

He spoke very *partially* in our favour. (= in a biassed way)

He has a well-known *partiality* for dry sherry. (= liking)

passed, past

We *passed* you in the street. Have you *passed* the exam?

It's five *past* two. She has a colourful *past*.

Many years *passed*. (= many years went by)

Many years *past* (= many years ago)

patent, patient

He's a quack, and talks a lot of *patent* nonsense. (= manifest, obvious)

Sorry to keep you – you've been very *patient*. (= forbearing, calm)

perceptive, percipient, perspicuous, perspicacious

A *perceptive* remark, a *perceptive* biography (= observant)

She was an unusually *percipient* person who could pick up all sorts of vibrations in a gathering, well outside the normal range of the senses. (= almost telepathic)

The judge gave a clear and *perspicuous* summing-up of the case. (= precise, comprehensible)

A *perspicacious* student of human foibles would notice this trait in her make-up. (= keenly observant)

perfunctory, peremptory

We exchanged a *perfunctory* greeting in the foyer. (= cursory, casual)

I was shown out in a most *peremptory* manner. (= imperious, brusque)

perpetuate, perpetrate

People who fail to learn from history *perpetuate* its mistakes. (= preserve and repeat)

Terrorist organisations sometimes *perpetrate* appalling crimes. (= commit)

persistence, perseverance, pertinacity

The *persistence* of her illness was a measure of its seriousness. (= continuation)

He showed great *persistence* in the dogged pursuit of his case. (= determination)

Only the *perseverance* of the crew saved the ship. (= effort against the odds)

The battle was waged with courage and *pertinacity*. (= doggedness)

perspective: see **prospective**

perspicuous, perspicacious: see **perceptive**

pertinacity: see **persistence**

phenomenon, phenomena

Phenomenon is singular, *phenomena* is plural.

pigeon, pidgin
The well-fed *pigeons* of Trafalgar Square (= birds)
The Lagos traders speak an interesting *pidgin*. (= mixture of colloquial languages)

plane, plain
He smoothed the surface of the wood with his *plane*. (= a tool)
The *plane* has landed. (= aircraft)
The rain in Spain falls mainly in the *plain*. (= flat ground)
She is a *plain* Jane. (= lacking in beauty)

plate, plait
A *plate* of food, a photographic *plate*, a metal *plate* (= dish or slide)
She wore her hair in two long *plaits*. (= pigtails)

poignant: see **pungent**

politic, political
His decision was not *politic* and offended many. (= wise)
I am not a very *political* animal. (= interested in politics)

pour, pore
The rain *pours* down, and tea is *poured*. (= flows)
He *pored* over the document. (= studied carefully)
The skin is full of tiny *pores*. (= holes)

practical, practicable
She's very *practical* and methodical. (= handy, businesslike)
Pollution has been eliminated as far as is *practicable*. (= feasible)

practice, practise
A medical *practice*; a quaint Japanese *practice* (noun)
Hamish *practises* his bagpipes every evening. (verb)

pray, prey
The congregation *prayed* for peace. (= asked God for)
The kestrel is a bird of *prey*. (= predator)

precede: see **proceed**

precipitate, precipitous
We tried to avoid any *precipitate* decisions. (= abrupt, hasty)
There was a precipitous drop of a thousand feet to the sea. (= sheer, like a precipice)

predict, predicate
I *predict* a win for Arsenal. (= prophesy, foresee)
The plan is *predicated* on these assumptions. (= based on)

prescribe, proscribe
The doctor has *prescribed* rest. (= ordered, recommended)
He has *proscribed* physical exertion. (= banned, forbidden)

presumptive, presumptuous
The *presumptive* diagnosis looks bad. (= probable)
It is *presumptuous* to intercede between spouses. (= forward)

principle, principal

Dishonesty is against his *principles*. (noun = code of conduct)

Tourism is one of our *principal* industries. (adjective = main)

The college *principal* is called Mr Nackyball. (noun = head)

proceed, precede

He *proceeded* to ask lots of questions. (= went on)

Let us go back to the *preceding* chapter. (= the one before, previous)

prodigy, protégé

Mozart was one of the best-known child *prodigies*. (= marvels)

Leicester was one of Queen Elizabeth's *protégés*. (= acolytes)

program, programme

The former is the US spelling, the latter is British English. The one exception, where the American spelling is always used in British English, is 'computer *program*' and its various 'computerspeak' spin-offs.

prophecy, prophesy

Noah knew the *prophecy* of the Flood. (noun)

People are forever *prophesying* the end of the world. (verb)

proscribe: see **prescribe**

prospective, perspective

He is a *prospective* Member of Parliament. (= would-be)

You can look at the problem from a number of *perspectives*. (= points of view, positions)

prostrate, prostate

He lay *prostrate* before her. (= stretched flat on the ground, helpless)

The *prostate* gland is an organ beside the male bladder.

protagonist: see **antagonist**

protégé: see **prodigy**

psychology, psychiatry

Psychology is the scientific study of the mind and of human behaviour.

Psychiatry is the branch of medicine which studies and treats mental disorders.

pungent, poignant

A *pungent* smell of bonfires filled the autumn air. (= sharp)

She gave a *poignant* description of her own deprived childhood. (= moving)

purposely, purposefully

She *purposely* tried to antagonise him. (= intentionally)

He walked *purposefully* towards the gate. (= resolutely)

rebound, re-bound

He hit the ball on the *rebound*. (= when it bounced back)

The family Bible was *re-bound*. (= given a new binding)

recipe, receipt
He had a marvellous *recipe* for fruit loaf. (= list of ingredients)
I got a *receipt* for each purchase. (= printed record)
recount, re-count
He *recounted* his story with humour. (= told)
The vote was so close that there had to be a *re-count*. (= further count)
recover, re-cover
She *recovered* very well from her illness. (= got better)
She stumbled but *recovered* herself. (= regained her balance)
She has *re-covered* the armchair beautifully. (= put on a new cover)
regal, royal
Burlington Bertie's bearing was so *regal* that neighbours called him His
    Majesty. (= splendid, king-like)
She may be a member of the *royal* family, but her conduct is less than
    regal.
reign, rein
Queen Victoria's glorious *reign* (= rule)
Give your horse free *rein*. (= straps for controlling a horse)
remittance, remission
Your *remittance* is now overdue. (= payment)
The *remission* of sins, of a jail sentence (= forgiveness, reduction)
repetitive, repetitious
His job is routine, *repetitive*, mechanical. (= characterised by repetition)
She has written a very *repetitious* account of her childhood. (= it
    contains unnecessary repetitions)
reversal, reversion
He suffered *reversal* after *reversal*. (= setback)
. . . a *reversion* to his former barbarous ways (= return)
review, revue
A *review* of progress, a *review* of the troops, a salary *review*, a book *review*
    (= critical study, assessment, inspection)
A Christmas *revue* (= show)
role, roll
What was the *role* of the prime minister in the affair? (= part)
Four buttered *rolls*, a *roll* of wallpaper, a *roll* of honour, a drum *roll*.
royal: see **regal**
saccharin, saccharine
I've no sugar but can offer you a *saccharin*. (= sugar substitute)
He flashed me a *saccharine* smile. (= artificially sweet, less than sincere)
sarcastic, sardonic
Sarcastic remarks tend to be positively cutting or sneering in intention,
    whereas a *sardonic* remark is more laid back and generally scornful.

sceptic, septic

Doubting Thomas was the original *sceptic*. (= person with lots of doubts)

Wounds are cleaned to prevent them turning *septic*. (= infected)

seasonal, seasonable

Seasonal greetings are greetings of the season. *Seasonable* weather is the sort of weather to be expected at a certain time of year.

sensitivity, sensibility

Calling *sensitivity* merely sense, Jane Austen wrote a whole novel to articulate the differences between these two words. By her book, *sensitivity* is the better characteristic, because it means 'having good judgment', awareness of others' feelings, and respect for them. *Sensibility*, on the other hand, is a slightly more public characteristic, implying an emotional delicacy which is impressionable and perhaps too easily – or too visibly – affected.

sentiment, sentimentality

He expressed little *sentiment* or emotion. (= feeling)

The whole affair was a display of mawkish and wallowing *sentimentality* whipped up by the popular press. (= emotionalism)

septic: see sceptic

serial: see cereal

sew, sow

She *sewed* a lace border round the wrists and hem. (= stitched)

The farmer *sowed* a crop of early grass. (= planted)

singing, singeing

They are *singing* their hearts out. (= making vocal music)

Drake is remembered for *singeing* the Spanish king's beard. (= scorching)

social, sociable

I've met him at *social* and business functions. (= communal)

She's an outgoing and *sociable* type. (= friendly)

sometime, some time

Come up and see me *sometime*. (= at some future period)

I may be gone for *some time*. (= a little while)

speciality, specialty

The first spelling is British English, the second is American.

stalactite, stalagmite

Icicle-shaped formations in limestone caves produced by a mixture of dripping water and lime. *Stalactites* hang down from the ceiling, and *stalagmites* grow up from the ground. (Remember: there is a *c* in *stalactite* and in 'ceiling', and there is a *g* in *stalagmite* and in 'ground'.)

stationary, stationery

Do not leave the bus until it is *stationary*. (= not moving)

He buys his office *stationery* from Smith's store. (= paper, envelopes, etc.)

story, storey
Tell me a scary *story*. (= fictional tale)
A multi-*storey* car park (= on several levels)
straight, strait
The car came *straight* at me. (= directly)
Your tie is not *straight*. (= hanging in a line)
The organisation is in desperate financial *straits*. (= circumstances)
The *straits* of Gibraltar (= narrow sea)
Note spellings of *strait*jacket and *strait*laced.
straightened, straitened
He *straightened* his tie. (= made it straight)
They live in very *straitened* circumstances. (= impoverished, restricted)
struck, stricken
The verb *strike* has two past participles. *Struck* is the general term, as in
   'The clock *struck* three' or 'The car was *struck* by lightning.' *Stricken* is
   confined to sickness and distress, as in 'panic-*stricken*', 'poverty-
   stricken', '*stricken* with fever', etc.
suit, suite
You wear a dinner *suit*, business *suit* or skirt, etc. (= matching jacket
   and trousers)
A *suite* is a set of furniture, or rooms, or a piece of music with a set of
   movements: a dining-room *suite*, a honeymoon *suite*, Bach's *Suite* and
   Variations.
swap, swop
Either spelling is acceptable.
swatted, swotted
He *swatted* the flies on the windowpane. (= hit at and squashed)
She *swotted* hard for her final exam. (= studied)
temerity, timidity
He had the *temerity* to ask for a pay rise. (= boldness)
His social *timidity* means he is terrified of company. (= shyness)
tense, terse
He looks worried and *tense* and taut. (= edgy, anxious)
His poems are *terse* little word pictures. (= spare, brief)
their, there, they're
The children were joined by *their* parents. (= belonging to them)
We went *there* on the way home. (= that place)
They're on their way. (= they are)
theirs, there's
The blue towels are *theirs*, not ours. (= belonging to them)
There's not much time. (= there is)
timidity: see **temerity**

to, too, two

Oh, *to* be in England . . . (infinitive)

Push the door *to*. (adverb, = 'shut')

He's gone *to* Paris. (preposition, 'in the direction of')

Try some vegetables *too*. (= also)

That's not *too* bad. (= very)

Two eyes can see better than one. (= number: 2)

tortuous, torturous

The old city was a maze of narrow, *tortuous* alleys. (= winding)

The prisoners were subjected to *torturous* conditions. (= hurtful)

troop, troupe

A *troop* of mounted police, cavalry, artillery etc. (= armed force)

A *troupe* of entertainers, acrobats, performers, trained animals (= company)

towards, toward

Both forms are correct, with British English favouring the -*s* ending and American English favouring the ending without -*s*.

two: see **to**

unaware, unawares

He was *unaware* of the danger. (adjective)

The bandit crept up on them *unawares*. (adverb)

unexceptional, unexceptionable

He is the author of several *unexceptional* novels. (= not very remarkable or interesting)

His behaviour was quite *unexceptionable*. (= blameless, i.e. there was nothing about his behaviour to which one could have taken exception)

uninterested: see **disinterested**

unreadable, illegible

The book was so verbose it was virtually *unreadable*. (= too dull to read)

My doctor's handwriting is almost *illegible*. (= indecipherable)

unwanted, unwonted

She feels very unloved and *unwanted*. (= not wanted)

He suffered a sudden, *unwonted* attack of panic. (= unaccustomed)

urban, urbane

Urban unemployment is a major problem. (= in cities)

He is the soul of *urbanity* and wit. (= sophistication)

venial, venal

The priest heard the confession of a variety of *venial* sins. (= minor, forgivable)

Many local politicians are *venal* and unscrupulous. (= open to bribes)

vicious, viscous
The shark can be a *vicious* killer. (= brutal)
The oil slick left a *viscous* black mess along the shoreline. (= glutinous, thick and sticky)

wave, waive, waver
They *waved* goodbye at the station. (= gestured with the hand)
. . . splashing about in the *waves* by the shore (= ripples of sea)
The formal application procedures were *waived*. (= not enforced)
Britannia rules the *waves* . . . and often *waives* the rules.
His faith has never *wavered*. (= faltered, hesitated)

whether, weather
I wonder *whether* it will rain. (= if)
The *weather* was very hot and humid. (= climate)

whose, who's
He was a man *whose* main hobby was music.
Who's been eating my porridge? (= who has)

wholly: see **holy**
windward: see **leeward**

wright, write
A *wright* is a craftsman (e.g. *wheelwright, shipwright*). The chief confusible between these two spellings is the word *playwright*, the name for a craftsman who makes plays. Many people make the mistake of spelling it 'playwrite', thinking of a *writer* rather than a craftsman of plays.

yoke, yolk
The colonial *yoke* was lifted in the 1960s. (= burden)
The *yolk* of an egg (= the yellow part)

Commonly misspelled words

abbreviate
abscess
abundance
abyss, abysmal
accelerate
accept, acceptable
access, accessible
accident, accidental
accommodation
accompany, accompaniment

accumulate
achieve, achievement
acknowledge
acquaintance
acquiesce
acquire, acquisition
acquit
actual
address
adequately

adieu
adjacent
admission, admittance
adolescent
advantageous
advertisement
advice (noun)
advise (verb), advisable
aerial
affect

aggravate
aggregate
aggressive
agreeable
aisle
alcohol
allege, allegation
allocate
allotted
almighty

alms
already
altar
alter
altogether
amateur
amount
analyse, analysis
ancillary
anecdote

ankle
annihilate
Antarctic
anticipate
anxious, anxiety
apology, apologise
apostle, apostolic
appal, appalling
apparatus
apparently

appearance
appendix
appreciate
approach
appropriate
approximate
arctic
argument
arrangement
ascend, ascent

aspirin
assassinate
associate, association
asthma
atheist
athlete, athletic
atmosphere
attempt
attendance, attendant
attitude

audible
audience
author
authority
autumn, autumnal
auxiliary
available
aviation, aviator
awkward
bachelor

bailiff
ballet
balloon
bankrupt
banjo, banjoes
bargain
basically
battalion
bayonet
bazaar

beauty, beautiful
becoming
begin, beginning
believe, belief
benefit, benefiting, benefited
besiege
bicycle
bigger, biggest
biscuit
bizarre

borough, burgh
boundary
bouquet
breath (noun), breathe (verb)
brief
brilliant
Britain
buccaneer
buffet
bulletin

buoyant
bureau
burglar, burglary
bury, burial
business
calendar
calibre
camouflage
campaign
canoe

career
careful
caricature
carriage
cashier
catarrh
catechism
category, categorical
caterpillar
caustic

cavalier
cedar
ceiling
cemetery
centre
challenge
champagne
changeable
chaos
character, characteristic

chasm
chassis
chauffeur
chocolate
choir
chorus, choral
Christian
chronic
cigarette
circuit

cite, citation
cocoa
collaborate
colleague
college
colonel
colonnade
colour, colourful
column
commemorate

commercial
commission, commissioner
committee, committed
comparative, comparison
compatible
competent
computer
concede
conceit
conceivable

concentrate
concern
condemn
confectioner, confectionery
connoisseur
connotation
conscience, conscientious
conscious
consensus
consistent, consistency

conspiracy
contemporary
continuous
controlled
controversy
convenient, convenience
coroner
corps
corpse
correlate

correspondence
corroborate
council, councillor
counsel, counsellor
counterfeit
coupon
courteous, courtesy
criticism, critical
cruel
cupboard

curious, curiosity
curtain
cynic, cynicism
dairy
debris
debt, debtor
deceive, deceit
decision
defence, defensive
definite

degradation
democracy
dependent
depot
descend, descendant
describe, description
design
despair, desperately
detach
develop, developed

device (noun), devise (verb)
diaphragm
diarrhoea
diary
different, difference
difficult
digestible
dilapidated
dilemma
dining

diphtheria
diphthong
disappear
disappoint
disastrous
discern
disciple, discipline
disease
disillusioned
dissatisfied

dissolve
dominant
donor
dough
duly
dungeon
dynamo, dynamos
dysentery
earnest
eccentric

eclipse
ecstasy
eczema
edible
eerie
efficient
eight, eighth
eliminate
embarrass, embarrassment
embezzle

emperor
emphasise
encyclopedia
endeavour
enough
enthusiasm, enthusiastic
entrance
envelope (noun), envelop (verb)
environment
equipped

estuary
etiquette
exaggerate
exceed, excessive
excellent
except
excite, excitement
excusable
exercise
exhaust

exhibition
exhilarating
existence
expense
experience
experiment
extraordinary
fallacy
family
fantasy

fascinate
fashion
fatigue
favour, favourite
feasible
February
fibre
field
finance, financial
focus

forcible
foreign
fortunately
forty
four, fourth
fourteen
freight
friend
fulfil, fulfilled
fundamental

gaiety
gallop, galloping
gauge
genius
gigantic
gnat
gnaw
government
grammar
grieve, grief, grievous

grotesque
guarantee
guard
guide, guidance
guitar
haemorrhage
handkerchief
handled
happen
happiness

ha**rass**

h**ea**rse

h**ea**ven

he**i**fer

he**i**ght

he**i**nous

he**ir**, heiress

he**ret**ic

her**o**, hero**es**, heroic

hi**cc**up

hin**dr**ance

hi**pp**opotamus

h**oe**, hoeing

hon**our**, honourable

hop**e**ful, ho**p**ing

hum**o**ur, hum**o**rous

hydr**au**lic

hyg**ie**ne

hy**mn**

hypoc**r**i**te**

icicle

ignor**ant**, ignor**ance**

illeg**ible**

i**ll**iterate

imagin**ary**

i**mm**ediately

impair

impertin**ence**, impertin**ent**

import**ance**, import**ant**

incident**a**lly

inde**fi**nitely

independ**ence**, independ**ent**

indispens**able**

inevit**able**

influ**en**za

ingen**ious**

ingredi**ent**

init**ia**tive

inno**c**ence

ino**c**ulate

insepar**able**

insta**ll**, insta**ll**ation, insta**l**ment

instinct

inte**ll**igent

inten**t**ion

int**e**rest

interfer**ence**

interp**r**etation

inte**rr**upt

i**rr**elevant

irrepar**able**

irresis**t**ible

i**rr**itate

i**s**land, i**s**let

iso**sc**eles

jealo**us**, jealo**us**y

j**eo**pardy

jewe**llery**

jubil**ee**

j**ui**ce, juicy

kee**nn**ess

kern**el**

khaki

ki**ln**

knowledge, **kn**owledge**a**ble

knuckle

lab**o**ratory

lab**o**rious

lab**our**

lab**y**rinth

lad**le**

l**au**gh, laughter

laundry

l**ei**sure

lett**uce**

l**iai**son

lib**r**ary

licen**ce** (noun), licen**se** (verb)

l**ieu**tenant

ligh**tn**ing (thunder and)

liquor
listen, listener
literary
lively
luscious
mackerel
magnificent
maintain, maintenance
maize
malicious

manageable
manifesto, manifestos
manoeuvre
mantelpiece
marriage, marriageable
martyr
marvellous
matinee
meant
measles

mechanic, mechanical
medicine
medieval
Mediterranean
melancholy
memorandum
messenger
mileage
miniature
miscellaneous

mischief, mischievous
mistletoe
monastery
mortgage
mosque
mosquito
motor
motto, mottoes
moustache
move, movable

muscles
myrrh
mystery, mysterious
naive
necessary
negligent
neigh
neighbour
niece
ninety

ninth
no one
note, notable
notice, noticeable
nuisance
occasion, occasional
occur, occurrence
offered
omit, omission
operate, operator

opponent
opportunity
opposite
ordinary, ordinarily
pageant
pamphlet
paraffin
parallel, paralleled
paralysis, paralytic
parcel

parliament
patience, patient
pavilion
peace
pencil
perceive
perennial
permanent, permanence
permissible
persecute

persist**ent**
perso**n**al
perso**nn**el
per**sua**de, persuasion
pharma**c**y, pharmac**eu**tical
pheno**me**non, phenomen**al**
phlegm, phlegmatic
photo, phot**os**
physical
physician

physique
piano, pian**os**
picni**c**, picni**ck**ing
pictures**que**
pi**e**ce
pig**eon**
pla**gue**
plat**eau**
playwri**ght**
pl**eas**ure, pleas**a**nt, pleasur**able**

pl**ough**
plum**b**er
pneumatic
pneumonia
pois**o**nous
pomegran**a**te
Portug**ue**se
po**ss**e**ss**, posse**ss**ion
potato, potat**oes**
practi**c**e (noun), practi**s**e (verb)

pre**cede**
pre**f**er, prefe**rr**ed
pre**j**udice
prelimin**a**ry
pr**e**vent, prevent**able**
privile**ge**
proc**ee**d
pro**f**ess, professor
progra**mm**e (unless computer
   program)
pron**ou**nce, pron**u**nciation

prop**a**ganda
prope**ller**
pro**s**ecute, prosecut**or**
psalm
psy**ch**ology
punct**ual**, punctuality
p**u**n**c**ture
pursue, purs**ui**t
qua**rr**el, qua**rr**e**ll**ed
quay

q**ueu**e
qui**e**t
qu**i**te
radius
ras**p**berry
re**a**lise
rea**ll**y
re**a**lm
rebel, rebe**ll**ion
rec**ei**pt

rec**ei**ve, receiving
rec**i**pe
reco**g**nise
reco**mm**end
re**f**er, refe**rr**ing, refe**rr**al, refe**ree**
refri**g**erator
reign
re**i**n
rel**a**tive
reli**e**ve, rel**ief**

remini**s**ce, reminiscence
ren**dezvous**
re**pre**sent
reserv**oir**
resi**g**n, resignation
resist**ance**
respons**ible**
rest**au**rant
rheumatism
rhinocer**os**

rhododendron
rhythm, **rhy**me
rog**ue**
sab**re**
sacrifice
sacri**le**gious
san**c**tify, san**c**tity
sat**ell**ite
sa**ti**sfy
s**au**ce, sauc**y**

scenery
scept**re**
schism
science
sculp**tor**, sculp**ture**
scythe
secondary
secret, secre**c**y
secret**a**ry
s**ei**ze, seizure

sent**e**nce
sep**a**rate
sepul**chr**e
s**er**ge**a**nt
sev**era**l
Shakespeare
she**ph**erd
sh**ie**ld
shi**n**ing
shr**ew**d

s**ie**ge
s**ie**ve
si**g**n, signal
signific**ant**
sil**houette**
sincer**e**ly
singe, sing**eing**
ski**l**ful
so**c**ial
solem**n**, solemnity

so**licit**or
solilo**quy**
solo, sol**os**
som**bre**
sor**c**ery, sorcer**er**
sove**reign**
spasm
spectacle
spect**re**, spectral
s**ph**ere, spherical

spon**sor**
stabi**li**se
st**alk**
station**ary** (not moving)
station**ery** (paper, pens, etc.)
statist**ics**
strat**e**gy, strategic
streng**th**
stret**ch**
substan**ti**al

sub**tle**, subtlety, subtly
su**cc**eed, succe**ss**
su**ffi**cient
s**ui**te
su**mma**ry, summarise
superintend**ent**
supervi**sor**
su**pp**ose
su**pp**ress
sur**ge**on

sur**r**prise
survey**or**
su**sc**ept**ible**
suspen**se**
sustain, susten**ance**
syllable
syllabus
symb**ol**
sy**mm**etry
synagog**ue**

synonym
syringe
tariff
tarpaulin
technical
teetotal, teetotaller
temperament
temperature
temporary
tendency

theatre, theatrical
thief, thieves
thigh
thorough
thought
through
tie, tying
tincture
tobacco
toboggan, tobogganing

tomato, tomatoes
tongue
tough
tragedy, tragic
transfer, transferred
tremendous
trophy
trousers
truly
tuberculosis

twelfth
typhoid
tyranny, tyrannical
umbrella
unconscious
undoubtedly
unique
unnecessary
until
usury, usurer

vacuum
value, valuable
vault
vegetable
vehicle
veil
vein
vengeance
veterinary
vicious

victuals
vigour, vigorous
villain
virtually
viscount
visible
warrant
weather
Wednesday
weight

weir
weird
wharf
whether
wholly
wield
wilful
withhold, withheld
woollen
wrestle, wrestling

xenophobe
xylophone
yacht
yield
yoke (bond or link)
yolk (of egg)
yours
zephyr
zinc
zoology

Check-up pages

This selection of exercises should not be taken too seriously. But I believe readers will welcome the opportunity to check their language skills. If a particular exercise seems particularly difficult, refer back to the relevant earlier section of the book. I take it for granted that most readers will use a good dictionary, where most of the answers may be checked.

1 Number

Change all the **singulars** into **plurals**:

I heard the noise in the tree.
The ship has struck a rock.
A lady's hat was on the peg.
The wolf is eating the rabbit.
The child ran to the window to see the fox.
The thief stole a valuable painting.
I kept the rabbit in a cage.
The sailor is swimming to his ship.
A cat – or a mouse – may look at a king.
I took a knife and fork.

2 Gender

Change all the **masculines** into **feminines**:

The son of a king is called a prince.
The heir to the property is a bachelor.
The tiger sprang at the bull and the fox ran away.
The governor summoned his manservant.
The duke was imprisoned in his castle by a wizard.
A steward brought my stepfather a glass of water.
'The bridegroom is my nephew,' said the headmaster.
'My brother is an actor,' said the waiter.
The emperor of Japan was our host and chairman.
Her husband is the proprietor of the hotel.

3 Verbs

Underline all the **verb phrases** in these sentences:

Good King Wenceslas looked out/On the feast of Stephen.
John is going home tomorrow.
The doctor should have spoken to you.
The plane will be landing around ten o'clock.
The crew have been safely rescued by a helicopter.
Come and see – the job is almost finished.
The supermarket was crowded with Christmas shoppers.
The sun has risen to its zenith.
Drink this medicine.
They fought the dogs, and killed the cats, and bit the babies in the cradles.

4 Phrasal verbs

Use suitable verbs from the following to fill in the **phrasal verbs** in these sentences:

hang break (used twice) *get turn* (used twice) *call give check keep* (used twice)

He _____ up angrily halfway through the phone call.
Some people seem to _____ away with murder.
Under prolonged interrogation, she _____ down in tears.
He _____ up on Monday and was offered a job.
The military police were _____ in to _____ up the demonstration.
She found it difficult to _____ up smoking.
Conference delegates have to _____ in at this desk.
Because of ill-health, he has had to _____ down an excellent job.
My neighbour _____ on working into her late 70s.
She _____ at her piano practice and became a famous pianist.

5 Prepositions

Fill in the **prepositions** in these sentences:

He's not accustomed _____ criticism.
Are you in charge _____ these dogs?
She's too clever _____ me.
The team is confident _____ victory.
What is their reaction _____ the plan?
Why are you talking _____ a whisper?
He is a native _____ Birmingham.
Please just glance _____ this letter.
Books are _____ sale _____ the basement.
You don't approve _____ him, _____ other words.

6 Parts of speech

What **parts of speech** are the underlined words or phrases?

These buns are <u>lovely</u>.
Who <u>rang</u> the bell?
He's <u>quite</u> a bright child.
She <u>leaves</u> by the six o'clock train.
He looked <u>beyond</u> the trees.
The child <u>seems</u> hungry.
She complained, <u>but</u> I ignored her.
You ought to <u>seriously</u> consider the matter.
<u>It</u> is going to rain.
I've got a red car and Fred's got a blue <u>one</u>.

The <u>professor</u> will see you now.
The choir sang <u>beautifully</u>.
<u>Dear me</u> – what has happened to you?
The beast in question is <u>an extremely fierce dog</u>.
Sarajevo, <u>capital of Bosnia</u>, has come under heavy fire.
I can see <u>something</u> in the distance.
I don't think he'll <u>get away</u> with it.
That's quite sensible, <u>isn't it</u>?
He walked <u>all the way</u> to the station.
He <u>came round</u> two hours after the operation.

A dinner <u>is being organised</u> in his honour.
He's <u>deliriously happy</u> with the result.
They live in a cottage <u>beside the beach</u>.
He's been <u>brought up</u> by an uncle.
He's eaten the lot. I have <u>nothing</u>.
She'll be with us <u>during November</u>.
The Taj Mahal is the <u>most beautiful</u> building in the world.
Nobody <u>ever</u> agrees with him.
My sister has written <u>me</u> a long letter.
Hydrogen <u>is mixed</u> with oxygen.

7 Phrases, clauses and sentences

Which are **phrases** and which are **sentences**?

A black and white cat.
That's quite all right.
Once upon a time.
Up the road and into the trees.
There's nothing wrong.

I enjoy a good film.
Fish and chips for tea.
Not on your life.
It's a funny old world.
Not in front of the children.

Here are some main **clauses**. Add a second **clause** to each to complete the sentence:

I went out into the snow _____.
_____ the dog will bark.
The cat's been sick _____.
Last week I painted the front door _____.
_____ the birds all flew away.
Lie down on that sofa _____.
_____ we got chips on the way home.
_____ the gerbil hid in a corner of its cage.
The elephants appeared suddenly out of the trees _____.
_____ Emma is no good at swimming.

Make these pairs of sentences into one **compound sentence**. Use **coordinating conjunctions** like *and* or *but* or *so*:

I like chips best. My brother likes pasta.
The rain came on. I put up my umbrella.
I offered a small donation. The secretary thanked me for it.
Mary went by air. The flight was delayed.
The ice cream looks nice. The trifle looks less than fresh.
They knew it was a long trip. They ate a good breakfast.
There was a loud peal of thunder. The children were frightened.
She caught a large salmon. She took it home for tea.
The taxi was summoned. Nobody left the party.
The college boiler broke down. The students were sent home.

Make these pairs of sentences into one **complex sentence**. Use **subordinating conjunctions** like *who, which, when, while, whereas, if, although, because,* etc. (The pairs can be moved around.)

I was angry with George. George was late.
How can you hear me? You're not even listening.
The boy wore a black tracksuit. He sat on my left.
I arrived. You were out.
I can't go. It's too expensive.
The dog barked. He heard a noise.
My brother likes pasta. I like chips.
She waited downstairs. I got ready hurriedly.
The explosive was found by a security man. It was in a plastic bag.
She looked very edgy and worried. Her companion was quite inoffensive.

Here are some **subordinate** and **coordinating clauses**. Add a good **main clause** to complete the sentences:

If you go down in the woods today _____
Although it was snowing _____
When Sleeping Beauty pricked her finger _____
While Goldilocks was fast asleep _____
Whenever the bell rang _____
_____ because I'm not old enough.
_____ and I go to bed.
_____ but that's the way the cookie crumbles.
Unless there's a marked improvement in his conduct _____
_____ and then we should see some results.

Underline the **main clauses** in these sentences:

Give him some more money, whatever he wants it for.
Show me the photos next time you visit me.
It's five years since we first met.
Suddenly I understood what he meant.
I have a dog which I'm very fond of.
She lives in Reading and works in London.
Sally's gone to Edinburgh but Andrew's gone to Glasgow.
When he arrived safe and sound, we were all relieved.
If you take the road that turns right at the traffic lights, you'll see a signpost that
    will direct you.
I was more interested in watching the game and in listening to the commentary than
    either of my companions seemed to be.

8 Word formation

Form **nouns** from these (e.g. *able, ability*):

able admire allow anxious arrive beg behave choose civilise create cruel describe
enjoy exhaust false famous fierce fragrant grow hate holy injure invite lazy live lose
mission move oppose please prosper punish real remember revive secure see serve
sick simple speak strong think warm weary wide worthy young

Form **adjectives** from these (e.g. *accident, accidental*):

accident affection anger attract Bible Britain child continent courage craft critic
custom destroy disaster duty exceed faith fashion favour forget giant grace height
inform introduce law love meddle metal music neglect north occasion parent pity
pride quarrel reason silk star success thirst thought tire union victory voice water
wood youth

Form **verbs** from these (e.g. *beauty, beautify*):

beauty circle civil courage critic dark false fat fertile full glass grief joy large long
magnet peril pure rich sharp simple solution speech success trial

Form **adverbs** from these (e.g. *able, ably*):

able bright courage critic destroy exhaust heavy hero joy just lazy ready resent succeed typical vain weary wise worthy wretch

Form **compound words** from these (e.g. *ache, headache*):

ache back berry black book cloth day door foot grand heart hedge house life man mill moon news night piece post rain sea school snow sun table water witch work

Underline the **prefixes** in these words (e.g. *amphitheatre*). Then try to say what the words mean:

amphitheatre antibiotic archangel bespectacled biography chronometer counterattack deactivate democrat disconnect downsize ecosystem equivocal forgo hypermarket hypodermic megalopolis metamorphosis millipede misjudge parasol perimeter polygon postdate submarine surcharge surname teleprinter tomorrow unclear unicycle upstream

Underline the **suffixes** in these words (e.g. *admirable*). Then try to say what the words mean:

admirable assistant baker Brazilian bushcraft computerese consultancy cookery damsel digestible dutiful farmhand fortunate girlish gossipmonger government hostess ignition interviewee Japanese kibbutznik letterhead machinery Marxism milkman minority modular narrator notify officialdom parliamentarian piracy privateer singer Spanish stationary threefold washable witchcraft workaholic youngster

9 Punctuation

Punctuate these sentences:

wheres the car asked the mechanic
her uncle said heres a cup of tea
mrs jones exclaimed what a dreadful storm
hes gone to the police station said james in a quiet voice
the girl suddenly shouted look
oh cried the child ive got no money for the bus
come here said the teacher coming replied george
the gardener asked have you seen my rake yes replied his mate i put it back in the shed
john asked have you time for a coffee sorry not tonight i replied im late for my train
when we get home said her father to the girl ill tell you the story of the pirate king oh good she replied are we nearly there
lets make a list of the places we want to visit first carthage second tunis third kairouan were going to need a good long holiday
he said that andrew who usually went fishing at weekends had gone to london instead

a tall woman walked into the shop removed her hood laid down her umbrella and handbag on a chair and drummed her fingers on the counter id like to buy a pair of black flat heeled shoes she said to the shop at large glancing round briskly for an assistant

in a climate like ours blue in comparison is one of the coldest most unfriendly colours one can use to decorate a room or at least that is my opinion

as the presidential motorcade swept along people from all walks of life office workers hairdressers shopkeepers school children all rushed out to the street cheering waving little flags and jumping up and down was it for joy or just to get a better view

10 Figures of speech

Complete these **doubles**:

To put on airs and _____
Everything is cut and _____
They fought tooth and _____
To be worn only on high days and _____
Membership is open to all and _____
The pros and _____ of the situation
The garden has gone to rack and _____
A danger to life and _____
He is at his mother's beck and _____
We strove for this outcome might and _____

Complete these **proverbs**:

Set a thief _____
When the cat's away _____
Too many cooks _____
One man's meat _____
Little children should be seen _____
Discretion is the better _____
Birds of a feather _____
A rolling stone _____
Every dog _____
Faint heart _____

Complete these contrasting **idioms**:

When the wolf attacked them, Steven _____ heels but Andrew _____ ground.
If you do that, it will be a feather _____ rather than a blot _____.
John was offered a promotion and I advised him to strike _____ hot, and not _____ grass _____.

Sally finds most maths problems plain _____, but Jane tends to find anything like that a very _____ nut _____.

In a crisis, Dorothy will take her courage _____ hands, but Ann will get cold _____.

11 Confusibles

Supply the correct words:

- *practice* or *practise*
  There is a football _____ on Wednesday.
  _____ what you preach.
  _____ makes perfect.
  Can we _____ the whole thing tomorrow?
  Do you _____ regularly? An hour's _____ a day is all you need to do.

- *advice* or *advise*
  What do you _____ me to do?
  I _____ you to see a doctor.
  Let me give you some expert _____.
  The Citizens' _____ Bureau offers a free _____ service.
  People love to _____ others, but they seldom follow their own _____.

- *all together* or *altogether*
  He did less and less work, and has now given up _____.
  They were huddled _____ in the climbers' bothy.
  Try to keep your tools _____ in one box.
  Such methods are not _____ satisfactory.
  _____, he has played in 44 international matches.

- *principal* or *principle*
  The _____ character was played by Kenneth Branagh.
  She has abandoned all her _____.
  Do you agree in _____ with the idea?
  The _____ will see you in his office now.
  The party is organised on Leninist _____.

- *alternate* or *alternative*
  We met on _____ Mondays.
  We need an _____ source of supply.
  There was no _____ but to increase the price.
  They _____ between hope and black despair.
  Can you suggest an _____ ending to the story?

- *forego* or *forgo*
  I was disappointed to _____ my summer holiday.
  Please read the _____ paragraph very carefully.

I acknowledge the ideas of Thorstein Veblen in the _____ analysis.
He has _____ smoking and drinking beer in his effort to get fit.
The result is a _____ conclusion.

- *practicable* or *practical*
  This information is of no _____ use.
  Noise levels have been reduced as far as is _____.
  I try to be more _____ than you.
  A white carpet in the kitchen is not exactly _____.
  His approach is down-to-earth and entirely _____.

- *lay/lie* or *laid/lain* or *laying/lying*
  She'll _____ anyone a bet on the Derby.
  I _____ down for a short nap.
  The leaves have _____ on the grass all winter.
  He gently _____ the book down.
  Snow is _____ thick on the moor.
  They are _____ a red carpet for the President.

- *passed* or *past*
  He's been in bed for the _____ few days.
  The train _____ through Perth at half _____ two.
  They say he has a rather murky _____.
  She _____ me a copy of the report.
  The plane _____ overhead with a roar.

- *inimical* or *inimitable*
  He dresses in a quite _____ manner.
  They are as _____ as oil and water.
  The Arctic environment is _____ to habitation.
  Her attitude is _____ to any form of opposition.
  Her _____ voice was audible outside the door.

- *course* or *coarse*
  They played golf on a 9-hole _____.
  The _____ of the war changed after Stalingrad.
  The grass by the shore was very long and _____.
  The wine was gritty and rather _____.
  I do hope he will stick the _____.

- *deadly* or *deathly*
  He's not joking – he's _____ serious.
  She swallowed a _____ dose of the poison.
  Her poor face was _____ pale.
  There's a _____ hush in the street tonight.
  After his outburst, there was a _____ silence in the room.

Underline the correct word of the two words in brackets.

You are not (*aloud, allowed*) in there.

The moon shone (*pale, pail*) across the sleeping town.

The jacket was made of (*course, coarse*) tweed.

Che Guevara was a famous Latin American (*gorilla, guerrilla*).

This murder is one of the (*grizzliest, gristliest*) in police records.

You are always (*losing, loosing*) something.

Large-scale British maps are produced by the (*Ordinance, Ordnance*) Survey.

Her front teeth are fixed to a dental (*plate, plait*).

The runaway horse came (*strait, straight*) at me.

Have you (*all together, altogether*) appreciated the urgency of the problem?

Your good (*advise, advice*) had no apparent (*effect, affect*) on his behaviour.

12 Spelling

● *-able* and *-ible*

There is no easy rule to follow when making adjectives with these **suffixes**, but we know that from *sense* we get *sensible*, while *admire* gives *admirable*. With the help of a dictionary, complete these:

practic . ble	excit . ble
access . ble	indispens . ble
prevent . ble	invis . ble
convert . ble	neglig . ble
approach . ble	advis . ble
incred . ble	permiss . ble
contempt . ble	cur . ble
respons . ble	irrit . ble

● **Homonyms** are words with the same sound but different spellings and meanings (such as *wave* and *waive*, *piece* and *peace* etc.). Confusion often arises with such pairs of words. With the help of a dictionary if necessary, write down a word with the same sound as the following, then define the pairs:

weight	hall
doze	vale
seed	maize
muscle	serial
marshal	sore
peak	threw
team	grate
gild	stare
sweet	paws
beach	time

board	rite
stake	cheque
hair	fair

- Sometimes it is possible to enlist the help of an easier spelling to help us with a harder one. For example, we all know that *ball* is spelled with two *l*'s. This should help to remind us to spell *balloon* with two *l*'s too. Use the easier words in the following sentences to help you to spell the harder ones correctly:

My birthday is *certified* on my birth _____*cate*.
The *bat*_____ of soldiers was ready for *battle*.
A _____*ette* is a small *cigar*.
On _____*mas* Day we remember the birth of *Christ*.
The job of a _____*ment* is to *govern*.
Some _____*cines* are not recommended by *medical* authorities.
A _____*ary* sometimes handles confidential and *secret* information.
We *com*_____ certain events and keep them in our *memory*.
Bronchitis is the name for inflamed _____*al* tubes.
A _____*ic* explosion is one which fills passers-by with *terror*.

- The **roots** of many derived words are not spelled exactly as the roots of the words from which they are taken. Thus a female *tiger* is not a *tigeress*, but a *tigress*. And a person with a sense of *humour* is not *humourous* but *humorous*. Add the **suffix** shown in brackets to the following words, and change the root appropriately. Check your answer with a dictionary:

wonder (-ous)	exclaim (-ation)
remember (-ance)	carpenter (-y)
sculptor (-ess)	glamour (-ous)
proprietor (-ess)	register (-rar)
winter (-y)	enchanter (-ess)
disaster (-ous)	curious (-ity)
encumber (-ance)	hinder (-ance)
vigour (-ous)	monster (-ous)
enter (-ance)	pronounce (-iation)
waiter (-ess)	impetuous (-ity)
labour (-ious)	repeat (-ition)
administer (-ation)	encumber (-ance)
vapour (-ise)	(de-)odour (-ant)

Index

Bold type indicates the main reference for a topic. *Italic* type indicates an exercise on that topic in the check-up pages at the end of the book.